Shamanism, History, and the State

Shamanism, History, and the State

Edited by

Nicholas Thomas and Caroline Humphrey

Ann Arbor

THE UNIVERSITY OF MICHIGAN PRESS

First paperback edition 1996
Copyright © by the University of Michigan 1994
All rights reserved
Published in the United States of America by
The University of Michigan Press
Manufactured in the United States of America
♾ Printed on acid-free paper

1999 1998 1997 1996   4 3 2 1

A CIP catalogue record for this book is available from the British Library.

Library of Congress Cataloging-in-Publication Data

Shamanism, history, and the state / edited by Nicholas Thomas and
  Caroline Humphrey.
        p.   cm.
     "Based on a conference that took place at King's College,
  Cambridge, in October 1989"—Acknowledgments.
     Includes bibliographical references (p.   ) and index.
     ISBN 0-472-10512-4 (acid-free paper)
     1. Shamanism—Political aspects. 2. Shamanism. 3. Religion and
  state—Case studies. 4. Cults—Political aspects.   I. Thomas,
  Nicholas, 1928-   . II. Humphries, Caroline.
  GN470.2S53   1994
  291.1'4—dc20   93-40589
                                                              CIP

ISBN 0-472-08401-1 (pbk. : alk. paper)

Acknowledgments

This volume is based on a conference that took place at King's College, Cambridge, in October 1989. For financial support, we are grateful to King's College, the British Academy, the Nuffield Foundation, and the Faculties of Classics and Anthropology and Archaeology at the University of Cambridge. Of the people who helped make the conference a stimulating event, we wish to thank Michael Taussig in particular.

Contents

Introduction

Nicholas Thomas and Caroline Humphrey

The forms of inspirational religious practice known as "shamanism" have provided a reference point for a huge literature in anthropology and religious studies and for an even wider field of popular texts on "alternative" religions and modes of consciousness. This book addresses an enduring and conspicuous lack in this literature, which has been heavily biased toward curing, trance, and medical aspects, toward characterization of what are supposedly general symbols or ecstatic techniques, and toward the shaman as a singular ritual practitioner. Here we approach the activities of shamans, and other inspirational practitioners, as political actors or mediators of historically constituted social contradictions and resistances.

Mircea Eliade's grand survey of "archaic techniques of ecstasy," which has long had the status of a key synthesis for this literature, was concerned at many points with stipulating what was or was not properly shamanistic. Though it ranged across diverse Asian, American, and Oceanic cases, some known through the most fragmentary of ethnographic reconstructions, it avoided associating particular varieties of shamanism or forms of shamanic practice with the peculiarities of political and social environments. It instead turned toward generalities, toward a general project of characterization.

> Healer and psychopomp, the shaman is these because he commands the techniques of ecstasy—that is, because his soul can safely abandon his body and roam at vast distances, can penetrate the underworld and rise to the sky. Through his own ecstatic experiences he knows the roads of the extraterrestrial regions. He can go below and above because he has already been there.

The danger of losing his way in these forbidden regions is still great; but sanctified by his initiation and furnished with his guardian spirits, the shaman is the only human being able to challenge the danger and venture into a mystical geography. (Eliade 1964:182)

The tenacity of this sort of characterization owes a good deal to what it means to us—the appeal of a wildness and transgression that is dissociated from the hierarchies and institutions of organized churches or scriptural religions. We associate it with an awesome environment; it seems individual, experimental, hallucinogenic. The magnetism of shamanism is not just a strand in pop religion or an aesthetic that has stimulated such avant-garde artists and cultural radicals as Joseph Beuys. It also has made some forms of shamanism peculiarly attractive as objects of scholarly investigation and has made others appear derivative, impure, or secondary. While Eliade's psychopomp is hardly a total fiction, this type, with its transgressive capacities, has long floated free from the central Asian societies in which it was originally documented. Like caste, taboo, and mana, shamanism is more of an exotic essence, a romanticized inversion of Western rationalism, than a scholarly category that can stand up to any sustained interrogation.

Though shamanism could be deconstructed through a genealogy of its uses in Western culture, we do not attempt to map out the range of Western academic and popular representations in this book. Though that has already been shown to be a productive exercise, our concerns are primarily to recover and analyse the diversity that essentialism has masked, and especially to recontextualize shamanic activities in their political contexts. In rehistoricizing shamanism, we take history as a relatively unproblematic framework rather than as a category that must also be deconstructed, but this strategy is motivated by a sense that the critique of Western representations of other (and past) societies should be complemented by more adequate and appropriate analyses of those societies, rather than supplanted by exclusively discursive reflection.

The anthropological literature is partially and unevenly influenced by the broader cultural preoccupation with the primordial and transgressive character of shamanism. The studies in this book depart from such preoccupation.

Our political and historical orientations prompted two general sets of questions: one concerning variants and transformations of shamanic powers within indigenous systems under conditions that are perhaps being rapidly altered by colonial expansion but are not directly structured by the projection of state power, and a second concerning the either antithetical or mutually consuming relations between shamanic activities and state cults. Our interests are dissociated from the singular type of *the* shaman. Even in entirely different traditions of writing on the topic, as remote from Eliade's religious history as structural functionalism, there is nevertheless (in for instance I. M. Lewis's work) an interest in a general model of "the shamanic career" and "the fundamental structure of shamanistic initiation," a comparative exercise that is seen to contribute to the "understanding of universal religious roles" (1986:89, 93). Given the diversity of political contexts in which shamanistic practices may be encountered, any such interest in universal roles must clearly suppress the political dimension, which is in any case marginalized by a focus on the structure of the individual practitioner's career.

Definitional debates over shamanism or spirit mediumship and types of possession have frustrated the comparative investigation of the ways in which shamanic agencies may constitute a field of political power or forms of political agency that react to or are incorporated by indigenous political dynamics and extensions of colonial or non-colonial state power. From this perspective, what may be significant are precisely the overlapping and mutability of various forms of contested ritual agency, rather than the clarification of what makes them distinct. The interpreter must begin by making distinctions and characterizations, usually on the basis of what is recognized or argued about locally, but these working typifications should be mere departure points for analyses of transformations and struggles over access to the divine, not end points of description. Because we do not aim to establish a new typology or classification of priestly-political agencies, the chapters in this book continue to employ terms that we suggest are problematic, such as *shaman*. We do not believe that inventing new labels would lead to more conceptual precision. We hope instead that the analyses within which our usage is embedded lead to a better understanding of the range of inspirational practices.

Rather than temporalizing shamanism through evolutionary language as a primordial or archaic form of religious activity perpetuated almost as a residue in the interstices or on the margins of more complex or "later" religions, we historicize shamanic activities by understanding their particular manifestations as results of historical processes. The processes include but are not limited to struggles and shifts between institutional and inspirational styles, interactions between societies in which shamanism may be identified as either indigenous or foreign and thus can mediate resistance or operate as a marker of ethnic difference, dynamics of state formation in which charismatic power may be appropriated and incorporated at the center or rendered peripheral and persecuted, and colonial confrontations in which shamanism becomes focal to resistance, particularly in the context of millenarian movements or cargo cults.

In analyzing shamanism politically and historically, we are not undertaking an entirely novel project. Writers who have already done this imaginatively and effectively include David Lan, in his book on the role of spirit mediumship in the liberation of Zimbabwe (1985), Michael Taussig, in his remarkable exploration of magic, memory, sorcery, and colonialism in southwest Colombia (1987), and Jane Monnig Atkinson, in her study of the shamanic performance among the Wana in Sulawesi as a public arena for the assertion and testing of reputation and leadership (1989). However, work of this kind has not been effectively integrated into the comparative discourse on shamanism and related topics, which remains preoccupied with psychological, symbolic, and medical aspects. We do not seek to substitute a sociological analysis for a cultural one. Instead we aim to draw these diverse orientations together in an account of representations and relations, of politicized meanings and efforts to monopolize certain forms of symbolic power and knowledge. We also seek to foreground comparison, not only by placing these diverse case studies together, but by presenting chapters (especially those of Thomas, Hugh-Jones, Hamayon, and Humphrey) that are comparative in themselves. We hope that this will enable readers to trace variants within regions that can be associated variously with political dynamics and patterns of colonial expansion.

We have been concerned with the following questions:

> In what ways are shamanic and inspirational activities subordinated to, incorporated into, or in competition with the "official" cults of kingship, the state, or an institutionalized

priesthood? In the absence of marked political centralization, how do they relate to other ritual agencies, such as the life-giving work of chieftainship?

In cases where there is a marked opposition between an inspirational and "official" cult, does the consolidation of state power lead to the marginalization of inspirational practitioners and the political suppression of cult activities? What relations conversely exist between political struggles and shaman-led cults in periods of social instability or state disintegration?

To what extent have shamanic activities provided contexts or focuses for anticolonial protest (colonialism being understood loosely as encroachment by any sort of state system, including socialist and precapitalist)? Are there also contexts in which shamanism consolidates or empowers a centralizing hierarchy or intrusive presence?

How does the symbolic content of shamanic activities change as the political contexts of shamanism and inspiration change? How are magic and cult activities appropriated and internalized by the state?

How do shamanic activities and related cults mediate differences between the indigenous and the intrusive, the central and the peripheral, the local and the exotic? What roles does the idea of shamanism play as an objectification of such differences?

One of our central questions thus concerns an antithesis between shamanism and various "official" or state priesthoods, but we do not argue that this is a necesary, general, or even predominant pattern. It is important to avoid replacing the essentialism of the properly shamanic (Eliade) with an essentialism of resistance, which could equally constrain our vision by privileging those forms of inspirational religion that are in an oppositional or subversive relationship with hierarchy, while eliding instances of the incorporation of shamanism in state power and cases where the "wildness" of shamanism may be a projection onto thoroughly domesticated practices.

Potentially, an enormous range of material might have been drawn into a comparative discussion of our questions. Our aim is to effectively broach the issues rather than resolve them, and because the questions are motivated by theoretical and analytical concerns rather than by a desire to present anything like a comprehensive account, we have not attempted global coverage or even a balance of regions in the case studies presented here. The omissions include Africa (although the dynamics of what has generally been labeled spirit possession rather than shamanism are obviously relevant), indigenous North America, and the inspirational dimensions of the European messianic movements consummately surveyed by Cohn (1970). We do, however, privilege two regions that have figured prominently in the wider literature on the topic: central and north Asia, and Amazonia. By including chapters that deal with these areas, we suggest how prior studies might be reinterpreted—even though the emphasis here is on new analysis, not critique—and at the same time expose differences of interpretation and approach. Hence, far from claiming any unitary new political, historical, or comparative approach to these topics, we suggest that their political and historical dimensions are available to be interpreted and argued about in a variety of ways.

Our effort to displace essentialism is signaled by the title of the first part of this collection, "Shamanisms." Each chapter in this part deals with variant forms of shamanism and their transformations in situations that in most cases straddle precolonial and colonial developments. Like other scholars in historical anthropology and ethnohistory, we avoid the notion that the arrival of whites into areas inhabited by "tribal" indigenous peoples is necessarily a radical break. Athough there are significant discontinuities, the differences and tensions internal to indigenous social systems are often manifested in responses to intrusion and the dynamics of colonial developments. In particular, where shamanic agencies are divided between two types of practitioners, the pattern in certain regions is that one kind may tend to become incorporated into colonized, neotraditional social hierarchies, while another may be marginalized and persecuted or may become central to messianic movements.

Thomas's chapter sets up terms for this kind of comparison by ranging widely across the ethnohistorically documented Polynesian societies. Though geographically dispersed, these share a common ancestral substrate, and in most cases, various ritual and political roles were divided between chiefs, shamans, and chief's priests. The broader pattern of evidence suggests an underlying rivalry between shamanism and the chiefly cult, and Thomas argues that the perceived failure of chieftainship led to its eclipse in some parts of the region by shamans with an expanded range of capacities. Hugh-Jones maps out a similar division between a horizontal shamanism involving trance and possession that is accessible to all adult men and a vertical shamanism based particularly on the transmission of esoteric knowledge within a small elite. In many Amerindian societies, the former type occurs on its own. But particularly in northwest Amazonia, these shamanisms may coexist in a relationship of contradiction and political tension that has developed in response to white intrusion. In some cases, messianic cults have been led by horizontal shamans and, associated with Catholicism, have been opposed by vertical shamans who are becoming Protestant pastors and preachers. Though the permutations in both the Polynesian and Amazonian cases are diverse and no simple formulae or rules can map the complex range of often poorly documented histories, certain basic tensions and alternations are manifest.

Hamayon identifies horizontal and vertical types of shamanism in Siberia, which she suggests are generally associated with hunting and pastoralist societies. Though this categorization and her consideration of the constraints on links between shamanism and state formation belong to an evolutionary approach that differs from the perspectives of most other contributors to this collection, the major differences are manifested in patterns of regional variation similar to those identified by Thomas and Hugh-Jones, particularly with respect to the development of the societies to the east and west of Lake Baikal after Russian colonization.

Gow's chapter moves in a different direction and raises an issue also addressed by Beard in her contribution. Gow directly confronts the notion that shamanism is a fully integrated element of indigenous culture that has been adapted as part of the resistance of impoverished urban peoples. He argues that shamanism in western Amazonia can be seen as a phenomenon that has developed in the symbolic economy of local racial categories. It parodies the debt relations of the *habilitacion* system and has a logic of taming forest spirits that recapitulates the mestizos' historical origins in the "taming" of the wild forest Indians by whites. This accounts for a particular association between shamans and mestizos—just as the latter live between cities and forests and are "river people," they are also masters of the paths between forest and urban dwellers. Although speculative and requiring further historical investigation, Gow's argument challenges us to reinterpret in a more historically situated way what appear to be quintessentially archaic or indigenous ritual phenomena. Historical anthropologists exploring other themes have established that hallmarks of non-Western sociality have been profoundly refashioned, or in some cases even created, through responses and interactions arising from colonial history, and the ideal types of shamanic activity may be equally susceptible to this sort of deconstruction and contextualization. The central Asian cases that provided Eliade's core examples might be considered in this light—a task taken up by Humphrey in her chapter.

The second part of this volume focuses more directly on the relations between inspirational religion and the state. Bayly's chapter deals with highly dynamic polities in south India in the period of commercial expansion prior to the establishment of British colonial rule. Under these circumstances, local manifestations of Islam and Christianity were far more fluid than subsequently, being received generally in the form of individualized saints' cults closely linked with warrior chiefdoms. Aspiring sovereigns needed to associate themselves with the cults as a resource, though by doing so they became key agents in the transmission of religions that were later much more clearly established and demarcated. The picture of unstable hierarchies constantly and violently reconstructed suggests a different relation between kingship or chieftainship and inspirational religion than that identified in Polynesia by Thomas. While Polynesian genealogical hierarchy was distinct from, and often in an antagonistic relationship with, cult practitioners, Bayly writes that in south India "the expansion of cults and the creation of new political realms were expressions of almost indistinguishable forms of power and authority." Perhaps the problem this raises for further research has to do less with shamanic and inspirational activities than with the political constitution of distinct kinds of hierarchical polities, some of which were far more open to inspirational power than others. As Bayly suggests, the more stable, colonially ordered states of the nineteenth century embodied more institutionalized and scriptural forms of religion and were not compatible with the inspirational activities that flourished earlier.

Bloch's chapter describes a case of inspirational religious practice among people at the bottom of the state hierarchy, a topic also addressed in the last section of Humphrey's paper. He asks why people of slave origin preserve a cult of Queen Ranoro, a mythical ancestor of Merina royalty, and why they do this in an idiom of ecstatic possession. He argues that the answer lies with the concept of ancestry, which is thought to fill up people during their lifetime, so that elders who are almost entirely taken up by the ancestral come to speak in a way that is empirically identical to their behavior when possessed for other reasons. Former slaves are cut off by their social position from receiving such regular ancestral blessing, which was policed by the state; but direct ecstatic possession could not be so restricted, especially in times of political turbulence, and the ex-slaves use of the cult of Ranoro to obtain the ancestral blessing for which they hunger. In this account, the "dancing mania" of the former slaves does not reject but mimics the values of the state. The mutability of the cosmological content of such cults is shown by the recent conflation of the ancestral with Christian blessing and of Queen Ranoro with the Virgin Mary.

The chapters by Barton and Beard return to a discussion of contested religious power at the core of the state, in this case in the Roman Empire. Barton shows how foreign, low-status astrologers came to play a crucial role in the struggle over access to knowledge of destiny. Various types of divination were associated with different political agencies within the state, but in the Late Republic astrology came to have popular appeal: it was regarded as proof that rule was decreed by destiny. "Thus," Barton writes, "as Constantine took the Christian god as his ally, Augustine took the macrocosm." The problem was that other people had access to astrology, too, not just the emperor. The greater the popular acceptance of astrology became, the more important its control was. By the fourth century, all forms of divination that were not public were prohibited on pain of death. This last theme, the policing of access to religious knowledge, or quasi-religious knowledge, not because it is wild or unseemly but because it is jealously guarded at the center of power, appears in three of our chapters, those by Bloch, Barton, and Humphrey.

Beard's chapter introduces another instance of the penetration of the alien into the center of Roman life—in this case, by the cult of the goddess Magna Mater. In this cult, flamboyantly foreign priests engaged not only in ecstatic dancing and flagellation but in the act of self-castration (performed in a trance of possession by the god Attis, a devotee of Magna Mater). The flagrant behavior and ambivalent

sexuality of these priests challenged the norms of religious officials and
the Roman ideal of maleness, yet the cult persisted for several hundred
years. Beard rejects chronological explanations (the gradual assimilation of the cult) and the idea of the wild as a challenge to the official.
These ideas of assimilation and challenge presuppose the separation of
ecstatic religion and the state. Beard's argument is that the cults provided a symbolic focus for the defining of the identity of the state. The
Roman Empire had no single religious system, but a series of often
inconsistent and mutually hostile systems, and the symbolic forms of
ruling power, in a context of rapid expansion, varied according to
time, place, and the nature of the process of domination. This variation blurred the distinction between ruler and the ruled. Beard argues
that there was an unresolved tension between Roman traditions and
the erosion of identity that occurred as political privileges were shared
with those outside. The claims and counterclaims experienced in relation to Magna Mater were in effect conflicts over how to define the
Roman.

Humphrey's chapter, which explores some of the political dimensions of shamanism within the Mongol and Manchu empires in north
Asia, brings out themes that are comparable to Bayly's findings on
south Indian kingship and to Barton's and Beard's work on ancient
Rome. At the time of the rise of the Mongol state, people who claimed
to communicate with, and thus to know the will of, Heaven were
not professional shamans but contenders for military supremacy. Such
a merging of religious and political authority seems to be characteristic of highly dynamic polities, as described by Bayly, and of the
early stages of state formation. An aspect of the establishment of the
dynastic and emperor-focused form of the state characteristic of north
Asia is the ability to make monopolistic claims to rule by the mandate
of heaven. Chinggis Khan acquired this when he succeeded in putting
to death the prophesier from a rival confederacy. Subsequently, the
Mongols did not stop referring to diviners on all important decisions,
but these people (often referred to in the literature as shamans) were
placed in client roles in relation to the ruler. Some were given the
honorific title *bagshi*, later also given to Buddhist priests, while others
were subject to restrictions or else gravitated to the courts of rival
contenders for heirship to the throne.

The second section of Humphrey's chapter discusses the more
stable context of the Manchu state after the conquest of China. Here

the shamanic cult at court rapidly became ritualized, merging with a sinicized cult of ancestors, and the great shamans who dealt with the external powers of nature were relegated to the margins of the empire. However, in a move not dissimilar in some ways to the Roman introduction of the cult of Magna Mater, Emperor Hongli had recourse to the practices of these "wild" shamans in his effort to revivify Manchu ethnicity in the eighteenth century. Here again we have the situation of a vast empire in a phase of rapid military expansion, when the issue of what it was to be a Manchu, hence a member of a tiny ruling elite, became crucial. The attempt to define a "true culture" by reference to those rural Manchus still living on the margins was unsuccessful: the Chinese tradition of the bureaucracy was too strong. But a patriarchal shamanic cult continued in the court until the end of the dynasty in 1911, while wild shamanism in the periphery has survived persecution under Manchu, republican, and communist governments. If the imperial dynasty thus used shamanism as a context in which to define Manchu-ness by reference to the periphery, the final part of Humphrey's chapter shows how a colonized people of the remote hinterland envisaged their shamanic ancestor spirit as masterfully flitting through the empire in a strange parody of imperial power.

This is an exploratory book. It does not offer a theory of shamanism but rather seeks to deconstruct this archetype. We find it more challenging now to loosen the classificatory paradigms that have slumbered through the decades since the publication of Eliade's book. The classic model of Siberian shamanism looks very different when it is seen in relation to competing political and religious practices in these same societies. What had seemed intrinsic features of shamanic activity can be perceived as contingent upon alternative strategies at particular historical junctures. Our starting point was the realization that political power, even in state systems, operates through ideas of fertility, blessing, ancestry, or knowledge of destiny, which are also the domains of inspirational agencies. We believe that these overlapping, shifting, mutually absorbing or mutually rebuffing agencies can only be properly understood through the analysis of particular historical situations, which may nevertheless suggest illuminating comparative parallels. This approach makes evident some features of cosmologies that are still puzzling—their mutability (in some respects) and persistence (in others). However, by focusing on the political import of what inspirational practitioners actually do, by critically discussing the possibilities that shamanic activities are in competition with cults of kingship and the state, as they may elsewhere be central to state formation, we hope to make shamanism visible in new ways, from the perspective of historical anthropology rather than that of ethnology.

REFERENCES

Atkinson, Jane Monnig
1989   *The art and politics of Wana shamanship.* Berkeley: University of California Press.

Cohn, Norman
1970   *The pursuit of the millenium: Revolutionary millenarians and mystical anarchists of the Middle Ages.* London: Paladin.

Eliade, Mircea
1964   *Shamanism: Archaic techniques of ecstasy.* Princeton: Princeton University Press.

Lan, David
1985   *Guns and rain: Guerrillas and spirit mediums in Zimbabwe.* London: James Currey.

Lewis, I. M.
1986   *Religion in context: Cults and charisma.* Cambridge: Cambridge University Press.

Taussig, Michael
1987   *Shamanism, colonialism, and the wild man: A study in terror and healing.* Chicago: University of Chicago Press.

Part 1. Shamanisms

Marginal Powers: Shamanism and Hierarchy in Eastern Oceania

Nicholas Thomas

The argument of this chapter is that diverse ritual and political relations can be understood not only in terms of the coherence of local systems but in relation to wider transformational patterns. Specific bodies of evidence can therefore be considered comparatively and particularly within regional contexts. In eastern Polynesia this perspective enables one to recognize a very broad counterpoint or conflict between a variety of forms of inspirational or shamanic agency and the centralizing force of chieftainship or kingship, which, as an encompassing ideology, tends to assimilate and incorporate all forms of important capacity. This opposition is recognizable in eastern Polynesia in myths, in individual disputes, in pre-European social transformations that can be inferred from linguistic and archaeological evidence, and especially in the broader pattern of differential social prominence and consequence. Most crudely, chiefs tend to be prominent where shamans are marginal and vice versa. However, the analysis cannot be convincing or effective if categories are taken to be fixed. The forms of agency are themselves mutable and subject to

---

This paper is a revised version of "Marginal powers: Shamanism and the disintegration of hierarchy," *Critique of Anthropology*, 8, no. 3. The changes made include both minor corrections and more substantial reformulations. The original paper included some rather speculative discussion of central and southeast Asian and Amazonian cases, which is rendered superfluous by other chapters in this volume. A complementary paper (Thomas, forthcoming) relates some of the material discussed here to theories of hierarchy and extends the argument to nineteenth-century and colonial Fiji.

various transformations according to political, historical, and cultural circumstances. It would be wrong to assume that shamanism is in any sense essentially antihierarchical or essentially dissociated from hierarchy. While the eastern Polynesian examples would lend support to such notions, it is clear from other cases discussed in this volume (see, for instance, the chapters by Beard and Humphrey) that it is equally possible for shamanic cults to be incorporated in state power or otherwise deployed by elites—for instance, in the elaboration of Roman identity discussed by Beard. In western Polynesia, the dynamics differ somewhat from the eastern Polynesian cases with which I start, and although there is some evidence that shamanic activities were clearly differentiated from chiefly or state cults, the relation of the latter to the former may be better characterized as containment rather than antagonism.

Polynesian Chieftainship and Shamanism

The ideology of chieftainship is not and was not exactly the same throughout Oceania. In much of Polynesia, however, some basic features are extremely widespread. Such effects as botanical growth and regeneration are traced to divine influences as well as to ordinary human work. Ancestor deities must be brought into certain relationships with this world and must periodically be offered sacrifices. Production (including successful fishing and such activities as auspicious house or canoe building) simply cannot happen without their presence or influence, which is what the seasonal rituals conducted by chiefs aim to secure.

The principle of birth order created a pervasive hierarchy, not just criteria for chiefly leadership. Rank within and between clans was based generally on a fiction of successive primogeniture, junior and senior members and junior and senior lines being more or less sacred according to their proximity to the firstborn ancestral line and the deities. The finer distinctions of rank among people generally were, however, far less significant than the irreducible qualitative difference between the chief and everybody else. The chief had a direct link with the gods: he (or occasionally she) stands for the gods among the people and for his people toward the gods. The access of people in general to divine agency is thus mediated by the chief. Chieftainship should then be understood not as a kind of leadership (that is, as a merely political institution) but as a whole cultural form that depends on and is manifested in life-giving ritual activity. Because the specific things, such as weather and growth, that this activity may be seen to control are of fundamental importance, the sense of indebtedness to the chief is generalized. Firth wrote that the Tikopia rites that constitute the cycle known as The Work of the Gods were "essential to maintain the fertility of crops and success in fishing, as well as the general welfare of the island as a whole" (Firth 1967:27) The link between the status of the chief and this work is explicit:

> In Tikopia eyes his overlordship and control are not only justified but natural, since it is he who is responsible for the people's welfare. He is their principle link with the ancestors and their only link with the supreme gods. He alone can perform the basic kava ceremonies which form the root of Tikopia religion. (1967:56)

Similar observations were made by George Vason, a Protestant missionary who lived (in a distinctly lapsed character) in Tonga between 1797 and 1801. The paramount chief, the Tui Tonga, was

> the priest of all the islands [the whole Tongan archipelago], and their mediator to converse with the Deity, and insure them plants, [and] was greatly reverenced throughout the island, and supported in splendor and dignity by the contributions of different districts. (Orange 1840:162; cf. Valeri 1990)

Although every Polynesian society was in some sense a chiefdom, and it is extremely likely on linguistic, comparative, and archaeological grounds that the rank-chieftainship-fertility complex characterized the societies of the first settlers who moved from western Oceania into the Fiji-Tonga-Samoa area (see Kirch 1984; Thomas 1990), this foundational and general character of Polynesian chieftainship should not obscure the fact that chieftainship was not everywhere unitary and encompassing. In some cases, usurping chiefs shared capacities with indigenous masters of the land; elsewhere, sacred chiefs withdrew (or were excluded) from action and left political matters to the leaders of junior lines. Some might be said to have been elevated to the status of kings; others were reduced to that of headmen or patrons. Hence, while it may be reasonably supposed that the institution of chieftainship had a particular character in the early phases of Polynesian prehistory, from which contemporary variants derived, analysis is no better served by essentializations of chieftainship than of shamanism. The chieftain had several facets— warrior, fount of life, political leader, and ritual master—that always entered into various combinations.

Before mapping out the associations between shamanic and chiefly agencies, some picture should be given of the "very eccentric class of people [who] lived apart in desert places"—as Hawaiian *kaula* were described by David Malo, a nineteenth century Christian Hawaiian writer (1951:114). A general picture is needed partly because inspired priestly activities in Polynesia and the Pacific as a whole have not generally been recognized as a form of shamanism in Oceanic anthropology, which has resulted in somewhat imbalanced interpretations of pre-Christian Polynesian religion. Loeb (1924) was one of few writers who did use the term *shaman;* Layard (1930) discussed its relevance in the Malekulan case. Important here is not the word employed but the fact that locally particular terms, such as *inspirational priest, prophet,* and *seer,* have precluded any broader perception of similarities in eastern Oceania. Like writers on millenarianism, analysts of shamanism in general might be accused of assimilating overly diverse cases to their subject matter (Guha in press), but in the Polynesian case, the reverse problem—the lack of any comparative vision—has been more conspicuous. An interest in the broader class of shamanic activities can be justified not only by the kindred character of the practices engaged in but by the fact that practitioners are known by some reflex of the proto-Polynesian term **taura* in nearly all cases. In accordance with regular consonant shifts, *kaula* can be equated with *taula* in Samoa and the Tokelaus, *tau'a* in the Marquesas, and *taura* in the Society Islands and Mangareva.

In many parts of Polynesia, *taura* were female and male inspired priests who acted as healers, oracles, and mediums, and they were quite distinct from another class of priests known as *tohunga*, who were specialists in traditions, ritual formulae, and an array of ritualized craft activities. The *tohunga's* position involved apprenticeship and acquired knowledge rather than an internal propensity or capacity that arose from possession. *Tohunga* might be described as official priests because they performed functions at ceremonies largely on behalf of chiefs. The way in which such a position was inherited resembled the inheritance of property; it was a social right based on membership of a family rather than on any essential connection between the person and the practice. Shamanism was sometimes inherited but more frequently arose directly from possession, from an act of selection attributed to a deity. When shamanic powers were inherited, the underlying notion seems to have been that a likeness of substance between kin or common propensity explained or made probable the deity's choice of the shaman's descendant. This is not clear, but there was no idea attested that a shaman had a right to pass on a privileged social position.

A number of early visitors to the Pacific described ecstatic performances involving possession by spirits or deities. William Mariner, who lived in Tonga between 1806 and 1810, gave the following general account.

> When he speaks, he generally begins in a low and very altered tone of voice, which gradually rises to nearly its natural pitch, though sometimes a little above it. All that he says is supposed to be the declarations of the god, and he accordingly speaks in the first person as if he were the god. All this is done generally without any apparent inward emotion or outward agitation; but on some occasions his countenance becomes fierce, and, as it were, inflamed, and his whole frame agitated with inward feeling. He is seized with a universal trembling; the perspiration breaks out on his forehead, and his lips, turning black, are convulsed; at length, tears start in floods from his eyes, his breast heaves with great emotion, and his utterance is choked. (Martin 1827, 1:101).

Similarly, in the Society Islands, the whole body of the *taura* was said to become convulsed "and inflated as if it was ready to burst." The god was supposed to descend into the *marae*, the temple, in a bird "like a heron" and then pass into the shaman's body at his call. The state of possession would end suddenly, and the *taura* would be motionless on the ground; at the same moment, "one of the sacred or Etooa [*atua*, deity] birds takes his flight from the Morai" (Haweis 1798:70; cf. Ellis 1832, 2:235–36).

Becoming a *tau'a* in the Marquesas involved a period of crisis, during which the future mediator between people and deities was abstracted from the ordinary human world and taken away by the *etua* (deities). The person would run furiously, emitting loud and incoherent cries and leaping and bounding up and down the valleys, collapse from exhaustion, and then begin to leap and run again with even greater vigor, as he or she entered into various states of more or less extreme possession. The possessed person would travel to other valleys, performing in the same way, and would report subsequently that gods had taken him or her among precipices and into deserted places. By some accounts, the initial possession of the *tau'a* could only be terminated through an offering. When this state of marked possession was over, older *tau'a* conducted the person to the *me'ae*, the sacred place, where official priests (*tuhuna o'ono*) recited chants that recognized the new *tau'a*. Subsequent possession was usually deliberately induced and controlled by the shaman. Some distinction was made between extreme or active states of possession, which were manifested by shaking, trembling, and hysterical symptoms, and a more general or perhaps passive condition, which characterized at least more potent shamans permanently: gods were said to reside in, or have eaten into, their guts.

The routine practice of the shaman could involve a number of activities, including various forms of curing, and oracles concerning war and the timing of feasts.[1] Most of these practices were only contingently linked with the fact that a *tau'a* might be possessed. The priest did not move into a trance to heal. A missing or captured soul might be lured back, but the shaman did not have the capacity to fly after it or to recover it from subterranean realms, as was the case in some other shamanic systems. The notion seems rather to have been that the presence of agency from the other world (the *po*) in the shaman enabled him or her to act in various ways as a manipulator of things and agents from the other world. Healing was very different metaphysically from being possessed, but there was a general structural similarity in that both invoked agents from the other world in the world of living and light. The person of the shaman was a nexus of interpenetration, and the shaman could act with respect to a variety of interpenetrations. Nobody else was situated in the same ambiguous yet empowered way.

---

1. The main sources here are Chaulet 1873, Lawson 1867, Lallour 1843–49, and Lesson, n.d. These are all discussed more extensively in Thomas 1990, which provides a fuller description of Marquesan shamanism.

Chiefs were also close to gods, but the nature of their proximity was quite different. The relation was one of genealogical continuity that enabled action on behalf of gods or humans at distinct moments. The chief stood for deities (and the ancestral line in particular) and could thus receive sacrifices or offerings, such as firstfruits, on their behalf. As a representative of society, the chief also could make sacrifices to the gods. The chief's role was a matter of signification rather than incarnation. Chiefs lacked the shaman's basis for practical work in the overlapping of *po* and *ao*.

In the Marquesas, there was a notable contrast between strong identifications between *tau'a* and gods and vague general links between chiefs and their ancestors. Offerings to gods were offerings to priests, who occupied the *me'ae* or sacred mortuary spaces. More significantly, some potent and aged *tau'a* were regarded as living *etua*, or gods, and lived in great seclusion, were thought responsible for the perpetuation of fertility and production, and were provided with human sacrifices. In a very early account of the Marquesas, the missionary Crook described a shaman named Tamapuameine in the following terms.

> Tamapuameine . . . is reverenced . . . as superior to all their other deities; & is firmly believed to dispense fertility to their Bread fruit trees, by his power over the Elements and the Seasons. He is now of a great age, & has from his childhood lived at [Hana-tetena, Tahuata], in a large house, surrounded with an Inclosure, called the 'A. In the house, is an Altar; & from the beams of the house, & the trees within the Inclosure, are human carcasses, with their heads downward, & scalped. . . . Of these, more are offered to him than any other Atua. (Crook 1800: 137–38)

Since there are few references in the sources to ceremonies associated with harvests or fertility of the kind well known from elsewhere in Polynesia, what Tamapuameine did to control weather or "dispense fertility" to the staple crop of breadfruit must remain obscure. The missionary observer could not help privileging the wildness and the violence of this heathenism over whatever he knew of its sense. Such practices as took place—if it was more than his presence, well-being, or favorable disposition that facilitated fertility—are likely to have been entirely different from the chiefly sacrifices that constituted such cycles as the Tikopian "work of the gods" described by Firth (1967), simply because the basis of the shaman's agency was different. It was unlikely that a living god would make sacrifices to himself or herself.

The content of the mystical process is less significant than the shaman's empowerment in this domain at all. The agency and efficacy of Marquesan shamans contrasts radically with the situation in most of Polynesia, in which the crucial and central fertility rituals were the responsibilities of chiefs and mostly constituted the basis of chieftainship. In the Marquesas, shamans seem to have acquired their potency at the expense of chiefs. This is underlined by the fact that human sacrifice was generally elsewhere intimately connected with chiefship. The principal occasions for sacrifice were chiefly life crises, which were significant because the chief or king was identified with the social totality, a point Sahlins has expressed in the notion of "hierarchical solidarity" (1985; cf. Valeri 1985). The chief generally played a direct part and had to consume the principal part of the victim's body, the eyes. While the *Bounty* mutineers were in Tahiti, they attempted to persuade people to abandon the custom, but were told that if this was done, "there [would] be no more chiefs" (Morrison 1935:207). In the Marquesas, in one narrow sense, there were no more chiefs. Although chiefs were seen as central to society and in some cases were strong figures who could direct affairs, especially in war, the capacities they had were not derived from any generalized ritual agency. Their followings were usually highly localized and depended as much on their landholding as their chiefship. Other landholders might frequently have been equally respected by their own dependants and followers. While chiefs never had any authority outside their own valleys (which often corresponded with tribal groups and were generally the geographic theaters of Marquesan life), prominent *tau'a* were recognized and propitiated by the populations of whole islands. While *tau'a* apparently needed to be installed by official priests, implying a persisting residue of ritual encompassment on the part of the chiefly cult, the significant deities of the *me'ae* seem often to have been dead shamans. Though the process was neither even nor complete, the growth of the ritual power of shamans seems to have mirrored the displacement of chiefs.

Chieftainship was eroded mainly as a result of a long-term process of ecological decline in the Marquesas Islands. From early phases of the islands' prehistoric settlement, burning associated partly with swidden cultivation reduced ground cover and permitted erosion. The potential productivity of slopes was considerably reduced, and an emphasis developed on the cultivation of breadfruit, which was vulnerable to periodic drought and, more particularly, to depradations during warfare.[2] A combination of social and ecological processes made periodic famine inevitable, which essentially meant that chiefs failed in their central ritual purpose. Individual chiefs were frequently expelled from their valleys in cases of despotic behavior and there is ample evidence for a more general if partial rejection. The processes arising from intense competition over resources tended to compound the fractured and unstable character of political groupings (Thomas 1985, 1990).

Transformations: Easter Island and Niue

The Marquesan case was not unique. It can be seen as one on a continuum in eastern Polynesian polities. Some were comparatively stable and displayed none of the fracturing of chiefly hierarchy apparent in the Marquesas. Others manifested more extreme developments along similar lines.

On Easter Island, genealogically defined rank declined substantially in importance, and an overtly competitive warrior-chief cult became central. Each year, the servants of prominent warriors competed in a race to swim out to a rocky islet and bring back the first egg of the *manu tara* or sooty tern. The winner's master became the *tangata manu*, or birdman, the paramount warrior chief for the fol-

---

2. The ecological conditions and determinations referred to here need to be qualified in significant ways. It should not be assumed that on small or inhospitable islands, one would always expect to find shamanism rather than chieftainship prominent. On some small islands, such as Tikopia (see Kirch and Yen 1982) and Mangareva, the presence of coral fringing reefs meant that soil lost from uplands was generally retained in alluvial fans that gradually spread into lagoons. Although lagoon resources might be deleteriously affected, available rich agricultural land might expand considerably. The problem of Easter Island and the Marquesas (among others, such as some of the Austral islands) was that any eroded soil would simply be washed into deep water: what was lost from upland slopes, potentially usable for swidden, was not gained in lowland terraces. More significantly, postulated here is a combination of ecological and sociopolitical processes: the other crucial element is the tendency to overproduce associated with expansive cycles of competitive feasts. These are less conspicuous in western than eastern Polynesia, as are, more generally, predatory warrior regimes and prominent shamanisms.

lowing year (Routledge 1917). Although the office of the king or chief (*ariki mau*) persisted, and although in some chants the chief continued to be credited with "making fertile the country," this seems to have been nothing more than a vacuous expression. That the head warrior was sometimes presented with certain firstfruits offerings reflects his specific encroachment on formerly chiefly capacties. In general, the *ariki mau* seems to have had very little authority and to have played no part in the birdman cult that occupied everybody's attention. The famous stone *ahu* statues, which—despite much diffusionist and less scholarly speculation—clearly represented deified chiefly ancestors, were abandoned and generally pushed over or defaced around the sixteenth century. Although this was probably done by enemy groups to each others' statues, the act reflects a more extreme rejection of chieftainship than seems to have taken place anywhere else in Polynesia (Kirch 1984:274–78).

Shamanic priests, known as *ivi atua*, or bones of the gods, played a prominent part in the birdman competition and cult. Though sources are inadequate and not mutually consistent, it appears that only warriors who had been dreamed about by a shaman could participate, and the principal deity of the cult, Makemake, was associated with priests. Healing practice involved a trance or ecstatic state that was induced through dizziness, and in which the priest spoke in a shrill voice identified with Makemake (Métraux 1940:325). One myth describes a shaman becoming annoyed after a family failed to give him fish, eel, and lobster, the latter two of which would have been prestige foods. He reacted by knocking over some of the *ahu* statues (Métraux 1940:87), which implies that the relationship postulated here for eastern Polynesia generally was one not simply of fundamental incompatibility but of specific antagonism that was explicit or nearly explicit in narratives, if not in consciousness. Myths from other areas give accounts of struggles between chiefs and shamanic priests. One from Rarotonga describes the poisoning by a chief of a cannibalistic priest with a propensity for demanding sacrifices of children while he was possessed (Gill 1880:99–100).

The island of Niue also underwent at least in the centuries up to about 1700, a process of political devolution, in the sense that chieftainship, if not other forms of hierarchy and inequality, were contracted.[3] Distinctions of rank and status became less significant,

3. See Thomas 1991:88–93, 229–30, for an attempt to explain the peculiarities

and chieftainship and hereditary priesthood disappeared altogether
(Thomson 1904:34–35). There was, however, a great deal of fighting,
and the office of *toa*, or head warrior, was important, although
arrived at on the basis of competence and performance. Given that
other conditions, such as a limited division of labor, were consistent
with evolutionary assumptions of broader trends in social development, it is not surprising that Loeb explains Niuean society by suggesting that the island was settled before the Polynesians "converted
to theocratic rule" (1926). Given that Polynesian chieftainship, rank,
and related institutions preexisted the settlement of Polynesia itself
and seem to have a long history in Austronesian social forms (see
Mosko and Jolly, forthcoming), the correct interpretation can only
be the reverse: that chieftainship and a more elaborate rank structure
existed at one stage but for some reason were not reproduced. Some
accounts, without providing adequate detail, suggest that chieftainship became discredited through the same process of repeated failures
of production that apparently took place in the Marquesas.

> They have no king. Of old they had kings, but as they were the
> high-priests as well, and were supposed to cause the food to
> grow, the people got angry with them in times of scarcity, and
> killed them; and as one after another was killed, the end of it
> was that no-one wished to be king. (Turner 1861:469)

It is not surprising that under these circumstances, *taula atua*, "a class
of people subject to inspirational spasms" (Loeb 1926:166), played an
important role, which was not restricted to healing practices.

> In a pre-war ceremony known as TUGI E MAMA (lighting the
> fires) the Taula-atua (shaman or priest) who was supposed to be
> the leader of the ceremony, first appeared in the fore-ground
> feverishly calling out in a language of his own to his gods, to
> come together and aid the troops who were about to enter the
> battle fields. (Etuata and Tamaki 1982:99)

Etuata and Tamaki disputed the term *shaman* (which Loeb

---

of Niuean colonial encounters through reference to the singularly "devolved" character
of Niue society.

employed): "In real Niuean thinking, the true functions of a taula-atua could be numerous" (1982:99–100). It is unproductive to have any rigid definition of shamanism, and obscurities can be introduced into comparative discussions if categorical separations are made between closely related inspirational activities. If, however, a continuum from a restricted healing role to a much wider range of capacities—which may seem to be outside the range of stereotypic shamanic capacities—is postulated, the probable prehistoric transformations can be understood. In fact, up until about 1700, the *taula atua* were thought to control the weather and crops, just as some *tau'a* did in the Marquesas. At about that date, a new line of chiefs or kings was reputedly installed from Tonga. They appropriated or recovered these powers for the chieftainship. Thus shamans had more or less extensive powers, which related variously with actual practical influence, according to the strength of chieftainship and centralized hierarchy at the time. It appears that as a kingship weakened, various functions and privileges, such as control over natural production and the right to demand sacrifices and occupy *marae*, might be taken over by inspirational priests. These processes could operate in both directions, but because, in most eastern Polynesian islands, socio-ecological deterioration was difficult to redress, transformations of unitary chiefdoms in predatory warrior-shaman regimes seem to have been irreversible, at least within the time scale up to European intervention. Hence, apparent and albeit partial reconstitutions of centralized hierarchy, as in Niue, were associated with some external intervention.

Under other circumstances, shamanic priests or those prone to possession were marginal. In the Society Islands, they were occasionally used as oracles in time of war but played no part in most major religious ceremonies, which took place at *marae* and were controlled by official priests. These sorts of priests were members of hereditary orders and were essentially servants of chiefs. The few passing references to the activities of *taura* in the Society Islands and of *kaula* in Hawaii underline the marginal status of their capacities. In both these island groups, there existed coherent and powerful chiefdoms. In Tikopia, where a strong ideology of chieftainship persisted in a much smaller polity, shamans (*taura atua*) were subordinated to the chiefs, and the inspirational activity was stripped of its force. On one ritual occasion, the chief told the medium what to

do, while the ecstatic dimension of the performance was clearly formalized and attenuated (Firth 1970:267, 269). Chiefs are jealous gods.
An encompassing chiefly unity does not admit much diversion or
dispersion of ritual power.

An inverse relationship between the coherence of a chiefdom and
the potency of shamans is found within as well as between Polynesian
island groups. The only parts of the Hawaiian archipelago in which
shamans were important were socially peripheral places, such as the
small island of Niihau on the western end of the Hawaiian chain.

> There are at Neehow many priests and, what we have not seen at
> any other of these Islands, priestesses, who all act as if they were
> inspired by some supernatural power, performing numberless
> strange and mad pranks. (Burney, in Beaglehole 1967:620 n. 2)

In the Marquesas, a broad contrast may be drawn between the
southern part of the group, which was more politically fractured and
egalitarian (with respect to the distribution of property among other
factors), and the northern part, in which a centralized chieftainship
existed on one island ('Ua Pou), and where a graded rank structure
had become prominent. On Nukuhiva, in the north, property was
more consolidated and certain elite families were more influential
than seems to have been typical of southern Marquesan situations.
But reports of deified shamans seem to have come mainly from the
southern part of the group, were Tamapuameine lived. Shamans there
had distinct privileges, such as exclusive rights over certain foods,
which did not exist in the north (Thomas 1990).

Valeri observed in the Hawaiian context that king and *kaula* each
represented "the totality in an opposing or competing form: the *kaula*
represents a totality directly accessible to the individual and thus in
opposition to the social hierarchy; the king represents a totality con-
substantial with the social hierarchy" (1985:139). Diverse outcomes
of this opposition or rivalry between different forms of access to
divine power are manifest across Polynesia, reflecting large patterns
of social transformation—the undoing of certain kinds of hierarchy
and their displacement by others. Hence, what is at issue is not really
devolution, or the reversal of a simple unilineal process. The marginality or centrality of shamans is, moreover, not simply an indicator
but an element of these processes. In eastern Polynesia particularly,

the antagonism between shaman and chief was sometimes evident in individual struggles. The pattern I have identified should be seen not just as a systemic model but ultimately also as the result of acts of struggle and accommodation, even if these events and shifts are mostly invisible in the prehistoric past.

The construct suggests that ancestral Polynesian society entailed a coherent chieftainship and marginal shamans with restricted capacities. This situation persisted on many islands, and in some cases shamans were evidently so rare or marginal that the sources make no mention of any kind of inspirational activity. But in general the crucial element of the pattern is not the presence or absence of shamanism but its status and character as a form of agency. Thus, in some cases, such as in Tonga, shamanic powers, thought occasionally conspicuous and ecstatic, were drawn into official chiefly rituals in a circumscribed and controlled form, or functions were restricted to an oracular role susceptible to deployment in the interests of chiefs. In these cases, there is no realized opposition or antagonism between shamanic and chiefly capacities, but rather a relation of complementarity between distinct forms of agency, one of which is clearly more encompassing and pervasively significant than the other.

Wider Implications

One of my concerns in this chapter has been to demonstrate that certain hierarchical forms, which have generally been regarded as basic elements of Polynesian culture, were not simply taken-for-granted features of people's implicit worlds. They may have been taken for granted in some areas, where chieftainship was obviously secure and supreme, but in the region as a whole, chieftainship, despite its fundamental character, was evidently contested and sometimes discredited. The political perceptions of Polynesians at the time of contact are irrecoverable, but a variety of facts, such as the mythic contests between chiefs and shamans, suggest that there was an explicit recognition that chiefs and shamans embodied alternate powers.

At another level, though, there was perhaps a kind of *doxa* that admitted no debate, that provided forms for explicit ideas without exposing itself to explication. The ritual efficacy of both chiefs and shamans stemmed from the notion that agriculture and other means of subsistency were subject to the control of deities, that could be and needed to be influenced or manipulated by people. Though this, as a cosmological tenet, is obviously an extremely general one that figures to some extent in many religious systems, the prior character of Austronesian cultures and the precarious ecology of many islands, which made periodic drought and famine tangible possibilities, gave the interest in life-giving ritual particular centrality. The concern to produce the fertility and plenitude that were too often lacking— though as much for political as environmental reasons—made both chiefly and shamanic agency consequential in broader terms. This point is perhaps too general to be informative, but its significance arises more from the question of how the analysis here might be extended or developed in other regions.

As other chapters demonstrate, antinomies between vertical and horizontal ritual agents, between shamans of one type and those of another, are discernable in many areas. Could these diverse religious systems be read in the same terms proferred in this chapter? In this context, the extreme generality of religious interests in life-giving forces could be misleading. I have argued that the concern with manipulating these forces in Polynesia was conspicuous and central. But the fact that the ideas are present to a varying extent elsewhere does not mean that they have the same centrality and that ritual contests are likely to have the same groundings. Elsewhere, obtaining spoils of war, accessing trade valuables, managing ceremonial exchange or rain, or suppressing witchcraft may figure more prominently in everyday concerns and in institutions central to social reproduction than the sorts of ritual work I have focused on in this chapter. A systemic and comparative analysis of certain hegemonic and peripheral powers can elucidate at once their local perculiarities and their underlying issues, but such comparisons cannot be explored unless there is a certain underlying coherence—whether arising from a common ancestral cultural substrate, a shared colonial experience, or the spread of social and religious traditions—that informs the actions and strategies of shamans and their rivals. What matters is not the nature of shamanism but what shamans do—whether they fail, succeed, eclipse others, or just get by.

REFERENCES

Beaglehole, J. C., ed.
1967   *The journals of Captain James Cook.* Vol. 3. Cambridge: Hakluyt Society.

Chaulet, P.
1873 Notices géographiques, ethnographiques et religieuses sur les iles Mar-
       quises. MS. Archives of the Congregation of the Sacred Hearts of Jesus and
       Mary, Rome.

Crook, W. P.
1800 An account of the Marquesas Islands. MS. Mitchell Library, Sydney.

Ellis, W.
1832 *Polynesian researches.* London: Fisher and Jackson.

Etuata, I., and P. Tamaki.
1982 The wisdom of Niue. In T. Chapman et al., eds., *Niue: A history of the
       island.* Suva: Institute for Pacific Studies.

Firth, R.
1967 *The work of the gods in Tikopia.* London: Athlone.
1970 *Rank and religion in Tikopia.* London: Allen and Unwin.

Gill, W.
1880 Gems from the Coral Islands. London: Ward.

Guha, R.
In press.   The millenarian space. *Canberra Anthropology.*

Haweis, T.
1798 Otaheitian priesthood. *Evangelical Magazine,* February.

Kirch, P.
1984 *The evolution of the Polynesian chiefdoms.* Cambridge: Cambridge Uni-
       versity Press.

Kirch, P., and D. E. Yen
1982 *Tikopia: The prehistory and ecology of a Polynesian outlier.* Bulletin 238.
       Honolulu: Bernice P. Bishop Museum.

Lallour, V.
1843-49 Notes sur les Marquises. MSS. Turnbull Library, Wellington, New
       Zealand.

Lawson, T.
1867 Sorcery. MS. Lawson Collection. Bishop Museum, Honolulu, Hawaii.

Layard, J.
1930 Shamanism: An analysis based on comparison with the flying tricksters
       of Malekula. *Journal of the Anthropological Institute* 60:525-50.

Lesson, A.
N.d. Iles Marquises. Documents divers. MS. Bibliotheque Municipale, Rochefort-
       sur-mer, France.

Loeb, E.
1926 The shaman of Niue. *American Anthropologist* 26:393-402.

Malo, D.
1951 *Hawaiian antiquities.* Honolulu: Bishop Museum.

Martin, J., ed.

1827 *An account of the natives of the Tonga Islands.* 3d ed. Edinburgh: Constable.

Métraux, A.

1940 Ethnology of Easter Island. Honolulu: Bernice P. Bishop Museum.

Morrison, J.

1935 *The journal of James Morrison.* Ed. O. Rutter. London: Golden Cockerel Press.

Mosko, M., and M. Jolly, eds.

Forthcoming *Transformations of hierarchy: Structure, history and horizon in the Austronesian world.*

Orange, J.

1840 *Life of the late George Vason of Nottingham.* London: John Snow.

Routledge, C. S.

1917 The bird cult of Easter Island. *Folklore* 28:337–57.

Sahlins, M.

1985 *Islands of history.* Chicago: University of Chicago Press.

Thomas, N.

1985 Property, hierarchy, and crisis in the Marquesas. *Social Analysis* 18:40–59.

1990 *Marquesan societies.* Oxford: Clarendon Press.

1991 *Entangled objects: Exchange, material culture, and colonialism in the Pacific.* Cambridge, Mass.: Harvard University Press.

Forthcoming Kingship and hierarchy: Transformations of polities and ritual in eastern Oceania. In M. Jolly and M. Mosko, eds., *Transformations of hierarchy: Power and process in the Austronesian world.*

Thomson, B.

1904 *Savage island: An account of a sojourn in Niue and Tonga.* London: Murray.

Turner, G.

1861 *Nineteen years in Polynesia.* London: John Snow.

Valeri, V.

1985 *Kingship and sacrifice: Ritual and society in ancient Hawaii.* Chicago: University of Chicago Press.

1990 Death in heaven: Myths and rites of kinship in Tongan kingship. In J. C. Galey, ed., *Kingship and the kings, History and Anthropology* 4 (1): special issue.

Shamans, Prophets, Priests, and Pastors

Stephen Hugh-Jones

In his book on Bororo cosmology, Crocker writes that "one of the characteristics of Amerindian shamanism is the surreal movement between 'high' and 'low' domains that contain antithetical cosmological principles. The idiosyncrasy of the Bororo consists in dividing capacity for this mediation between two agents" (1985:313). In this chapter, I will show that dual shamanism is more widespread than Crocker imagines and that it can be used to illuminate some differences in shamanic phenomena and social organization between various Amazonian societies and some of the processes of historical change that have taken place within them. I draw on comparative material but base my argument on data from northwest Amazonia. I will also attempt a more satisfactory integration of this material with accounts of various millenarian movements. It has long been recognized that the messiahs who lead these movements were shamans. However, accounts of Tukanoan shamanism sometimes treat these movements as if they were rather localized and temporary aberrations on an otherwise tranquil scheme of traditional practice and belief. I present new data on these movements that shows that their impact was more widespread, more fundamental, and more long lasting than is often supposed.

Amazonian shamanism can be roughly divided between two ideal

Field research on which this paper is based was carried out at various times between 1968 and 1991 by C. and S. Hugh-Jones and was variously supported by the Social Science Research Council (now ESRC); King's College, Cambridge; the British Museum; and Central Television. This support is gratefully acknowledged. Also acknowledged are Robin Wright's helpful comments on an earlier draft.

types that I will call vertical shamanism (VS) and horizontal shamanism (HS). Though all forms of shamanism combine knowledge with inspiration, in VS the predominant component is esoteric knowledge transmitted within a small elite, while in HS the emphasis is more democratic, depends less on "saying" than on "doing," and involves the more classic shamanistic features of trance and possession.

In many Amazonian societies, HS occurs on its own. It appears to be associated with more egalitarian, forest-oriented societies with an ideological emphasis on warfare and hunting. Secular power is often separated from sacred power, and shamans are morally ambiguous and may have relatively low status and prestige. Shamanism is individualistic, open to all adult men, frequently involves widespread and relatively free use of hallucinogenic substances, and is only peripherally involved in the ritual reproduction of society. Mythology is also relatively unelaborated, and myths are often subject to idiosyncratic elaboration by different tellers. As examples, I have in mind such societies as the Yanomamo and Achuar.

In a few cases, notably the Bororo and the Arawakan and Tukanoan groups in northwest Amazonia, HS occurs together with VS. Sometimes a single person combines aspects of both types; sometimes they are divided between different individuals. VS appears to be associated with more complex, ranked societies, often characterized by an Amazonian version of descent, and with less emphasis on warfare and hunting. Secular and ritual powers are often merged and limited to a few powerful men, often shamans of the VS type, who are morally unambiguous, enjoy high prestige and status, and play a key role in social reproduction through elaborate ancestor-oriented life crisis rituals involving bullroarers or sacred flutes and trumpets. Their knowledge is relatively closed and is founded on an elaborate, dogmatic mythological cannon. No trance or possession is involved, and where hallucinogens are used, the shamans typically give them to others rather than using them themselves. Although the evidence is admittedly thin, it is enough to suggest that where VS and HS coexist, the relationship between them is not simply the complementarity that Crocker describes. It also appears to contain an element of contradiction and political tension that is interwoven with more complementary, abstract cosmological principles.

The historical situation of interethnic contact, a complex and shifting ground of alliance and conflict within and between different segments of white and Indian society, creates tension and contradictions. Certain features of the northwest Amazonian crisis cults can be seen as one more visible (and thus documented) manifestation of a working out of these contradictions, an ongoing process involving an intellectual effort to interpret and accommodate competing claims and ideas and a practical effort to readjust politico-economic relations. The thesis of Wright and Hill that such movements represent "a reorientation of social and economic relations in which the refusal to co-operate with the external, dominating order of the white people became elevated to the status of a sacred cosmological postulate" (1986:51) is attractive both for its truth and its liberal sentiments. Nonetheless, the argument is still phrased in terms of two blocs, white people and Indians, pitted against each other, and it fails to take into account the internal divisions and tensions within white and Indian society and the external ambiguities of simultaneous antagonism and alliance, autonomy and dependence, between these two blocs considered as wholes. Of particular concern is the status of the *caboclos* of mixed white and Indian descent. Some messiahs came from among this sector, and historical records show caboclos vacillating between support for Indian messiahs and support for colonial authorities. Some dynamics of these contradictions can be glimpsed in the details of the movements, in the subsequent history of the groups involved, and in their contemporary beliefs.

The cults themselves, which grew up toward the end of the last century, were related to Catholic missionary activity. They principally involved shamanism of the HS type, sometimes in combination with VS. At times they were opposed by secular political leaders and by shamans of the VS type. Today, among the Arawakan-speaking peoples to the north of the Vaupés, where Protestant missionaries have broken the Catholic hegemony, VS and HS coexist and messianism is a living force. In the Tukanoan-speaking Vaupés area, still dominated by Catholic missionaries, shamans of the HS type have all but disappeared, leaving only VS shamans who have taken on some of the roles and attributes of HS.[1]

Though my division between two manifestations of shamanism

---

1. Among the Bororo, the opposite has happened: *aroe*-shamanism of the VS type has disappeared while *bope*-shamanism of the HS type persists. In a general fashion, Crocker (1985) relates this change to the impact of Brazilian society but does not consider the specific role of the Salesian missionaries in this process.

has received concrete expression in two different roles, one of which has now virtually disappeared, my aim is neither to reify such distinctions nor to produce a synchronic typology. My concern is rather to explore the relation and dynamic interplay between two principles or modes, in this case manifest in shamanism, that receive expression in the synthesis of sameness and difference, inside and out, kin and affine, alliance and descent, endogamy and exogamy, and vertical and horizontal that is typical of Amazonian societies (see Overing 1983–84).

Dual Shamanism

Shamanism is like acting or playing music—received knowledge and training combined with originality, skill, and performance. To know what you are saying and doing, you must learn from others, but to be any good, you must add something of yourself. Within shamanism, these two aspects—power and knowledge, achievement and ascription—call to mind the traditional distinction between the shaman and the priest. The shaman derives his powers from direct contact with spirits through possession and trance; he is a part-time specialist who acts alone and concentrates his efforts on curing. The priest earns his credentials through specialized training; he is a full-time specialist working for the community, a member of an organization who officiates at regular, collective ceremonies as a ritual specialist (see Turner 1972). Though traditionally associated with different social types, such formal distinctions correspond with my own distinction between VS and HS and with certain indigenous categorizations of shamanic phenomena and roles.

Duality connected with shamanism has been widely reported from different parts of Amazonia. Perhaps the most common is the ambivalent nature of the shaman himself—shamans may use their powers for good or ill. This ambivalence has been described either as sociopolitical—shamans should kill their enemies in other groups and cure their friends in their own group—or as the product of apprenticeship—shamans who master their emotions and aggressive desires use their powers to cure, and others who fail to exercise self-control become sorcerers. In relation to the Tukanoan Desana, Buchillet (1990) proposes a third intepetation for this ambivalence, namely, that it obeys the internal logic of the construction of shamanic knowledge in which the ability to cure and the ability to kill appear as inseparable and complementary elaborations of mythic speech distinguished by their rhetorical construction and symbolic conditions of use. A second kind of distinction, involving relative degrees of knowledge and power, can be used to rank shamans in a formal or informal hierarchy. In these cases, increasing power often goes hand in hand with increasing ambivalence—more powerful shamans may be better curers and also potentially more dangerous than their lesser counterparts.

A further set of distinctions are based on the different activities, functions, spheres of competence, and sources of power that are ascribed to different shamans and to dualistic cosmological principles to which they relate. Here we find the division into distinct shamanic roles, VS and HS, a pattern found among the Bororo and the Arawakan and Tukanoan peoples of northwest Amazonia. This pattern is displayed in table 1. The following notes are designed to bring out the major features of this pattern and do not provide an exhaustive account of northwest Amazonian shamanism.[2]

The Arawakan Wakuénai Baniwa living in the Içana and Guainia basins in the frontier zone of Colombia, Brazil, and Venezuela distinguish between *malirri*—shamans proper—and *malikai liminali*—the owners of chants. Relying on hallucinogenic snuff, rattles, magical stones, and crystals, shamans retrieve lost souls and treat illness by physical manipulation of the patient's body—blowing tobacco smoke, massage, and sucking out harmful objects and vomiting them away. In some cases they also employ the technique of water throwing, ascending to the sky in trance to seek the aid of the ancestors. They are highly active, move about a lot, and use their snuff-heightened senses to locate harmful substances in the bodies of their clients and lost souls in the world outside.

The shamans intersperse their work with sitting on a stool and singing songs that describe the shaman's actions and experience and that refer to the fate of the patient's conscious, individual soul. They

---

2. This table is an idealized abstraction of the data concerning the Arawakan and Tukanoan groups as a whole. I am aware that it does not correspond exactly to local variations reported in the ethnographic literature. On Arawakan shamanism see Hill 1983 and Wright 1981, 1992; on Tukanoan shamanism see Bidou 1983, Brüzzi Alves da Silva 1962, Buchillet 1983, 1987, 1990, Hugh-Jones 1979, and Reichel-Dolmatoff 1975.

TABLE 1. The Payé and the ~Kubu: Horizontal and Vertical
Shamanism Compared

HORIZONTAL SHAMANISM—PAYÉ	VERTICAL SHAMANISM—~KUBU
TRAINING	
—In forest, ecstatic, use of parica snuff.	—In house, reflective, use of yagé.
—Physical transmission of powers; emphasis on personal experience.	—Verbal transmission of powers; emphasis on learning esoteric canon.
—Nonhereditary transmission with payment for teaching.	—Patrilineal transmission with no payment for teaching.
CURING	
—Outside house physically active, direct contact with patient.	—Inside house, physically passive, no contact with patient.
—Uses rattles, stones, and audible, self-reflexive songs.	—Blows on food/drink as vehicles for inaudible nonreflexive spells.
—Action on physical manifestations of illness inside body.	—Action on causative agents located outside body.
—Retrieves lost individual conscious soul.	—Protects collective unconscious soul.
—Retrospective curing of lesser illness.	—Prospective divination, prophylaxis; curing of life-threatening illness.
ATTRIBUTES	
—Powerful.	—Knowledgeable.
—Associated with hunting, fishing, and warfare; with Jaguar, thunder, lightning, and Scorpius.	—Associated with forest fruits and gathering; with Tapir and Pleiades.
DUTIES	
—Provides game and fish; ensures animal fertility.	—Provides fruits; ensures vegetable fertility. Renders game safe to eat.
—Ad hoc activities on behalf of individuals; no marked ceremonial role	—Regular activities on behalf of community. Major ceremonial role in rites of passage.
—Horizontal relations with outsiders: affines, enemies. Reciprocal exchange.	—Vertical relations with insiders: kin, ancestors. Lineal continuity.
SOCIAL STATUS	
—Younger, physically active, feared.	—Older, physically inactive, respected.
—Lower status; complementary to secular political roles.	—Higher status; overlaps with secular roles.
—Aggressive, morally ambiguous.	—Peaceful, morally unambiguous.

work outside the house in the company of their patients, sometimes in conjunction with other colleagues, and their services are handsomely rewarded in advance—guns and sewing machines are mentioned as payments for treatment of the more serious illnesses. Their powers are graded. The most powerful and most feared are the "snuff-jaguars" or "jaguar owners," master shamans who alone have the power to bewitch others in revenge for sorcery attacks by "poison owners," shamans who use their powers for evil ends. Such powerful shamans as these became the millennial prophets of the last century and are considered to be saviors and "like Christ" today, though it is sometimes claimed that there are no longer any such powerful shamans still living.

By contrast, the chant owners, who also conduct the major rituals surrounding birth, initiation, and death, use only chants and tobacco smoke in their cures. They blow these over gourds of liquid that are given to the patient to drink. They work alone, inside the house, sitting motionless in a hammock, and they have no direct contact with their patients. Employing neither trance, hallucinogens, nor other paraphernalia, they cure entirely through continuous singing and through the verbal manipulations of disease-causing entities that their songs effect. Though they act as vehicles of travel, these songs refer not to the singer but to the fate of the patient's unconscious, collective soul. These chant owners are highly respected and morally unambiguous senior elders who alone can cure life-threatening illness.

This same pattern is true also of the Tukanoans of the Vaupés region, southern neighbors of the Baniwa, who divide shamans into two major categories yai—"jaguar" or payé—and ~kubu—"priest."[3] I will refer to these two as payé and ~kubu. The curing activities of the Tukanoan payé, similar to those of his Arawakan counterpart, are neatly summarized in the following text.

---

3. A similar pattern is reported for the Piaroa. Shamanic activities are divided between the "owner of blowing" and the "owner of prayers." The former inspire fear; have access to the spirit world, where they consult good spirits and fight with enemy shamans and bad spirits; and can diagnose illness. The latter blow spells prescribed by the former and inspire no fear. The owners of blowing are clearly more powerful than the owners of prayers: though the owner of the house, Kaplan's *ruwang* (1975), can be either, a community might have several owners of prayers but only one owner of blowing, and all the latter are owners of prayers as well (Mansutti Rodriguez: 1986 12–13).

When seeing the diseases the shaman takes "fish-yagé." When he is intoxicated he begins to sing. When he is singing thus he ascends to the rainbow. The shaman carries a rattle adorned with the feathers of the oropendola bird. With this rattle he attracts all things. He attracts all the splinters and stones toward himself. With the rattle and with his shaman's stones he banishes the disease. Then he blows with his cigar that contains the spell. The splinters and stones become visible to him. In these cases he simply grasps them and throws them away. (Reichel-Dolmatoff 1975:94)[4]

These payés employ powerful hallucinogenic snuffs (Virola and Piptadenia) and a special kind of *yagé* ("fish yagé"), which they use to acquire their visionary and ecstatic powers and to see inside their patients' bodies and recapture their lost souls during curing. The ancestors of these payés obtained their powers—snuff, aggressive spells, and a magic club—from the master of thunder, and today they are closely associated with thunder and lightning and with the aggressive powers of the jaguar—the more powerful are able to transform themselves into such animals at will. They often live an isolated, solitary existence in small houses located in headwater areas deep in the forest. Such men are greatly feared and are accused of sorcery by their rivals and by ordinary people. Historically these payés also played an important role in warfare, acting as leaders, inciting others to go on raids, and providing magical paint that made the warriors aggressive and invincible. In this connection, Barasana elders tell of the exploits of Rumbling Jaguar, a shaman who was also a great curer and prophet.[5]

---

4. A small gourd rattle, different from the one used in ceremonial dances, is the insignia and essential tool of the Tukanoan payé, the vehicle of his travels. This rattle and other equipment—snuff tubes, quartz crystals, and other magical stones—are illustrated in Allen 1947:578.

The ~kubu's equivalent of this rattle is a long, feather-ornamented ceremonial lance with a swelling in one end into which small stones have been inserted. During dances, he uses this rattle to mark transitions in time. His equivalent to the payés crystals is a large white cylindrical quartzite pendant ("jaguar stone") worn hanging from his neck.

5. The aggressive activities and powers of payés have a particular link with the period of the year known as the Caterpillar Summer (Reichel-Dolmatoff 1975:111,

Novice payés are trained, sometimes in groups, living in isolation with a master shaman. The office is not hereditary, and a powerful payé may transmit his knowledge to nonrelatives from other groups in exchange for payment. The training involves fasting, vomiting, and sexual abstinence, and the novice must obtain a number of spirit weapons and tools of office. Some of these are physically transmitted from his master; others he must obtain for himself. Hallucinogenic substances play a central role in this training, giving the novice his first visionary experiences and allowing him to experience and master the trance state. Emphasis is also placed on individual qualities of persistence and endurance and on the individual's capacity to experience and interpret things for himself (see Reichel-Dolmatoff 1975:76–83).

Within this broad category of payé are distinctions based on differences of technique, source of powers, and specific domain of action, and on relative powers and knowledge. For the Desana, Buchillet (n.d.) reports a division between the "jaguar"—associated with the sky, thunder, and the use of Virola snuff—and the more powerful and dangerous "jaguar of aquatic animal-spirits"—associated with water, the underworld, and the use of a hallucinogen made from the roots of *sakaka* (Conaraceae?).[6] Though Barasana shamans do not use Virola snuff or hallucinogens of any kind in curing,[7] they distinguish between the lower-grade *rude* or *huti reagi* ("one who blows and throws illness away") and the more powerful and knowledgeable *oko yuegi* ("water thrower").[8] The former are often younger men and normally cure less serious illnesses. They do their curing outside the house at night, blowing tobacco smoke over their patients' bodies and sucking and

115–6). This season, ruled over by the constellation Caterpillar Jaguar (roughly equivalent to Scorpius), is one of danger and sorcery and was also the season of warfare. Caterpillar Jaguar (Scorpius) stands in complementary opposition to ~ Yokwaro (Pleiades), the latter having a marked association with the ~kubu. (Hugh-Jones 1982).

6. Echoes of this division are found in Desana shamans' use of both special fish yagé and Virola bark snuff for curing. Barasana shamans, who eschew such substances, say that fish yagé belongs to the fish spirits and Virola belongs to the tree spirits.

7. Reichel-Dolmatoff's report of Virola use among the Barasana (1975:163) is incorrect—the snuff concerned would have been ordinary tobacco snuff. His report of the use of yagé in shamanic curing (1975:133) would not apply to the contemporary Barasana either.

8. Goldman reports a similar distinction between "blowers," who cure minor ailments and "water throwers," who deal with more serious cases (though the latter have lower status). In this case, water throwers are like the classic payé: they use rattles and hallucinogenic snuff and are associated with jaguars and thunder.

physically manipulating them to extract pathogenic substances. The latter are generally elder men whose role may overlap with that of the ~kubu. They cure more serious illnesses and operate only in the hot midday sun, using water scented with aromatic leaves, which they throw over the patients' body. The water acts as a sieve that trawls through the patient's body removing spines, bundles of fur, or feathers, which the shaman throws away amid much blowing, flicking of fingers, and clapping of hands. The reflection of the sun in the water provides the medium for the shaman's ascension to the sky to consult with ancestral spirits and to seek their aid.[9]

For the Desana, the payé also plays an important economic role, using hallucinogenic snuff to visit the master of animals to obtain game and fish and to enable him to tell the hunters and fishermen where to find their catch. In exchange for the animals, the payé must pay an equivalent number of human souls. The relations between the master of animals and human beings and those between hunters and the animals they kill have a markedly sexual character (see Reichel-Dolmatoff 1971).

As the powers of the payé rest on the ecstatic use of hallucinogens, those of the ~kubu rest on an exhaustive and accurate knowledge of a lengthy and internally differentiated corpus of esoteric knowledge contained in myth. No credence or credit is given to any innovations he might seek to introduce into this canon. His task is to interpret and regulate the contingencies and flux of daily life by relating it to the changeless, transcendent order that myth displays and guarantees.

Selection for this role occurs at birth, and training begins at an early age. Inside the *maloca* and sitting on a stool by his father or paternal uncle—the knowledge is transmitted patrilineally—the aspirant ~kubu listens to portions of myth, committing each one to memory and reciting them back again as proof of his learning. Having mastered the stories, he must learn a series of spells for divination, protection, curing, and aggression, and a lengthy series of chants used in collective ceremonies. He must learn the secrets of how each spell or chant articulates with its relevant segments of narrative. The emphasis is on tranquil reflection, listening, learning, knowing, and

9. Incidents in myth describing characters ascending to the sky via reflections in water and descending to earth on strings provide the conceptual key and primordial basis of these powers (see Hugh-Jones 1979:274–75, M.4.A and B).

understanding, an emphasis encapsulated in the stool on which he sits. To prepare for this knowledge, the aspirant must fast and purify his body. He is given small quantities of yagé (Banisteriopsis) to help him learn.[10] After initiation, as he takes part in collective dances, he takes more yagé, but later on, as a ~kubu, he no longer depends on it. Instead he gives it to other men to enable them to dance and chant and to appreciate an otherworldly dimension that he inhabits through his thoughts alone. Training and learning last long into adult life, and not until a man is an elder and begins to officiate at collective ceremonies does he acquire the status of ~kubu. Full recognition of this status comes only when he conducts the ceremonies centered around sacred flutes and trumpets representing clan ancestors and involving the initiation of young men into a secret men's cult (see Hugh-Jones 1979).[11]

The powers of the ~kubu—to render food safe, to diagnose and cure illness, to divine the future, to protect people from danger, to conduct major rituals, and to mediate contact with the ancestors—rest on verbal spells. Most adult men share some of the attributes of the ~kubu in that they know some spells that they use, in the context of their family, to deal with the everyday problems they confront. What distinguishes the real ~kubu is his total mastery of a much wider range of such spells, his knowledge of their associated mythology, and his ability and willingness to use this knowledge to interpret and control events for the benefit of a wider community of which he is the focus and, often, the leader.

For the Vaupés Indians, many, perhaps most, illnesses are held to be the result of eating food, especially the meat of large animals

---

10. The slower, more cerebral effects of yagé are quite different from the violent and dramatic effects of Virola. Yagé's effects are essentially visual and auditory and help in learning—the taker sees and hears what he knows. When Barasana men invite each other to chant together after taking the drug, they often say, "Lets go and learn."

The effects of Virola are altogether more physical and bodily: the taker experiences direct and ecstatic sensations of death, flight, possession, and the like. These subjective differences in sensation correspond to differences in the main active chemical constituents of Banisteriopsis (harmine) on the one hand, and of Piptadenia and Virola (beta-carboline and triptamine alkaloids) on the other (see Schultes and Hoffman 1979).

11. The presentation of the *sari* feast, which also involves sacred flutes and trumpets, likewise marks the attainment of the status of *ruwang itso'fha*, or the high status of priestly shaman and territorial leader, among the Piaroa. See Kaplan 1975:54.

or fish, that has not been properly treated. The ~kubu is the expert at the treating procedure. Prospectively, he blows spells to render food safe to eat; retrospectively, he blows them to remove the effects of the failure to carry out this procedure properly. The spells are normally blown silently into some vehicle—food, drink, coca, cigar, paint, nettles—which is ingested by the beneficiary or applied to a part of the body. In this sense the ~kubu's role is complementary to that of the payé—he makes safe what the other provides.

The role of the payé as provider of fish and game is also complemented by the ~kubu's role as provider of forest fruit. Though I have heard no mention of tapir transformations by the ~kubu to match the jaguar transformation of the payé, the tapir figures in various Barasana myths as a ~kubu and as the owner and master of tree fruits. Game or fish and forest fruits are the prime foci of two different and complementary ritual modes, one involving exchange between affinally related exogamous groups of equal status, the other involving internal relations within the clan and a stress on hierarchical relations between individuals. Rituals in the latter mode, conducted by the ~kubu, promote the fertility of forest fruits and form part of the secret clan-based ancestor cult mentioned above.[12]

The curing activities of the payé involve trance and vertical ascents and descents between different cosmic layers; the spells of the ~kubu imply more horizontal travel, in thought, to different places on this earth. His spells have three essential ingredients: a list of animal, plant, and other spirits together with their harmful attributes; an inventory of geographical locations associated with each category of spirit; and a set of verbal commands—I wash, I break, I throw down, I cool down and soon—which put into effect his powers and neutralize those of the animal or spirit concerned. As the spell progresses methodically down the list, the ~kubu travels from place to place cleansing and neutralizing the different dangerous attributes and powers he encounters.

Though the ~kubu has an important role in the prevention and cure of illness, his prime function is to effect the transitions—birth, initiation, and death—that ensure the socialization of individuals, the

---

12. For the myths see Hugh-Jones 1979:M.6A.287, M.7.J.299. On the ritualization of forest fruit see Hugh-Jones 1979. The division between two distinct ritual modes among the Barasana and other Tukanoans is closely paralleled by a similar division among the Arawakan Wakuénai (see Hill 1984).

passage of generations, and ordered relations between the ancestors and their living descendants. Such transitions are dangerous, and the ~kubu must ward off the dangers involved—here his protective role comes to the fore.[13] Though he may fail to provide adequate protection—a failure that, in serious cases, may lead to a life-threatening wasting away and sapping of vital energy caused by the ancestral spirits—his intentions are not normally called into question. The ~kubu is the upholder of the moral order and is not normally accused of sorcery.

The Payé and ~Kubu in their Social Context

Hill (1984) has argued that the two forms of Wakuénai social organization, division into geographically dispersed exogamic phratries of equal status and into hierarchically ordered sibs making up each phratry, serve as alternative modes for orienting social and economic behavior with respect to the natural environment. The Wakuéani are culturally very similar to their Tukanoan neighbors, and Wright's arguments would apply to them as well. The first, *natural social mode* leads to an opening-up that culminates in ritual exchanges of food and affinal alliances between exogamic groups. It is associated with, among other things, (1) hunting, fishing, and agricultural activities; (2) complementary male and female productive activities; (3) open, indirect exchange between competing affinally related phratries of equal status; and (4) symmetrical or homogenous relations among individuals, with little or no specialization. The second, *ritual-hierarchical mode* involves a contraction of the social order and an emphasis on hierarchical ranking between the sibs of each exogamous phratry. It is associated with, among other things, (1) the synchronization of social and economic behavior with the ripening of forest fruits and with human physiological processes; (2) polarization of male and female activities; (3) closed, direct exchange between kin divided into hierarchically ranked groups; and (4) heterogenous, differentiated relations among individuals, with specialization according to ritual criteria.

---

13. This protection was once embodied in ceremonial shields owned and used by the ~kubu. Though such methods are no longer in use, the ~kubu still uses his powers to construct invisible protective fences around his community and its people.

These two modes are distinguished as ideal types for analytic purposes, and in practice they are not rigidly differentiated.[14] In part they also overlap with my own analytic distinction between horizontal and vertical shamanism, represented in this instance by the payé and ~kubu. Compared to that of the ~kubu, the position of the payé is relatively more open and democratic, involves somewhat less specialization and a greater element of achievement and competition, and is strongly associated with the outwardly directed activity of hunting and with the antagonistic relations between groups implied in warfare and sorcery accusations. The ~kubu is associated with rituals involving forest fruits and life-crisis ceremonies and has a particular association with the *Yurupari* ceremonies, where the vertical relations between the living and their ancestors and the hierarchical ranking of clans is ritually expressed (see Hugh-Jones 1979).

In northwest Amazonia, the clans in each exogamic group are hierarchically ranked according to the model of the birth order of a set of male siblings and are typically associated with different ritual roles. Among the Barasana, the top clans are chiefs, followed by dancers and chanters, warriors, shamans, and last, servants. Similar systems have been reported for other Tukanoan groups. A curious contradiction exists, however, in the position of the shaman within this system. ~Kubus usually enjoy a position of power as the formal political leaders and headmen of their communities (as chiefs), but their position in the formal clan hierarchy comes near the bottom (acting as servants to these chiefs). The shaman clans have junior ranking partly because just as the youngest sibling is seen as mediating between generations, the shaman, too, has a mediatory role (see Hugh-Jones 1974:126).

The ambiguous position of the shaman can also be related to a certain instability or tension between the hierarchical and egalitarian tendencies that are manifest in northwest Amazonian social organ-

---

14. In the case of the Barasana, these two modes also correspond to two major cycles of mythology, one dealing with the creation of the sacred flutes and trumpets used in clan rituals and with the ancestral or *he* people who are represented by them (see Hugh-Jones 1979:M1, M5, M6), and the other dealing with the origins of alliance and intergroup exchange that were the prerequisites of the development of truly human society (Hugh-Jones 1979:M7). White people figure only in a third cycle, which is also much concerned with the origins of the powers of the payé. ~Waribi, the hero of this cycle, is the father of white people and the originator of messianism (see Hugh-Jones 1988).

ization, in which repeated and sometimes hotly contested assertions of relative rank between different clans conflict with a more general egalitarian emphasis, both the formal equality between exogamous groups and the de facto equality of the individuals within them outside the context of ritual.[15] These tensions are a version, peculiar to northwest Amazonia, of a much more general and often reported tension in Amazonian societies between dangerous, potentially powerful relations (of warfare, hunting, exogamy) with the outside and with the other, and safe, potentially sterile internal relations with one's own kind, kin and ancestors (see Overing 1983–84).

In addition to his de facto position as political leader, the ~kubu is by definition an elder. The Wakuénai and Desana refer to him as "grandfather" and distinguish him as such from the payé. This testifies to the ~kubu's position of seniority and respect. The role of the ~kubu as a specialist in myths and chants overlaps with that of the chanters and dancers who occupy a position in the hierarchy just below that of the chief; the Wakuénai equivalent for the Barasana term ~kubu is malikai liminali, "the owners of chants." Although the role of chanter is formally distinguished from that of ~kubu, all individual ~kubus known to me in the Pirá-Paraná region are also specialist chanters. This shows the importance of distinguishing between the formal categorization of different ritual roles associated with ranked sibs and their de facto allocation among different living individuals.

I also tentatively suggest that the ambiguity surrounding the status of the shaman can be resolved and understood if we relate it to the division between the payé and the ~kubu. The shaman as younger, physically active payé normally enjoys a relatively low status and limited power, a position that corresponds to that of the shaman in the formal ranking, sib-linked ritual roles. The shaman as elderly, reflective, and priestly ~kubu enjoys a relatively high status as political leader, a position that implicitly corresponds to that of the chief. Further, where the payé and ~kubu occur together, the potential for tension or conflict exists between them and will be increased if the payé begins to assert a more prominent leadership role. Such a sit-

15. Societies like those of northwest Amazonia "have not developed into theocratic chiefdoms due to the strongly egalitarian, or "bottom up," ethos of everyday social life that counterbalances the ongoing production of highly specialized ritual hierarchy" (Wright, 1992, 14).

uation probably arose during contact with colonial powers, when payés became the prophet-leaders of millennial cults.

The Early Millennial Cults

During the latter half of the last century, the Indians living in the frontier zone of Colombia, Venezuela, and Brazil took part in a series of messianic movements, led by shaman-prophets claiming a divine mission and identifying themselves with Christ. Though these movements were centered around Arawakan ritual specialists from the Guainia and Içana basins, their effects spread southward to the Vaupés region and involved Tukanoan Indians both as adepts and followers and as leaders of their own cult activities. Though each movement has been identified with a particular leader, the cultural similarities and frequent contacts between the different Arawakan and Tukanoan groups of the area, the similarities in the reported details of the movements, their connections in time and space, and the common socioeconomic circumstances related to contact with outsiders suggest that they formed part of a much wider and more widespread state of religious ferment that affected the region as a whole.

So far, the anthropological studies of these movements have focused exclusively on material from Venezuela and Brazil (see Hill and Wright 1988, Schaden 1983/84, Wright 1981, Wright and Hill 1986). Published material from the Colombian Vaupés and data from my own field research among the Barasana provide new insight into these movements and confirm that they were more widespread than is commonly supposed. Before presenting the Colombian material I will give a brief synthesis of some of the better known cases.[16]

As far as is known, the movements began around 1857 with the preaching of Venancio Aniseto Kamiko (also called Venancio Christu) and continued into the 1880s. The leaders of these movements— Venancio Aniseto Kamiko (Baniwa, 1857–58), Alexandre Christo (Tukano, 1858), Aniseto (Baniwa, 1875 and following), and Vicente Christo (Arapaço, 1878 and following)—were shamans with extraor-

---

16. Though the data does not always support such generalizations, for reasons of brevity I shall generalize between cases. For the details of each movement, the interested reader should consult Wright 1981.

dinary powers of clairvoyance, transformation, and curing. They claimed that in visions they ascended to heaven and had direct communication with the dead, with spirits, with the saints, and with the Christian God and various indigenous figures—Tupana, Yáperikuli, Oaki—who are often identified with him. The prophets claimed to be Christ, and some of their followers took on the names of the saints—Santa Maria, São Lourenço, and Padre Santo.

These prophets preached that the Indians should cease to work for the white people. The white people would be expelled, and a great fire would bring an end to the present world and mark the start of a paradise free from exploitation and oppression by outsiders, free of the illnesses they brought, and with an abundance of food to end the starvation and misery brought on by colonial contact. In preparation for the new order, to hasten its arrival and to guarantee their salvation, the faithful were told to fast, abandon work in their gardens, and bring presents and gifts of food for their leaders.

The prophets organized mass meetings in special houses where they preached in front of crosses and conducted baptisms, confessions, marriages, and divorces. At these meetings, carved wooden images of Christ were used, and the people danced and sang, carrying small wooden crosses in their hands and singing, "máariye, máariye" ("heron, heron")—a common refrain from a genre of sacred dance music found among the contemporary Arawakans and Tukanoans (see fig. 1). The prophets predicted the coming of the Catholic missionaries and claimed responsibility for their arrival, but in taking over the role of the priests and employing Christian imagery and symbolism, they implied that the missionaries were now redundant. In other respects the gatherings appear to have had much in common with caboclo saint's day festivals and with indigenous dance feasts (*dabukuri*) where food is exchanged between affinally related groups.

The shaman-prophets were also famous as curers. As part of their cures, they anointed people's bodies with magical substances and covered them with leaves. They also went into trance and acted as mediums, ascending to the sky to bring down the spirits of the dead so that they could communicate with the living and assist the shamans in curing the sick. The dances themselves also protected people from disease and brought them health.

With their revolutionary promise of freedom from oppression and injustice, and with the Indians in open rebellion, the movements

FIG. 1.   Page from bilingual Tukanoan/Spanish booklet produced by the Servicio de Salúd, Mitú, Comisaría del Vaupés, Colombia, as part of a campaign against tuberculosis (author and artist unknown). The drawing shows people dancing with crosses while payés shake bunches of leaves and employ visionary techniques as part of their curing. The caption reads: "The payés knew nothing of TB and began to find out where it came from. They put drops of liquid from a plant obtained from Waimasa (the spirits) in their eyes so that they could see the disease through their visions."

were bound to arouse the suspicions and hostility of the local white traders, missionaries, and government officials. As they became more militant, the leaders were banished or put in prison, and the villages of their followers were raided by parties of soldiers who burned down the houses, stole anything of value, and sent the inhabitants fleeing to the forest. Over a period of some twenty-five years, as each movement was suppressed, the agitation went underground, flaring up again at a later date and in a different place.

Discussion

Features of these movements show clear parallels with the indigenous shamanism and religion of the area and with elements of Christianity.

Superficially, a number of features of the movements—crosses, hymn singing, confessions of sin and pleas for forgiveness, baptisms, marriages, and the figures of God, Christ, and the saints—appear to be direct borrowings from Catholicism. However, these elements were often mediated through the folk beliefs of the local caboclo population and were reinterpreted in the light of indigenous beliefs and practices.

Venancio Christu was well versed in Christian ideas, having been brought up by a preacher and having spent his childhood among caboclos. To begin with, he called himself a saint, and many features of his movement and of those that followed show clear parallels with the local saint cults. Some of the prophets' assistants took on the names of saints, the offerings of food made to the shaman-prophets parallel those made by caboclos to saints in return for protection and redemption from sin, and saints figured prominently in the cult songs as promising forgiveness of sins.

The rites of baptism performed by the cult leaders combined aspects of Christianity and Indian religion. Like the confessions and singing that went with them, these rites promised redemption from sin and suffering. The epidemics and outbreaks of new diseases that came with colonial contact were interpreted in terms of sin, but the Indians' notion of sin had clear affinities with their own understanding of disease causation. In this area, illness is often diagnosed in terms of breaches of food taboos, a point that clarifies why fasting was so important and why some cult leaders forbade the consumption of meat and chilli peppers (see Buchillet and Galvão, n.d.).

In addition to their parallel with the shamanic practice of water throwing, these baptisms have resonances with indigenous naming practices. Personal names, conferred by shamans of the VS type, are the seat of the collective ancestral soul that each individual acquires soon after birth. The appropriation of the most powerful names from Christian mythology appears to have been part of a more general strategy of wresting control of new religious forces and assimilating them to those already known to the Indians. The name Christu was an important aspect of the shaman-leaders' own power, and they used this power to bestow the names of the saints on their followers.[17]

---

17. Two cult leaders, Vicente Anizetto Kamiko and Anizetto himself, shared the same name.

Indians often ask foreigners other than priests to bestow names on their children. Historically traders often fulfilled this role, and some Indians kept little figures of

Identifying themselves with Christ, the prophet-shamans claimed that they could ascend to the sky to speak with deities. Contemporary Tukanoan and Arawakan Indians often liken powerful jaguar shamans to Christ or to figures in mythology identified with him, and the shamans themselves claim that, in curing, they ascend to the sky to speak with indigenous ancestors or Christian deities. Such ascents are talked of in terms of a "death" and "rebirth."

The shamans often interpret critical illness as a divine calling, and their ability to survive such illnesses is treated as an important index of their supernatural powers. Venancio Kamiko began his prophecies following his recovery from illness and attributed his recovery to a divine calling. The prophets are reported to have imposed obligatory fasting on themselves and their followers and to have ordered them to withdraw from productive activities. In this area, fasting and withdrawal from work figures prominently in shamanic training, in the treatment of illness, and in preparation for ritual activity. The gifts that the prophets ordered their followers to bring likewise parallel the payments made to shamans for curing and other services.

More directly, indigenous accounts of the movements often state explicitly that the prophet-leaders were shamans of the ecstatic or HS type. The Brazilian Desana refer to these leaders as "payés of the cross" and describe how they used hallucinogenic snuff in their cults and how they obtained from the sky holy water that they used in curing (see Buchillet and Galvão, n.d.). The use of this water is explicitly linked with the shaman's practice of water throwing. Evidence also suggests a correspondence between the hand-held crosses used by the prophets and their followers in their meetings and the gourd rattles used by the shamans in curing and by the dancers at feasts (see fig. 1).

The details of the messianic gatherings show clear parallels with more traditional dance feasts. In both contexts, singing and dancing figure as key transformatory devices mediating between mundane and spiritual existence. In the mythology of the area, ancestral spirit

---

saints in special nichelike boxes for them to use on these occasions (see Koch-Grünberg 1909/10: 185).

Indians in the Pirá-Paraná region still bear names like Christu (Christo), Sãtiago (Santiago), Pau (Paulo), Poro (Paulo), Atuni (Antonio), and Maria, which they associate directly wtih the early messianic cults.

beings became human as the result of singing, dancing, or drumming. In the case of feasts, singing and dancing temporarily transform the state of ordinary people back into that of spirits. In the case of messianism, this singing and dancing was meant to transform the people and their world into a permanent state of immortality in a paradise inhabited by the ancestors, with abundant food, no work, and no suffering—a transformation that would reverse the original creation.

The ability to foretell the future is also a feature of shamanism in this area. The prophets foretold the ending of the present world, sometimes in a cataclysmic fire, sometimes in darkness accompanied by violent storms, and sometimes by the world being turned upside down. The theme of the ending of the world and the coming of a new order figures prominently in local mythology, most notably in the myth of Jurupary, who was burned to death in a universal conflagration. The fire was the origin of both the sacred flutes and trumpets used in clan ancestor cults and of human sickness and suffering. Following the fire Jurupary ascended to heaven, where he lives in a world free from suffering. The Indians' stories of the prophet leaders describe how they ascended to the skies to make contact with these ancestral figures and how, following their deaths, they too became immortal beings in heaven.

The Background to the Movements

By the beginning of the nineteenth century, the Tukanoan and Arawakan Indians living along the Río Negro and along the lower parts of its major western affluents, the Içana, Guainia, and Vaupés, had already had considerable contact with colonial society. Slave raids in the first half of the eighteenth century had depleted the population of the upper Río Negro, and though on a much reduced scale, they were still happening at the time of Wallace's visit in 1850. Missionaries, soldiers, and merchants had made repeated efforts to settle the Indians in nucleated villages, some located near centers of agricultural production far downstream. The Indians were also exposed to new diseases against which they had little resistance, and they suffered waves of epidemics from the late eighteenth century onward.

At the end of the century, the collapse of the plantation-based economy on the Río Negro brought a period of relative peace for the still surviving Indians. They abandoned the downstream villages and returned to their homelands to reconstruct their society, a process involving the revival of traditional forms and the integration of elements of new technology and ideology. They became increasingly dependent on steel and other foreign goods, and the sporadic activity of the missionaries and contact with the caboclo population exposed them to orthodox and folk Catholic beliefs, which they interpreted selectively in the light of their own ideas and experience.

This brief period of relative calm was soon shattered by the rise of a mercantile economy based on a combination of debt bondage and various kinds of taxation, forced labor, and outright slavery. Harried by traders and soldiers, the Indians built boats, made ropes, produced farinha, and extracted products from the forest—all for scant, if any, reward. In addition to exploitation, they suffered hunger and disease, the loss of children taken away to be "civilized," and the theft of their food and property. It is no wonder that they rebelled and sought hope in the missionaries' teachings.

It is important not to slip too readily into presenting Indians and white people as two opposed blocs. The relations between Indians and colonists and between the different components of the colonial society contain many tensions and ambiguities. Neither white people nor Indians can be treated as unambiguous and unitary categories. On an expanding frontier, the terms *White, Indian,* and the intermediary *caboclo* are relative and contextually defined. But this is not simply a matter of verbal categories. Venancio and the other prophets were men with considerable experience of colonial society. Some of their followers were caboclos, and the traders and soldiers these prophets opposed were either acculturated Baniwa and Baré or of mixed descent.

Furthermore, some Indians acted as the agents and allies of the colonial powers, either out of their own self-interest or because, as official appointees, they had no choice. These middlemen, from groups classed by the colonial powers as "settled" or "civilized," were charged with negotiating resettlement, administering a tax on farinha, providing child and adult labor, and organizing punitive slave raids against the more isolated *gentios* of the interior. Like their contemporary counterparts, the men who carried out these orders were in an ambiguous position liable to generate tensions within the group. A hint of such tension is contained in the oral history of the

Hohódene, a Wakuénai sib, where different chiefs debate over whether or not to follow a mestizo trader and relocate downstream, a debate that leads to the splitting up of the group (see Wright and Hill 1986:38).

Some of these middlemen became powerful chiefs in their own right and amassed large amounts of wealth, both indigenous valuables captured in raids on their neighbors and manufactured goods supplied by the traders in exchange for slaves, labor, local produce, and even the sexual services of their women (see Coudreau 1887:148). They were feared and hated by the more isolated groups. The Uanano tell how they joined their Baniwa allies in raids on the headwaters of the Tiquié and Papurí (see Chernela 1983:445–48). From the other side of the fence, the peoples of the Pirá-Paraná and Apaporís tell of a terrible period when they were raided by the cannibal Barea Gawa, who carried off men, women, and children to the Río Negro, from whence they never returned.

Like the traders, these middlemen exploited the ambiguities between kinship obligations, indigenous barter, and capitalist credit that often underlie debt bondage across ethnic frontiers (see Hugh-Jones 1992). The Indians' demand for manufactured goods was also, and still remains, an essential part of a system that creates dependency and converts it into gross exploitation. The vehement rejection of exploitation through debt bondage emerges clearly as a theme of the Arawakan millennial movements (see Wright and Hill 1986). Its counterpart, the theme of dependency on manufactured goods, is clear in the cult activity in the Pirá-Paraná region, where elements of Christian belief were linked with the acquisition of merchandise. Similar ideas may have played a part in the Arawakan movements as well. A hint of them occurs in a Desana account of Vaupés millennialism in which Camillo (=Vicente Kamiko) is described as God living in a well-lit house in the sky that is filled with food (both Indian crops and white peoples' food, like rice and beans) and all kinds of goods.[18]

Alongside internal friction caused by alliances between Indians and outsiders is evidence of tensions between those engaged in cult activity and others who avoided such involvement. One reason for

---

18. The text states, "He had everything: concertinas, a violin." When the colonial authorities arrested Vicente Christo's three assistants, Padre Santo, Santa Maria, and São Lourenço, among the things found in their possession were three old shotguns and two old violas (Wright and Hill 1986).

these tensions may have been that the cult activities attracted military reprisals that others wished to avoid. There is evidence that some Indians rejected the message of the prophets and doubted their claims and authority. Wright (1981:296) mentions Tukano and Tariana chiefs who were in conflict with Alexandre Christu on this score. The claims and pretensions of the prophet shamans are also likely to have led to conflict and jealousy between them and other shaman rivals. Tensions between the shaman-prophets and other Indians and doubts about the truth of their message also emerge as a theme in accounts of cult activity in the middle Vaupés and Pirá-Paraná. Using the label "sin," these prophets preached against the *brujos*, or evil shamans; and when the prophets died, their deaths were put down to poisoning by jealous rivals (see Buchillet and Galvão, n.d.).

Further ambiguities can be seen in the position of the missionaries vis-à-vis both Indians and traders. On the one hand, the missionaries set themselves up as protectors of the Indians against the abuses of traders and soldiers. This protective role is seen most clearly in their opposition to the slave raids against the Makú and other more isolated Indian groups. They also engaged in trade with the Indians, supplying them with manufactured goods in return for labor and local products, a role that brought them into sharp conflict with the local traders, or *regatões* (see Coudreau 1887:149, 153). Padre Coppi applied to Manaus for official permission to expel both traders and payés from the region by armed force, and in his diary, he devotes as much space to harangues against the former as he does to diatribes against the latter (see Coppi, n.d.).

On the other hand, the missionaries themselves imposed a harsh regime and were involved in the slave trade (see Spruce 1908:355), in the enforced relocations of Indian settlements, and in the "civilization" of their inhabitants. Most importantly of all, they waged a vigorous campaign against the Indians' religion in general and against the shamans in particular. At stake was the issue of who were the legitimate representatives and controllers of supernatural power. The shamans saw the missionaries as their counterparts and rivals and accredited them with the same powers. For them the Christian God was their own Jurupary, the Indian culture hero, whose virgin mother Amaru was none other than the Virgin Mary. In conducting baptisms and marriages as part of their messianic activities, they were taking over the priest's functions and implying that the missionaries' presence and pretensions were redundant. When priests arrived to investigate Alexandre's movement, those involved sent a message saying that "they did not need Padres for they already had their own" (Wright 1981:293). For their part, the Padres saw the shamans as satanic imposters and their cult of Jurupary as Devil worship.

These tensions came to a head in the 1880s when the Franciscan missionary Padre Coppi installed himself at Ipanoré, a Tariana village described by Coudreau as "par excellence a village of payés" (1887:152). As the climax of his attack on native religion, Coppi publicly exposed the sacred Jurupary masks to the women and children of the village. In the uproar that followed, the missionaries were expelled from the area.

Coudreau, from whom the information on this incident comes, also provides some glimpses of religious tensions within Indian society itself.

> The payés do not agree about this Tupan; some, but few, celebrate feasts in his honour: it is he, they say, who created everything that exists. But many among them do not agree that the Tupan of the White people is the same as their own.
>
> They consider that one and the same Tupan cannot serve for two races. When they are drunk they are arrogant in their affirmations. "Our God," they say, "is more powerful than that of the White people." But here it is above all Jurupary who they have in mind. Quite coolly, those who interpret the mythology establish a kind of vague hierarchy: Jurupary, the Terrible; the Indians' Tupan, the Good one; the White man's Tupan, the Powerful. But they are more keen to take charge of the latter than they are frightened of him. (1887:193–94)

Following the exposure of the masks, these tensions became acute. Different shamans had competing visions: to one, Tupan appeared with a message that the Indians should submit to the priests and renounce their traditional feasts; to another, Jurupary said, "Tell the people of the Uaupés that I am not so stupid as to tell them to abandon me"; to yet another, he appeared saying, "The mysteries have been profaned, you serve our enemies or you do not care, the great Jurupary, the powerful, the terrible is angry with you" Coudreau 1887:200).

With the exposure of the masks, the cult of Jurupary and the messianic activity of dancing with crosses were now firmly opposed, a split that threatened the Indians' religion and the position of the shamans. Powerful shamans, in close touch with divinity, had claimed that God or Tupana, a figure equated with the creator of the world and father of Jurupary in Indian mythology, had sent missionaries with shamanic powers at their own bequest. These same missionaries were now attacking the cult of Jurupary. It is highly probable that this opposition between messianism and Jurupary found resonances in the division between the ecstatic jaguar shaman and the priestly ~kubu. The messianic prophets were primarily jaguar shamans of the HS type, and the dominant figures in the ancestral cult of Jurupary were ~kubus.

There has not simply been straight opposition between Indians and white people in which elements of Christianity, appropriated and reinterpreted by Indian shamans, were used as a protest against colonial forces. Instead, such protest emerged as part of a much more complex pattern of tensions and contradictions that also created internal divisions in Indian society. I suspect that some of these tensions involved the relation between the payé and the ~kubu.

Without better data, it is impossible to say exactly how these tensions were related to the changing fortunes of indigenous shamanism through time. All we really know is that after its initial outburst in the second half of the last century, messianism declined along the major rivers exposed to more intense contact; that it persisted much longer in the more isolated headwater areas; and that since the decline of millennialism, jaguar shamanism appears to have declined in importance throughout the region as a whole.

I suggest that the decline of messianism is directly linked with that of jaguar shamanism and that both are related to the establishment of permanent and effective Catholic missions in the first decades of this century. Where Catholic missionaries became firmly established, the priests asserted their control over Christian symbols and ritual and over the religious life of the Indians and directly attacked the more visible activities of the jaguar shamans. In these areas, ~kubus have continued to practice, though their activities are reduced in scope and carried on in a semiclandestine fashion. In the more isolated headwater areas, where direct missionary influence dates from the late 1960s, jaguar shamans appear to have come to prominence during a short period of cult activity and then to have undergone a similar decline, with some of their functions and attributes being taken over by the ~ kubus, who continue to flourish today.

In the Arawakan area to the north of the Vaupés, from the 1940s onward, the hegemony of the Catholic missionaries was challenged by a highly successful missionary campaign led by the American evangelist Sofia Müller of the fundamentalist New Tribes Mission and, to a much lesser extent, by the World Evangelization Crusade. Today, some 80 percent of the Arawakans are *creyentes*, or "believers," with the rest nominally Catholic (see Journet 1988:23). Though there were probably many reasons underlying the extraordinary enthusiasm with which the Baniwa took to evangelical Protestantism (see Journet 1988:23–40), one important factor seems to have been their earlier history of messianism. According to Wright, Sofia's message was couched "in almost the exact same terms as the early messiahs" and has given rise to "a movement with strongly messianic and millenial overtones." Lead by native pastors, these Protestant converts are overtly opposed to shamanic practices. Despite this opposition, jaguar shamans are still most active, and small-scale millenial movements still broke out in the 1950s and 1960s (Wright 1981:85–87).

Cult Activity in the Middle Vaupés Area

Although the movements described above had their focus among the Arawakan groups immediately to the north, they spread southward among the Tukanoan Indians living in the basin of the Río Vaupés. Alexandre Christo, a Tukano Indian and the second prophet, lived near the mouth of Japú Igarapé at Juquira, between the Tariana settlements of Ipanoré and Jauaraté, and his movement attracted many of the more isolated Indians from the surrounding forests. Vicente Christo, an Arapaço, was based in the headwaters of Japú Igarape, and his movement had influence throughout the Vaupés area. Further cult activity took place in the Papurí area and up along the Río Tiquié into the headwater area toward the Río Pirá-Paraná.

Although the data on these cults is fragmentary, it seems clear that they were in the same general idiom and related to those already described. It is not possible to assign precise dates to these latter cults, but the evidence of contemporary Indian informants suggests that they came after the downstream movements described earlier. Buchillet and Galvão (n.d.) provide a genealogy of the leaders of the movement, which I shall use to order the data.

According to Buchillet and Galvão, Camillo (Vicente Christu) taught Alizente (Alexandre) and Tomaso. Tomaso then taught Vicente and a Tukano called Joaquim Parakata, who announced that, as the present earth was rotten and full of sickness, he would create a new one by turning it upside down. Three generations later, a miraculous child called Maria appeared among the Desana of the Makuku, an affluent of the Papurí. The story of Maria is well known throughout the Vaupés (see also Anon. 1970:23–24, Builes 1951, and Kumu and Kenhiri 1980:86–87).

Maria was the daughter of an old woman also called Maria. Some stories say that she had no father; others say that she witnessed her own conception. With water from a crystal goblet, the old woman anointed the young Maria's eyes so that she had visions. The child, who was called a saint, prophesied the arrival of the missionaries and, in the presence of a cross, began to preach about heaven and hell and sin and salvation and to sing special songs. People came from miles around to hear the child, and the old Maria organized gatherings at which the faithful brought flowers for the young girl and danced around a cross ornamented with leaves.[19]

At an early age, the child cried a lot, made a cross, and began to sing strange songs. Later she made her father prepare a drum and a special cross of red hardwood and persuaded her female friends to get their fathers to do likewise. Initially the adults disapproved of her songs and doubted what she told them. "You are talking rubbish when you speak like this," they said to Maria. "You are lying and just want to frighten us" (Buchillet and Galvão, n.d.). But when she told them that her songs had been taught her by Christ and would release the people from their heavy burden of sin, they agreed to learn the songs, which could also make the souls of the dead ascend to heaven. The elders now began to believe in Christ, who was in the sky, but who would one day appear among them. Her fame spread from the Papurí to the Vaupés, Tiquié, and Pirá-Paraná, and people came from miles around to hear her.

---

19. At the time of Builes's visit in 1950, the hardwood cross was still standing on the site of the maloca where Maria lived. Buchillet's data mentions the Salesians moving this cross to Jauareté.

The white people sent her a box containing a flag and other ornaments used by the caboclos for their saints' day festivals. In it they put a curse that caused a measles epidemic among her followers. After the epidemic, Maria announced the end of the world, a time when all sinners would be turned into animals with horns and be eaten by jaguars and spirits. She added that deer and cows had once been people who were punished for their sins, a theme that reappears in a Barasana text. Maria was finally poisoned by jealous neighbors, and after her death, the cult ceased. But her songs, the songs of the Holy Cross, are still fresh in the memories of the older men, who still sing them to enthusiastic shouts of "Viva Santa Cruz."[20]

Maria was followed by a Tukano prophet called Lino Sêwa or Santo Lino, who also had a following that extended from the Papurí to the Vaupés and Tiquié. He lived at Termite Rapid, the site of the first Montfortian mission on the Papurí. He told everyone to make their own cross, taught them sacred songs, and preached that all his

---

20. According to Builes (1951), her songs went as follows:

1. María, María, ori!
(Mary, Mary flowers).

2. María, María, oriá
oriá, oriá.
(Mary, Mary flowers,
flowers, flowers).

3. Santa, santa, santa,
María, santa, santa.
(Holy, holy, holy,
Mary, holy, holy).

4. María, santa mano
Virgo, perdone pecadores,
perdone pecadores,
perdone pecadores.
(Our holy Mary
Virgin, forgive (us) sinners,
forgive (us) sinners,
forgive (us) sinners).

More or less identical songs were recorded by C. Hugh-Jones in 1982 in a Tukano village on the Tiquié below Parí-Cachoeira and known to the Barasana of the Pirá-Paraná. Other verses of these include:

Orire dupeoda Santa María,
Orire dupeoda Santa María.
(Put down the flowers, Holy Mary,
Put down the flowers, Holy Mary).

San Menitu María, San Menitu María,
María San Menitu, María San Menitu,
Perdona di perdona.
(Saint Benedict María, Saint Benedict Mary,
Mary Saint Benedict, Mary Saint Benedict,
forgive (us), forgive (us)).

followers would ascend to heaven. He also effected many cures with medicines of his own creation and was responsible for an extraordinary flush of flowers in the local forests (see Brüzzi Alves da Silva 1962:320–21). This Lino Sêwa is almost certainly the same as Yewá, a prophet who used a magic mirror given him by God to foretell the arrival of the missionaries (Kumu and Kenhiri 1980:87).

Buchillet and Galvão (n.d.) talk of a prophet called ~Yehuri. ~Yehuri also lived at Termite Rapid and was probably the same person as Santo Lino. He was a water-throwing shaman whose cult used parica snuff and blessings of holy water obtained from the sky. ~Yehuri announced the end of the world, a period of darkness when jaguars and spirits would punish all sinners by eating them, the Indians would become white people, children would give birth, and babies would be born hairy and would speak from their mothers' wombs as a sign of their divinity.

~Yehuri was followed by another Tukano, Raimundo. Raimundo's father was a payé who wanted to teach him to become a shaman by giving him parica snuff. Initially Raimundo had no visions and appears to have resisted his father's wishes. Later he accepted the call, and having made a hardwood cross, which he set up in front of his house, he began to predict the coming end of the world in a similar vein to his predecessors, much to the annoyance and jealousy of other shamans, who tried to kill him with sorcery. In addition to preaching, Raimundo gave his followers parica, but they failed to have the same visions.

Raimundo was finally poisoned, and Buchillet's informant ends his narration with the following words:

> Raimundo was the last. This talk ended with him. Parica ended with him too. The people who talked of these things no longer exist. That was of another time. . . . When Raimundo was older he had this to say: "I did these things but I couldn't stand the strain. When people want to do these things, many people come together. They listen and after hearing much they get tired and jealous." (Buchillet and Galvão, n.d.)

These words neatly summarize the decline of both messianism and the use of hallucinogenic parica snuff, the mark of the payé.

Cult Activity in the Pirá-Paraná Region

Information on messianism in the Pirá-Paraná region comes from two brothers, Pasico and Pau, living close to the headwaters of the Rio Tiquié. The Barasana refer to Vaupés messianic cult activity as "Bitter's songs" (*Sie basa*) and tell how they were taught the songs by "Bitter" (*Sie*) or ~Waribi, ("He-who-went-away"). ~Waribi, a trickster figure and culture hero well known throughout the Vaupés under various different names, is the source of shamanic powers and is responsible for the creation of the first people. He is also identified with Christ: rejected by the Indians, he departs from this earth and creates white people, their possessions, and their powers, together with the ills and suffering they bring (see Hugh-Jones 1988).

Pasico's story of messianism tallies well with the information provided above and brings together the time dimensions of mythology and history. Not just a factual description, it combines details of the cults with an account of how ~Waribi returns to offer the Indians a second chance—freedom from suffering and, by implication, access to the material wealth that he created and gave to the white man. This second chance is conditional on their acceptance of his message.

Pasico's story comes at the end of a long myth. Before it begins, ~Waribi has rid the world of the last evil creatures and cannibals left over from earlier times. Pasico's (much edited) story continues as follows.

> "There's going to be no more of that," said ~Waribi, "now there are going to be beautiful people." He was about to create the ancestors, all the peoples of the world, with his songs. "Now I'm going to sing my song," he said, "the song of the heavens, of the heavenly water."
>
> He went up into the sky to fetch a small gourd of special water. He was going to pour it over himself and wash off all the dirt and pollution he had picked up in his earlier travels. This was the first baptism, what the priests do today.
>
> Now he was ready to begin his songs, so he called all the people to him. He did this where he came to earth, where they first sang Bitter's songs, on the Vaupés at Bitter's beach, at Bitter Jaguar's mountain. The Tukano were the first to hear his songs, then he taught our people at Huriti, where there is another of

his mountains, the place where he sang. He called our ancestor Yeba, and he was prepared to listen. He called the Bará, the Tukano, the Arapaço, and even some of the Tatuyo, and they all listened. But the Taiwano, other Tatuyo, and the Cubeo wouldn't listen. ~ Waribi taught the other groups, the Tuyuka, the Tukano, and the Bará. Lots of people came to hear the songs he taught.

From the Tukano the dance spread from group to group up the Tiquié. Many different peoples sang these songs, but the ~ Yake ~ Hidoria [a Barasana clan] wouldn't. They said, "It's all rubbish, white people's stuff. They are singing the white people's songs." The ~ Hidoa ~ Sida [a Tatuyo clan] didn't sing them either, nor the Makuna—they didn't know about them and said they were rubbish. The Tanimuka and Yukuna, all those downstream peoples, they had nothing to do with it. It came this way, up the Tiquié. And ~ Waribi had come from that way too, in the beginning. It came up as far as here and then stopped. That's how they knew about those dances—because ~ Waribi had left the knowledge with them.

There was much debate as to whether or not to listen to him. Yeba, the Barasana ancestor, asked him, "What are your songs like anyhow? I'm going to sing my own songs, our people's songs," he said. Others said to ~ Waribi, "You're a stranger, not one of us." "I am good," replied ~ Waribi. "I'm not lying." But lots of people doubted him and said he was lying. They said, "I'm having nothing to do with him. He's a liar, a brute, a bastard. He knows nothing." When they said these things, he sent them away. "You go and stand over there," he said, cursing them, causing them to fall down, and making their feet and hands stiff. He turned them into wild beasts—caimans, tapirs, deer, and jaguars. "People like that are not meant to hear my words," ~ Waribi said. They missed their chance to become people. "It's your own fault," he said to them. The ones who refused to listen to him were turned into animals with horns and with paws like animals or dogs. Everyone was frightened, so they all came. That's what my father said.

~ Waribi brought special water for baptism with him; it was meant for them to use today, too. Stone Flycatcher [a mythical character identified with the Holy Ghost] was there with him.

He said to the people, "His songs are good; listen to them. His message is good; he's against people aguing, fighting, and killing each other. He's already got rid of all those who fight and kill and who eat people."

"What are you going to sing about?" they asked him. "I shall sing about my mother," ~Waribi replied. "Lets hear it then," they said. "One of you must respond as I sing," said ~Waribi. A man from the Waiya ~Koaboda clan [Barasana] stood not listening to him, and others, the ~Hadera [a Barasana sub-group], were also not attending to him and were acting as if they did not want to see him. "What are you doing?" asked ~Waribi, "This is for everyone to learn, for all the people." This happened at ~Badaitara House, at Huriti, an ancestral site on the Apaporís.

~Waribi had a special drink with him, Bitter's wine. Yeba sipped a little bit of this drink. Then all the people came into the house to hear him teach, and they were pleased by what he told them. There were also other people who were with his mother. "My mother has not disappeared," said ~Waribi; "here she is with me."

But others still said, "It's all lies; he's tricking us. He wants to put an end to fighting and killing. He's going to finish us all. Let's kill him." But he replied, "You can't do that. I cannot be killed. I am from the heavens." "Well, we'll see about that," they replied, eager to kill him. Others said, "Don't kill him." They were Indians, who liked him and wanted to hear his message.

Then he began to sing. The people listened, but they couldn't sing his songs. That's why today, too, we do not know you white people's songs. First ~Waribi taught them the song about Paul.

"Pau ~sato, Pau ~sato,
sa Kiritu, sa Kiritu,
yi dopena ~Satiagu,
Pau ~sato, Pau ~sato, Pau ~sato,"

he sang. "So that's how it goes," they said.

"Should we sing it too?" they asked themselves. Haruhi the Dancer said, "I'll sing his song. How does it go?" he asked. "I'll tell you bit by bit," ~Waribi replied, adding, "Keep quiet you lot. If you want to talk you must go outside." That's why today, too, the priests always tell people to stop talking.

Then ~Waribi sang some more:

"~Baría ~sato, ~Baría ~sato,
ridopena ~Satiagu,
~Baría ~sato, ~Baría ~sato, ~Baría ~sato."

He was singing about his mother, the Virgin Mary.

Then he sang about flowers:

"Gori ~sato, gori ~sato,
~Sata ~Baría, gori ~sato."

"Ah! So that's how it goes," they said. "I'll see if I can do it too," said Yeba. "Look at him singing along like a woman," they said. "I'm no woman," said Haruhi the Dancer. "Yeba can sing along with him if he likes, but I'm going to sing my own songs." He wanted to be an Indian. "Yeba's just pretending. He's not ~Waribi's son. He's not his younger brother," they said, jeering at Yeba, who insisted on singing along with ~Waribi.

Then ~Waribi sang again:

"~Sa Kirítu, ~Sa Kirítu,
ridopena ~Satiagu, ~Sa Kirítu,
~sato ~Baría, ~sato ~Baría."

Then ~Waribi said, "I'm going to baptize you. I'm going to wash you with this heavenly water." He washed Yeba so he was like a white man. "Let's follow him," said Yeba. "We should all take part in the dances, the children, the old people, all of us. That's what he wants." And that's how the old people first began to sing these songs, the ones he taught them.

But Haruhi the Dancer and others rejected the songs, saying that the Indians should sing their own songs. "Those are not our songs. Our songs make us live. They give life to our hearts. We are forest people."

At a place on the Tiquié, ~Waribi made Bitter's flesh and Bitter's drink. The drink was pineapple wine, which came from

a plant the Star people had planted. The people drank the pineapple wine from little gourds, saying, "It's really Bitter's blood."
In their drunken vision, they saw Bitter as a man. He came along
and baptized them. That's what my father told me. It was really
strange.

~ Waribi brought green plantains and made little round flat
cakes, which he roasted on the griddle for them to eat just like
what the priests give out today. But they wouldn't eat them.
Then he made rice, in tiny pieces and very white. "They must
be tobacco seeds," they said, not knowing what they were. So
~ Waribi took it away from them, saying, "They don't know
me," and he gave them to the white people, so only they have
rice now. He also offered them the tobacco with very big leaves,
but because they didn't recognize it, he gave it to the white people
too. The old people said that he hid everything away from us.

The people came with flowers of all colors—red, yellow, green.
They came singing into the house carrying crosses of red hardwood. In the middle of the house was a big table for the wine.
The man who led it all was a shaman, someone like me who
knows and thinks. They sang with him as he stood by a cross
over there. He wore a hatlike thing made from woven palm leaf,
like a priest's hat. He was like a priest. He also wore a vestment
made from a strip of white bark cloth pleated like our bark cloth
dance aprons. And he had another longer strip on top, very fine
and soft with designs painted on it. He didn't wear feathers—
that's quite another thing, nothing to do with this. It was not
like one of our dances. They did not dance; they just sat in the
house and sang and put the flowers they brought in pots of water
on the table, lots of them.

They did this at special times like the white people's fiestas.
And if they failed to do it, it was very bad; there was lots of
illness. They did not drink yagé; they just sang together. The
shamans told them not to fight each other, not to be angry and
not to argue. They preached what ~ Waribi had taught them.

The leaders were shamans, and they gave people names from
these dances: Pau from Saint Paul, Maria from Santa Maria,
Christ, and Santiago, too. But then our fathers, especially the
men of the ~ Hadera, said again that we should not do this

because it was a White peoples' thing. "They are White people, beasts. We should not associate with them. It's all lies and nothing to do with us. We should do our own dances. We should dance in macaw feathers and paint," they said—they were really against it all.

Our people did not do their own dances in those days; they sang the ~Waribi songs instead. They were not shamans, and they didn't drink yagé either. They said yagé was horrible, like the white people do today. The other people, the Tatuyo and the people from downstream, said, "They must be white people, ~Waribi's children, that's why they sing Bitter's songs like the white people do." But the elders said, "We are people, too; we are not white people. The white people are the ones who know how to make axes, knives, and clothes. We are just imitating them."

Then, after that ~Yake ~Hido ~Baki [the ancestor of a Barasana clan], their elder brother, said, "You are of my group. You are real people. Why don't you do your own dances. You know how to dance, too." So he taught them the dances and gave them ancient tobacco, and then they too knew how to sing and dance, they who had once sung the Bitter songs. Our grandfather Sira the Dancer began to sing our own songs, the forest peoples' songs. He was the first to sing. They snuffed the old people's snuff, and they were shamans. Before that there were no chanters and no ~kubus, only people who did Bitter's songs. Today we are ~kubus, and we know our stuff. And that's how it is today, too—they sing their own songs. This is what my father told me they did. His fathers and grandfathers saw them do that, but he never saw it himself.

Pau's account adds some important details about the rites themselves, their aims, and the shaman's curing sessions that went with them. The songs were brought by emissaries from the Tukano and Bará. Each group had its own ceremonial center named after a saint—Pauro Buro after St. Paul for the Bará, Atuni Tukuro after St. Anthony for the Tatuyo—where people would gather bringing bunches of flowers. In addition to crosses, they made statues of *Sie* or *Oaki* (Jesus/God), which they set up in the house. The people sang their songs both kneeling and walking around the statues, and in addition to priestlike robes, the shamans in charge wore crowns of thorns made from vines.

The aim of the rites, Pau says, was to bring white people and their goods back from the edge of the world, where ~ Waribi had sent them when he created people (see Hugh-Jones 1988). At the time, the Barasana were in need of steel axes and machetes, clothes, and other white goods that were in short supply. There was conflict over these activities, because other shamans were using their powers to keep the white people at bay. To command the spirits of white people to come and to bring them down to earth, the shamans blew spells onto a book painted with red paint and into a gourd of beeswax. The gourd was the gourd now used in the men's cult of flutes and trumpets (see Hugh-Jones 1979). When people were created, the ancestors had been offered a better gourd that guaranteed them immortality and contained the power to make the manufactured goods. The Indians' ancestors had refused this gourd, which was then taken away by white people. When they blew spells on the gourd, white people arrived and talked with the people.

The rites also involved curing and protection from illness. To effect their cures, the shamans used bunches of leaves as rattles and went up into the sky on ladders or vines to call the ancient jaguar shamans who live alongside ~ Waribi and the spirits of white people. Their abode is like a white people's town, with many houses and constant light. The old jaguar shamans would come down to earth dressed in jaguar-skin cloaks. While they were down below, the shaman remained up in the sky. When they had finished their cures, they would swap places once again. For protection from illness, the shamans also carried out baptisms using Bitter's special water. The shaman called Rumbling Jaguar is especially remembered as having cured illness in this manner, as having been involved in the Bitter Dance, and as having encouraged people to fight each other and to attack the white people. For this reason he came into conflict with Sira the Dancer, who advocated peace and a return to the Indians' own way of singing and dancing.

Discussion and Conclusion

Northwest Amazonian millenarian movements were more widespread than has hitherto been supposed. They spread progressively from

Arawakan groups living along the larger northern rivers and having relatively intense contact with colonial society, to more isolated Tukanoan groups living in headwater areas to the south and west. Although the cults shared a number of features in common, conformed to a common pattern, and formed part of a wider whole, significant variations have been correlated with different local socioeconomic circumstances and different degrees of external contact. Despite a common concern with salvation from the ravages of introduced disease and epidemics, the strong element of anticolonial protest, hostility to white people, and rejection of debt servitude manifest in the earlier movements is absent as they spread further south. In the headwater areas, where missionaries were absent and traders rarely ventured, the cults appeaar, in part at least, to have been directed toward obtaining exotic goods that were in short supply.

Another difference is the extent to which shamanic prophecy gave rise to genuinely popular movements. Allowance must be made for the difference between hostile opinions of missionaries and government officials expressed in colonial documents and the relatively benign and sympathetic accounts of present-day Indians. Even so, the leaders of the downstream movements achieved a lasting fame as master shamans and prophets and met with considerable success in generating widespread movements of revolt. Shaman-prophets in the upstream areas, although attracting a wide audience, also met a strong element of doubt and skepticism among ordinary people and outright hostility and jealousy from other shamans.[21] However, jealousy and tensions between rival shamans were not absent from the downstream movements either.

These differences are partly the product of two ends of a temporal sequence known to us through very different kinds of evidence. They are also correlated not only with different local socioeconomic circumstances and intensity of contact with outsiders but with variations in the pattern of dual shamanism in the two areas. There appears to be a difference in the relative importance of the ~kubu and payé as one moves from south to north or from Tukanoan- to Arawakan-speaking areas.

---

21. The only case of a female prophet also comes from the upstream area. A further difference appears to have been a great emphasis on prophecy concerning the arrival of the Salesians and Montfortian missionaries among the upstream cult leaders.

In the Pirá-Paraná area to the south, no one is recognized as a jaguar shaman, and no shaman uses the payé's insignia of parica snuff and gourd rattles, but the ~ kubu continues to flourish, apparently in his full traditional role. These ~ kubus are quite dismissive of the supposed powers of jaguar shamans. They know about parica snuff and about shaking maracas or bunches of leaves, but they find these practices threatening and faintly ridiculous. They emphasize that they are not part of their own group's ancestral heritage but belong to groups further to the north and south. This superior but slightly fearful attitude is reflected in the fact that when ~ kubus wish to run down their rivals' power and knowledge or to imply that they harbor evil intentions, they may refer to them as *yai* or "jaguar." Here, ~ kubu is being opposed to *yai* as good is to bad. Barasana ~ kubus do use techniques, such as water throwing and sucking out pathogenic objects, that are typically associated with the payé, so the division between the two types is not absolute. But they are adamant that real jaguar shamans are a thing of the past, the last ones having been active at the time of the millennial cults. I have no reason to doubt them because there is little evidence of a strong tradition of payés. And because missionaries did not arrive among the Barasana until the late sixties, the payé's disappearance can hardly be attributed to missionary activity.

Along with ~ kubus, payés figure quite prominently in the ethnographic literature on the Tukano and Desana to the north of the Barasana, and jaguar shamanism appears to be especially prominent among the Cubeo, the group physically and culturally closest to the Arawakans further north. But these other Tukanoan groups also claim that the real payés have all but gone. Such claims may partly be a matter of nostalgia, but they also appear to reflect historical reality. Even in 1900, an old shaman was already complaining to Stradelli that "today there are no longer any payés, we are all curandeiros ('curers')" (Brüzzi 1962:278). Indians and anthropologists attribute the decline of the payé to suppression by Catholic missionaries—the highly visible collective seances of the payé were an easy target for the priests. Though also affected by contact, the discreet, solitary, and essentially verbal activities of the ~ kubu were easier to conceal.

The tradition of jaguar shamanism is strongest and most developed in the Arawakan area. Here, despite a long history of Catholic missionary activity followed by evangelical missionaries who waged an incessant and energetic campaign against shamanism, we find not only the fullest and most elaborate ethnographic records for this type but the survival of "jaguar people masters," the most powerful payés of all, right up to the present day. The relatively greater importance of the payé among the Arawakans is related to another difference, namely, their greater cultural emphasis on warfare and trading. Groups of Arawakans waged war on the Tukanoans and raided them for slaves right up to the time of the first messianic cults, and today they continue to supply them with all the manioc graters they use.

Throughout this chapter, I have tried to integrate what is known about messianism more fully with discussions of northwest Amazonian shamanism and to suggest why, despite much talk about them, there are so few powerful payés left in the area today. Part of the answer has, I think, already been given: jaguar shamans became especially prominent as the prophet-leaders of millennial cults. Among the Tukanoans these have subsided, and with them the true jaguar shaman has all but disappeared; among the Arawakans, where there is still strong messianic fervor, jaguar shamans maintain a stronger, if increasingly tenuous, presence. Although some prophets displayed some of the attributes of the ~kubu, the evidence suggests that they were above all payés. If my argument about the relatively greater weighting of the payé's role among the Arawakans is correct, this and their earlier more intense exposure to the pressures from colonial society would be consistent with the fact that millenialism evolved earlier and was more pronounced among them. But I think we can go further than this.

I have suggested above that rivalry, jealousy, and mutual accusations of sorcery are integral features of horizontal shamanism. I also suggested that such rivalry is a much less marked feature of relations between elderly, priestlike ~kubus whose position depends less on virtuoso performance and public acclaim than on wisdom acquired through years of learning and experience. That payés deal primarily with individuals and that their role relates more to the external relations of warfare and hunting also accords with this pattern. The payé is charged with horizontal, or foreign, relations. The ~kubu's main concern is with the reproduction of the group—the passage of generations through time—and with vertical relations between the living and the ancestors that are internal to the clan.

I suggest that the arrival of white people, their relations of alliance and exploitation with different sectors of Indian society, their diseases, their wealth, their powers, and their beliefs exacerbated and increased certain contradictions already present in Indian social organization, one aspect of which was the relation between the payé and the ~kubu. Where sacred and secular powers are merged and limited to few, powerful elder men who are the foci of communal life and whose knowledge is closed, secret, and couched in an esoteric language, the presence of shaman-prophets attracting a large and mixed following and using hallucinogenic drugs for access to supernatural powers is likely to have been threatening.

The elder and more conservative ~kubus, whose inward-directed powers rest on received canon, would have been ill-adapted to cope with the threat posed by white people. Initially, the balance would have been tipped in favor of the more flexible and individualistic payés, who were charged with dealing with outside forces. Using elements of folk Catholicism appropriated and reinterpreted for their own ends, the prophets formulated an effective ritual response and orchestrated collective opposition to the colonial powers.

Millenial cults, armed resistance, and retreat into isolated headwater zones played important, but temporary, roles in the survival of northwest Amazonian Indians. In most of the Tukanoan area, the arrival of permanent Catholic missions brought a certain amount of protection, but this protection had its price—the missions were opposed to shamanism and other manifestations of Indian religion. This opposition appears to have resulted in a decline in the role and significance of the payé. In the areas exposed to direct missionary presence, the ancestor cults were abandoned, and the ~kubu, taking on some of the functions of the payé but with a much reduced role, effectively went underground. What was once shared between the ~kubu and the payé now appears to be shared between the ~kubu and the Catholic priest. In the more isolated areas, the ~kubu has maintained his position. He coexists with younger men who he may dismiss as ineffective payés, but some of whom he knows will be the ~kubus of tomorrow.

Among the Arawakans, where the payés were stronger, a more active millennial tradition persisted. The arrival of the evangelists, with their apocalyptic preaching and hostility to both priests and traders, triggered a new millenarian movement of mass conversion to Protestantism led by converts. Journet suggests that Arawakan evangelism "should be considered as a complex form of acculturation, favouring the return to traditional moral values within a framework borrowed from the dominant culture" (1988:35). One aspect of this is a displacement of the payés by a new form of religious leadership that, though hostile to all forms of shamanism, appears to be a transformation of the role of chant-owner. The new religious leaders are the pastors, whose authority is founded on their ability to read biblical texts, and who also act as secular leaders or chiefs.

Placing shamanism within a wider structural, regional, and historical frame reveals insights that are not apparent when it is seen simply as a traditional practice in an isolated, local context. The role of the shaman is sometimes defined in contradistinction to the priest or chief. Like the relation between their Bororo equivalents, the relation between the payé and the ~ kubu is complementary and linked with antithetical cosmological and sociological principles. But this relation also contains the potential for rivalry and tension. How these contradictions work out in practice depends on the particular historical circumstances of the groups involved, their internal relations and cultural biases, and their relations with the external forces that impinge on them.

REFERENCES

Allen, P. H.
1947   Indians of south-eastern Colombia. *Geographical Review* 37:567–82.
Anon.
1970   Desanos: Vaupés-Colombia. *Almas* 34, no. 360:17–25 (Aug.).
Bidou, P.
1983   Le travail du chamane: Essai sur la personne du chamane dans une société amazonienne, les taluyo du Pirá-Paraná, Vaupés, Colombie. *L'Homme*, 23 (1):5–43.
Buchillet, D.
1983   Maladie et mémoire des origines chez les Desana du Uaupés (Brésil). Ph.D. diss., University de Paris, Nanterre.
1987   "Personne n'est là pour écouter": Les conditions de mise en forme des incantations therapeutiques chez les Desana du Uaupés Bresilien. *Amerindia* 12:7–32.
1990   Los poderes del hablar: Terapia y agresión chamanica entre los indios Desana del Vanpes brasilero. In *Las Culturas Latino-Americanas a Traves de Su Discurso*, ed. E. Basso and J. Shearer. Quito: Abya Yala.

Buchillet, D., and Galvão, W.
N.d.   Genealogia dos messiah Tukano e Arawak do alto Río Negro. Typescript.

Brüzzi Alves da Silva, A.
1962   A civilização indigena do Uaupés. São Paulo: Linográfica Editôra.

Builes, M. A.
1951   *Cuarenta dias en el Vaupés.* Yarumal.

Chernela, J.
1983   Hierarchy and economy among the Kotiria (Uanano) speaking people of
       the northwest Amazon. Ph.D. diss. University of Michigan, Ann Arbor.

Coppi, G. I.
N.d.   Breve historia de las Misiones Franciscanas. Typescript.

Coudreau, H. A.
1887   *Voyage à travers les Guyanes et l'Amazone. La France equinoxiale.* vol.
       2, Paris: Challamel Ainé.

Crocker, C.
1985   *Vital souls: Bororo cosmology, natural symbolism, and shamanism.* Tuc-
       son: University of Arizona Press.

Hill, J.
1983   *Wakuénai society: A processual-structural analysis of indigenous cultural
       life in the Upper Río Negro region of Venezuela.* Ph.D. diss. Indiana
       University.
1984   Social equality and ritual hierarchy: The Arawakan Wakuénai of Vene-
       zuela. *American Ethnologist* 11:528–44.
ed. 1988   *Rethinking history and myth: Indigenous South American perspectives
       on the past.* Urbana: University of Illinois Press.

Hill, J., and R. Wright
1988   Time, narrative and ritual: Historical interpretation from an Amerindian
       society. In J. Hill, ed., *Rethinking history and myth: Indigenous South Amer-
       ican perspectives on the past.* Urbana: University of Illinois Press.

Hugh-Jones, S.
1979   *The palm and the Pleiades: Initiation and cosmology in northwest Ama-
       zonia.* Cambridge: Cambridge University Press.
1982   The Pleiades and Scorpius in Barasana cosmology. In A. F. Aveni and
       G. Urton, eds., Ethnoastronomy and Archaeoastronomy in the American
       Tropics *Annals of the New York Academy of Sciences* 385:183–201.
1988   The gun and the bow: Myths of white men and Indians. *L'Homme* 106–
       7:138–56.
1992   Yesterday's luxuries, tomorrow's necessities: Business and barter in NW
       Amazonia. In C. Humphrey and S. Hugh-Jones eds., *Barter, exchange and
       value: An anthropological approach.* Cambridge: Cambridge University
       Press.

Journet, N.
1988   *Les Jardins de Paix: Etude des structures sociales chéz les Curripaco du*

Haut Río Negro. Ph.d. diss., École des Hautes Études en Sciences Sociales, Paris.

Kaplan, J.
1975   *The Piaroa: A people of the Orinoco Basin.* Oxford: Oxford University Press.

Koch-Grünberg, T.
1909–10   *Zwei Jahre unter den Indianern.* Berlin: Weismuth.

Kumu, P., and T. Kenhiri
1980   *Antes o Mundo Não Existia.* São Paulo: Livraria Cultura.

Mansutti Rodriguez, A.
1986   Hierro, barro cocido, curare y cerbetanas: El comercio intra e interétnico entre los Uwotjuja. *Antropológica* 65:3–75.

Overing, J.
1983–84   Elementary structures of reciprocity: A comparative note on Guianese, central Brazilian, and north-west Amazon socio-political thought. *Antropológica* 59–62:331–48.

Reichel-Dolmatoff, G.
1971   *The Shaman and the Jaguar.* Philadelphia: Temple University Press.

Schaden, E.
1983/84   Los mesianismos en la América del Sur. *Maguare* 2, no. 2:11–22.

Schultes, R. E., and A. Hoffman
1979   *Plants of the Gods: Origins of hallucinogenic use.* London: Hutchinson.

Spruce, R.
1908   *Notes of a botanist on the Amazon and Andes.* London: Macmillan.

Turner, V.
1972   Religious specialists. In D. Sills, ed. *The International Encyclopedia of the Social Sciences.* London: Macmillan.

Wright, R.
1981   The history and religion of the Baniwa peoples of the Upper Río Negro Valley. Ph.D. diss., Stanford University, Stanford, California.
1992   Guardians of the cosmos: Baniwa shamans and prophets. *History of Religions* 32(1): 32–58.

Wright, R. and J. Hill
1986   History, ritual and myth: Nineteenth century millenarian movements in the northwest Amazon. *Ethnohistory* 33(1):31–54.

Shamanism in Siberia: From Partnership in Supernature to Counter-power in Society

Roberte N. Hamayon

When dealing with shamanism from the point of view of its relationship to power, one is faced with three facts agreed on by all specialists:

1. Shamanism is only present as an all-embracing system in archaic, tribal, or noncentralized, societies. Therefore shamanism is generally considered to be elementary or primitive as a symbolic system or form of religion.

2. Shamanistic phenomena are also found in centralized societies, which points to the adaptive character of shamanism. However, though shamanism is primary in archaic societies, its manifestations in centralized societies are not only fragmentary and altered but peripheral or even opposed to the central authorities; this is a sign of the structural weakness of shamanism. Related to this simultaneously adaptive and vulnerable property of shamanism as a system is the latent availability of shamanic practices in all types of society; this availability becomes manifest especially in crisis periods, when such practices easily revive or emerge.

The use of the term *supernature* (instead of supernatural world or realm) is meant to express the conception found in the most archaic societies of Siberia, where it is coextensive with nature, that is, where it is constituted of spirits animating natural beings and phenomena.

I am grateful to Caroline Humphrey for her help in writing this chapter in English.

3. Whether in tribal or centralized societies, one encounters an absence of shamanistic clergy, doctrine, dogma, church, and so forth. Therefore shamanism is usually characterized as a politically and ideologically limited or deficient system. In other words, although shamanic phenomena are found in state societies and may even play a role in state formation, shamanism as such is not found in the position of a state religion.

A series of related questions now arises. Do these facts express only historical chance, or do they constitute a feature inherent in the structure of shamanism? Is shamanism intrinsically unable to evolve and form itself into a church? Are shamanic societies unable to develop into state societies without having their shamanic practices and practitioners pushed away into the fringes? To pursue this matter further, how should we analyze and interpret the historical cases when shamanistic societies have been transformed from tribal into state organizations? And how should we appreciate the related changes in their religious life?

The purpose of this chapter is neither to discuss this question in general nor to analyze anew questionable historical cases, but to provide for a common discussion with some arguments directly deducible from the basic principles of shamanism, such as are found in archaic—namely, Siberian—societies. My use of the term *shamanism* refers only to its presence as a central symbolic system. This implies the co-occurrence of two criteria: (1) the shamanic institution is a constitutive part of social organization, and (2) the shamanic institution is in charge of the regular life-giving rituals, destined to ensure the reproduction of society and of its natural resources.[1] The adjective *shamanic*[2] is used in reference to representations such as (1) the idea of spirits (the spirits being in a similar relation to animals, plants, natural places, or phenomena, to that which the soul of man

---

1. This type of ritual is the only regular one performed by shamans in strictly shamanistic societies. It is the most important from a political point of view, the most relevant for the study of the relations between politics and religion, and a crucial stake in the process of state formation. This applies also to the life-giving supernatural entities themselves. A religion can be said to be working at the state level only so far as it rules the life-giving rituals.

2. *Shamanistic* refers to the practicians and practitioners (those who perform the rites and those for whom the rites are performed).

has to his body, which allows for direct contact with them),[3] and (2) such activities as healing, divining, and prophesying, which are dependent on particular circumstances or entailed by disturbances, whatever their position and value in society and ritual life. Such representations and practices may be present whether shamanism is central or not.

This chapter is based on an extensive study of Siberian data (R. Hamayon 1990) that attempts to highlight the basic principles of shamanism in this area. A comparison of Siberian societies leads us to distinguish three types of shamanism, of which only the first two correspond to shamanism in the full sense of the term as defined above. These three types are defined in an analytic way. Particular societies do not necessarily strictly correspond to any one type. For instance, the first type, which is intended to characterize the system found in the most archaic societies, those inhabiting the Siberian forest and living mainly by hunting, is called here "hunting shamanism" or "the shamanism of hunters," although these peoples generally also have domesticated animals. The latter are kept primarily for the purpose of hunting their counterparts that are still wild. Likewise, the second type, "pastoral shamanism" or "the shamanism of pastoralists," is found in societies inhabiting the borders of the forest and steppe regions, whose members still hunt occasionally. In both cases, the conception of supernature, and of humanity's relationship with it, retains features of both types. My classification of a given society as corresponding to one rather than to the other type means simply that this type of shamanism prevails in it. In the third type, shamanistic phenomena are already peripheralized. Each type is logically rooted in the foregoing one.[4] The basic principles of shamanism evolve from a political point of view, an evolution with implications for the questions dealt with here.

Hunting Shamanism: An Exchange with Animal Spirits

According to beliefs of the hunting societies of the Siberian forest, the animal species by which humans gain their living (mammals,

---

3. The notion of direct contact with spirits is directly connected with this conception of spirits as being similar in essence to the soul of man, which moreover distinguishes them from gods.

4. This does not imply that the first type gives root automatically to the two following types and only to them.

birds, fish) are animated by spirits. It is necessary to make an agreement with the spirits to hunt animals or take fish (that is, one must act on supernature to take resources from nature). This making of agreements is the main function of the shaman, whose specialty is maintaining relationships with spirits. His task is described as obtaining from the spirits good luck or fortune for the hunters of his community, that is, promises of game for the coming season. The shaman's action on the spirits is a prerequisite for the hunter's action on the animals. Relationships with animal spirits are conceived of as similar to relationships within society. Thus, human actions (obtaining good luck and then killing game) must occur in the framework of an exchange relationship and must be balanced by a compensation.

This human-animal exchange prospect accounts for the shaman's status as an in-law in supernature: to acquire the necessary legitimacy for the performance of his task, he must ritually marry the daughter (or sister) of the game-giving spirit,[5] so that he can act in the supernatural world as a rightful husband and not as an abductor. This exchange prospect also accounts for the following conception, spread all over the Siberian forest region: according to this idea, humans eat the meat of game animals in the same way that animals' spirits feed on human flesh and blood. This is the reason why sickness (experienced as loss of vitality) and death in the community as a whole are understood as a just payment for its successful hunting life in both the past and future. This is also the reason the spirits are considered to be ambivalent: they give life but must take it back sooner or later. So it is with the shaman, whose task is carrying out the exchange process with them. This last idea accounts for the characteristics of the shaman's behavior and practice. His activity consists in making himself identical with his "in-laws"; his costume makes him similar to the main game animal;[6] he imitates its behavior, first in the manner of a husband (he jumps, prances, cries, and snorts), second in the manner of a killed animal (he falls down, as if he were dead). His practice is pragmatic and personalized. This is not a liturgy to apply but an art to exert, and it implies seducing, negotiating, and even tricking.

---

5. The generic figure of the game-giving spirit is represented in the form of the main game animal, an elk or reindeer in Siberia.

6. His headgear is adorned with antlers. Symmetrically, the female he married is sociologically made into a wife.

The exchange law between humankind and the world of natural and supernatural beings makes them partners as well as game for each other. Being similar to the human soul in essence and on a par with humans as alliance and exchange partners, spirits are not transcendent. They are feared but not worshiped. They are respected only as far as is required by the exchange process and by its institutional framework (that is, by the alliance relationship made concrete in the shaman's ritual marriage).

Such a dualistic principle is reflected in the very conception of nature considered from a geographical point of view. Nature is a nutritious milieu (as opposed to a series of locations), seen in depth and on a horizontal plane with humankind. More precisely, the forest is one milieu to which also belong at one and the same time mammals and birds; a tree is considered to be one thing from roots to top. Waters are another example, every river being the same from source to mouth. Man keeps dualistic relations with each of them separately, and the shaman is concurrently said to marry the daughter of the fish-giving spirit as well as that of the game-giving one.

This dualistic principle is also at work in social organization. Society is divided into moieties, and alliance relationships obey a direct exchange rule that unfolds between moieties or clan subdivisions within moieties. Moreover, hunting is performed according to the social rules of collaboration with in-laws.

Although relationships are dualistic from the structural point of view, they are not so from the functional one. The two partners are ultimately both taker and giver to each other, but they are ideologically either taker or giver, not both at the same time. Positions in the alliance or exchange process are not reciprocal but oriented. Taking and giving are not given the same value. From the hunter's point of view, taking comes first ideologically and requires heroism. Giving, which implies having something to give, may be prestigious, but it is scorned because the one in a giver's position is going to be deprived of riches, game, a daughter, vitality, or life. Peoples in Siberia identify themselves with a taker's position, and consider the giver's as the partner's position. Moreover, between taking and giving, a time lag occurs, whether an actual delay or a ritual separation. This time lag allows for acting on the timing, manner, and amount of giving, that is, for introducing a mediation. This ideological distinction turns a reciprocal exchange into a three-stage process entailing hierarchized positions for the partners. Though the relationship between partners remains objectively reciprocal in general, it is subjectively hierarchized at each stage of the exchange process. This pattern, which opens the way to hierarchy, also limits its extent, preventing it from becoming a permanent feature: social positions are meant to remain alternate. Each man in each moiety is alternately in the position of a wife taker and wife giver toward the other moiety.

This pattern raises a special question concerning the social position of the shaman, who is in charge of the community's exchange with the animal spirits of its environment as a whole. His art as a shaman is to take (fortune) as much and as soon as possible and to give back (human vitality) as little and as late as possible. It consists in profiting by the time lag between these two stages, that is, in working on the third, mediatory stage. This is a source of power for the shaman. Is this power likely to become centralized in the political sense? The answer is negative. The shaman's exercise of power is controlled by the community. If the hunting season is not successful, the shaman who has performed the ritual is thought to be no longer able to seduce his supernatural wife sufficiently to obtain much game from her, and he will be replaced by another one at the following ritual. Also, the shaman depends on the community for acquiring the tools of his power—his costume, drum, and other paraphernalia—and for keeping them "animated," or inhabited by spirits (the ritual aimed at obtaining the promise of game also works for "animating" the drum). The shaman's power is strictly dependent on his efficiency. He enjoys authority not by being a shaman but by proving useful as such. Although the dualistic principle at work in hunting societies gives place to a mediatory action, it prevents such mediation from becoming institutionalized and thus maintains shamanism in a form that is basically inconsistent with a centralizing ideology, hence with state formation.

Pastoral Shamanism: A Heritage
from Humanized Spirits

The archaic pattern of shamanism discussed above is modified together with changes in the way of life. Stock breeding induces a preference for transmission within the world of the self rather than for exchange with the world of the other: herds and pasturelands are inherited (whether as true property or only by usufruct rights).[7] This goes together with important changes in social organization. We observe a move from direct to indirect exchange rules, from residence with in-laws to patrilocal residence, from moieties to clans. Patri-filiation relationships become more important than alliance relation-ships in social structure and life.[8] Accordingly, the view of nature and supernature changes.

Nature is no longer a milieu that gives food directly, but becomes a collection of locations that make production of food possible. Con-sequently nature is no longer conceived on a single horizontal level, but on several levels hierarchized along a vertical axis. Henceforth a tree is distinguished according to its root, trunk, and top, referring to different levels, and similarly a river is divided up according to its source, course, and mouth. A mountain that looks down on the pasturelands of given descent groups (segments of clans) is considered the geographical mark of these groups' territory and the dwelling place of their ancestors. For these descent groups, such a mountain constitutes a token of their legitimacy as such, establishing them as having rights over the lands, and it also provides a concrete place where they can get into contact with their ancestors, to ask them for everything that favors successful grazing, especially rain, and for all kinds of protection from rival groups. The ancestors, though human, are often assimilated to the mountain itself (and considered to be its spirits), just as in hunting societies the game-giving spirit, though animal, is the spirit of the forest itself. Together with the mountain, the ancestors constitute a category of life-giving supernatural entities. However, what they give is not subsistence as such but the conditions for producing it. They favor their descendants in as much as these take part in the collective ritual performed on the side of the moun-tain. They punish them for transgression of patrilineal rules and ethics, by sending them diseases, especially skin diseases (which are visible and therefore a public shame).

The collective ritual dedicated to the ancestors abounds in invo-

---

7. Inheritance is patrilineal all over Siberia. However, although hunting societies are very similar to each other, pastoral societies are not. The pattern of shamanism outlined in this section of the chapter is mainly based on data referring to the Exirit-Bulagat of the Buryats, living to the West of Lake Baikal.

8. Although both relationships are always present, one may have precedence over the other from both a structural and a functional point of view.

cations, offerings of milk products, and sacrifices of domestic animals. All these marks of worship of the ancestors are offered as a compensation for the "grace" implored from them. Addressing human entities, humans make use of their own language;[9] addressing superiors, their attitude is that of worshipers; breeding domestic animals,[10] they avoid becoming the food for the spirits in the exchange process. Thus, the appearance of human entities as a life-giving supernatural category, along with verticalization of space and hierarchization of relationships, goes together with the development of prayer and animal sacrifice.

Furthermore, rituals to ancestors are not as a rule conducted by shamans, whose only specific role concerns the sacrificial meat, a part of which is given to every participant. Invocations and offerings are usually performed by the elders of the groups involved or by specialists closer to priests than to shamans. In this field, the shamanic institution, while still having a specific function, is as such submitted to clan law.[11]

However, another supernatural category plays a part in the life-giving process. This is the founder of the tribe, who is animal by essence but human by function, inasmuch as he begets the forefathers of the clans.[12] He originates from the animal part of the supernatural world and takes a place above the ancestors in the human part of it. His activity as a life-giving entity is entirely due to his animal

---

9. Addressing animal spirits, the hunter imitates the cries and appeals of wild animals.

10. Unlike game animals, domestic animals are in continuity with the man who breeds them and therefore may serve as a substitute for him.

11. The pattern of social organization is mixed among the Exirit-Bulagat and the pastoral Tungus. The clan works as a unit only for exogamous purposes; it does not have a common territory. On the contrary, a local unit is generally constituted of segments of at least two different clans, which may marry each other. Therefore, because the ritual to the ancestors dwelling on the mountain is intended for the local unit, it is not strictly speaking a clan affair; most of the time, it is performed jointly by members belonging to two or more clans.

12. Such is for instance Lord Bull, the founder of the Exirit-Bulagat tribe of the Buryats (his appearance as a bull is similar to the appearance as an elk or reindeer of the game-giving spirit, all of them being horned or antlered ruminants). In the same way, the Tungus supernatural entity Buga, initially the game-giving spirit, preserves its appearence as an elk (consistent with the meaning of *buga*, elk or reindeer in Tungus and Mongol) even though it is called grandfather, old man (or grandmother, old woman), among pastoral groups. Humanization opens the way to transcendence.

origin: as an animal, he is supposed to embody fertility, and he is treated as an animal in fertility rituals (see also Humphrey 1973). The shaman is specifically entitled, on his behalf, to transmit fertility to the community. This is the only regular shamanic ritual in pastoral life. It is very obviously marked by imitations of animal behavior connected with fertility. Furthermore, the role of this figure as tribal founder—his role as a human being—is expressed only in myths and is in no way connected with obtaining fertility. All this is illustrated by the figure of Lord Bull, the founder of the Exirit-Bulagat tribe of the western Buryats.

The presence of such a character is crucial for the presence of shamanism as a constitutive institution in society. His animal origin is the basis for a continuing partner relationship between humans and life-giving supernatural entities. This partnership implies the persistence of a dualistic worldview, which in its turn implies the limitation of power in society. However, the pattern of shamanism in pastoral societies is mixed, because life-giving supernatural entities are divided into two categories implying two types of relationships. On one hand, pastoral shamanism retains the main feature of hunting shamanism—relationship with an animal entity—but the life-giving role of this entity is reduced to providing the principle of fertility. On the other hand, pastoral shamanism implies conditions dependent on human entities for this principle to work. Thus, the primary reciprocal relationship with animal supernature is subordinated to a nonreciprocal relationship based on patrifiliation and dependence on human entities, which is echoed in society by the subordination of shamanic to clan institutions. This is subordination as to the objectives and results of the shaman's relationship to this animal entity, not as to the means, which by that fact escape the field of human descent relationships.

We may speak here of a process of "affiliation of alliance," that is, the integration of alliance relationships into the patrifiliation rule. For example, although the shaman still has a supernatural wife (of animal origin), he is considered an heir of his ancestors. The reason for this is that the supernatural wife is considered to love men and elect them as shamans always in the same line, which makes her inheritable from generation to generation. This in turn changes the conception of the shaman's legitimacy. Thus, although fixed hierarchical relationships are allowed to develop, they are prevented from evolving into centralization. This limitation occurs only so far as fertility is still thought to depend on an entity of animal origin, that is, inasmuch as this vital principle is ruled through an alliance between entities different in nature, not through a filiation between entities of same nature.

In spite of the presence of this animal figure, the dualistic aspect of the worldview in Siberian pastoral societies is not the same as it is in hunting societies. In particular, roles and positions no longer alternate between the two parts but are fixed. The adoption of pastoralism and patrilocal residence is correlated with the affirmation of the senior/junior opposition as socially relevant. However, the dualistic principle is preserved inasmuch as status and moral values do not go together. Thus, among the Western Buryats, although the senior has higher status, the junior has higher value. The junior's position is deprived of prestige and is socially dependent, but it is nevertheless associated with heroism, manliness, courage, and efficiency. Lack of understanding and deficient action are attributed to the senior's position. Is such a dualism likely to evolve so that it becomes compatible with a form of centralization and state formation?

This question is made particularly acute by the appearance of hierarchized supernatural entities in some of the Siberian pastoral societies. For instance, among the Exirit-Bulagat of the western Buryats developed a supernatural category that was neither human nor animal but cosmic, situated above the founder of the tribe, Lord Bull, and called *tengeri* ("skies"). These are only mentioned in invocations, and they are not really of great concern in shamanic rituals; only in myth is Lord Bull said to be the son of one of them. However, these "skies" are conceived of as divided into two camps endlessly fighting one another, although one is senior and the other junior. Thus, dualism is still at work at this upper level. A parallel exists here with the fact that the tribe is submitted to the Russian Empire but is still in itself a collection of rival clans, without any centralizing tendency.

The Limit of Oriented Dualism or
the Threshold of Shamanism

Is the process of verticalization of relationships able to attain the degree of centralization characteristic of state formation together with the maintenance of shamanism as such? Let us take the case of the Buryats and compare the different fates of the tribes living to the west and east of Lake Baikal. To make this comparison particularly relevent to our purpose, let us recall the very acute question asked by Caroline Humphrey in "The Uses of Genealogy," where she asks "why a centralized acknowledged hierarchy based on patrilineal descent could arise and remain among the nomadic Khori (=Xori, the Buryat stockbreeders living east of Lake Baikal], when it did not among the Ekhirit-Bulagat [=Exirit-Bulagat, living in the west partly by agriculture]?" (1979:256). This difference is all the more surprising because the Buryats on both sides of the lake had been encouraged to unite around chiefs by the Russian administration, which was eager to have permanent interlocutors among the local populations. However, this fostering of hierarchy was successful only in the east.

Another feature that illustrates the difference is the fact that shamanism remained strong in the west, among the Exirit-Bulagat, but was superseded by Lamaist Buddhism in the east, where this religion developed a church and a clergy. In the west, shamans were still men, who enjoyed a ritualized initiation to their office and who were invested with regular tasks in life-giving rites, that is, in the rites intended to reproduce the world order. Thus, in the west, sha-manism was still a constitutive institution in society. In the east, shamans were mostly women, for men deemed it more profitable (in prestige, riches, and social position) to become Buddhist lamas. Access to the shamanic function was late in life and informal, that is, not ritualized. Whether they were men or women, shamans per-formed divination, healing, and other such rituals that depended only on circumstances and aimed at repairing disorders, but shamans did not play a role in regular rituals. In this eastern case, shamanism was no longer present as an institution indispensable for the repro-duction of society. Rather, it was a profession, and a relatively low-valued one. In the west, shamanism was an institution closely bound to the clan. But in the east, shamanic practices and practicians were socially peripheral and considered to be opposed to power. Their activities were on the whole devoted only to private matters, and they focused on rites implying relationships with people who were victims of foul ("unnatural" or premature) deaths or who had violated social rules, and whose wandering souls were then accused of causing troubles among the living. In this way, shamanism was concerned with relationships within society rather than with its natural environment. Thus, on the whole, eastern Buryat shamanesses were stamped with notions of subversion and transgression.

Some related differences exist in the conception of spirits, especially in ideas about life-giving figures. The most prominent life-givers are not the same on the two sides of Lake Baikal. Whereas the western Buryats have Lord Bull, the eastern Buryats have no animal figure. Their main fertility-giver is the White Old Man, spirit-master of lands and waters, a human, represented as mounted on a deer or having a deer at his feet. He is a syncretic figure, invested with a regular role at life-giving Lamaistic rituals at sacred cairns on mountains, called *oboo*. Among the other supernatural figures, the cosmic category called *tengeri* ("skies") now has a more important place in syncretic rituals and representations. Significantly, in the east, they are no longer divided into two opposed camps, as they were in western Buryatia (though they are not united either).[13] Moreover, they are more or less assimilated to, or confused with, Buddhist deities called *burxan,* which is illustrated by the expression *burxan tengeri* used in many syncretic ritual texts. Similarly, there developed a category of demons and monsters living in the underworld. Neither the upperworld nor underworld beings maintained relationships with human beings similar to human relationships (that is, by marriage or descent), as had been the case with animal and human categories of supernatural beings.[14] These upperworld and underworld beings are no longer spirits but gods and devils, ontologically different from the human soul. Furthermore, the principle of ambivalence characteristic of hunting shamanism gives way to bipolarization: the upper pole of the vertical axis is thought to be entirely positive, and the lower one is entirely negative. Status and value henceforth go together.

---

13. As is the case of the thirty-three *tengeri* in the Mongol epics of Geser, more or less borrowed from the thirty-three skies of Indra, or in the case of Mongke tengeri ("Eternal Sky"), an ideological concept connected with the emergence of Chinggis Qa'an's empire among the Mongols, see Beffa and Hamayon 1990. The term *tengerism* is used precisely to refer to the fact that state formations among the Turco-Mongol societies of inner Asia had the notion of "sky" (heaven) as a privileged ideological support. The question of this notion being borrowed from China is open.

14. It is interesting, in the context of religious change under the pressure of Lamaism, that the chief of the underworld, Erleg xan, has a horned head, which recalls the antlered or horned heads of the game-giving spirit of the forest of hunting societies and the fertility-giving figure of semipastoral societies.

Conclusion

Although the historical context of the Russian Empire makes it impossible to decide on the basis of Siberian data whether shamanism is likely to combine with state formation, the dualistic principle inherent in shamanism is a structural obstacle to this, in spite of its possible evolution toward hierarchization. So far as state formation implies centralization, it cannot emerge from a shamanistic society unless shamanism has been led to fragment into a series of separate practices carried out by marginalized specialists. The question of dualism is twofold. One aspect concerns the dualistic forms of power at the top of centralized societies. This could be investigated through a thorough study of the possible shamanic features present in such dualistic forms of power, such as, for example, a sacred kingdom where the king assumes alternately two opposed functions, or a kingdom with an appointed fool playing an influential role in relation to the king. The other aspect concerns the type of relationship between mankind and supernature, that is, whether or not this is dualistic, implying reciprocity.

A second related hindrance exists to state formation in shamanistic societies: the shamanic mode of action, which is implied by the dualistic principle at work in organizing relations with supernature, can be characterized as pragmatic. Pragmatism is entailed by the type of relationship involved in this dualistic framework—an alliance or exchange relationship between partners. This makes shamanic practice an art to exercise, as opposed to a liturgy to apply. Thus, pragmatism is not to be seen as a deficiency and does not imply the lack of rules and regularities. Rather, it appears as a deliberate refusal of dogmatism. Shamanic societies, and shamans in nonshamanic societies, reject the use of writing for strictly shamanic matters; this goes together with the absence of a church or a clergy. On the whole, shamanism seems to refuse its own codification, because this would hinder the play of partnership with supernature—a partnership always available, so far as it consists in turning imaginary entities into partners with whom to exchange and negotiate, and which does not a priori exclude from its scope anything related to human life.

A third obstacle is constituted by the very nature of what shamanic activity claims is "fortune" or "good luck." Whether the focus is game, rain, fertility, mental health, love, success in trade, affairs, travel, or something else, the common element is the dependence on individual talents and the escape from the ordinary rules of any centralized organization.

REFERENCES

Beffa, M. L., and R. Hamayon
1990   The concept of *tenger* in *The Secret History of the Mongols.* In *Proceedings of the International Conference for the 750th anniversary of The Secret History of the Mongols,* Ulan-Bator.

Hamayon, Roberte
1990   *La Chasse à l'âme: Esquisse d'une theorie du chamanisme siberien.* Nanterre: Société d'ethnologie.

Humphrey, Caroline
1973   Some ritual techniques in the bull-cult of the Buriat-Mongols. Curl Lecture. In *Proceedings of the Royal Anthropological Institute.*
1979   The uses of genealogy: A historical study of the nomadic and sedentarized Buryat. In *Pastoral Production and Society.* Paris and Cambridge: Editions de la MSH/Cambridge University Press.

River People: Shamanism and History in Western Amazonia

Peter Gow

Throughout western Amazonia, illness is cured by shamans who use the hallucinogen *ayahuasca*. When this shamanic tradition is described among indigenous tribal peoples, for example, by Chaumeil (1983) on the Yagua or Harner (1972) on the Shuar, it is treated as part of an unbroken pre-Columbian cultural tradition. In the small and isolated communities of native Amazonian peoples, ayahuasca shamanism is supposed to be fully integrated within the organic totality of traditional culture. But when the same practices are observed in the poor barrios that stretch out around the cities of Pucallpa and Iquitos, things are clearly more complicated. Several writers, such as Luna (1986), Dobkin de Rios (1972), and Chevalier (1982), have addressed this issue and interpreted urban ayahuasca shamanism as an import from tribal peoples that is now responding to the chronic economic insecurity and alienation of the urban lumpen proletariat. Chevalier, in his study of a small town on the Pachitea River, writes of the urban condition,

> shamanism . . . becomes the site of a constant rebellion led by the
> forces of a totally alien domain—those of the Campa universe—

My research on the Bajo Urubamba and on other areas of western Amazonia was supported between 1980 and 1988 by the then Social Science Research Council, the Central Research Fund of the University of London, and the Nuffield Foundation. I thank Cecilia MacCallum, Stephen Hugh-Jones, Graham Townsley, Michael Taussig, Elvira Belaunde, Laura Rival, Penelope Harvey, Peter Wade, Joanna Overing, and the editors of this volume for their comments on earlier versions of this chapter. I also thank J-P Chaumeil for his detailed reply to the chapter. I have not integrated his suggestions, because I hope to generate a wider debate on the issue.

which recognizes neither the distinct existence of "this material world" nor the disembodied supremacy of other-worldly spirits. (1982:423).

The civilization of the mestizo world, in the process of destroying tribal cultures like that of the Campa, has taken over their shamanic traditions of the vanquished as a "vision of silent despair."

I believe this approach is false historically and ethnographically. I argue that *ayahuasca* shamanism has been evolving in urban contexts over the past three hundred years, and that it has been exported from these towns to isolated tribal people to become the dominant form of shamanic curing practice in the region. It evolved as a response to the specific colonial history of western Amazonia and is absent precisely from those few indigenous peoples who were buffered from the processes of colonial transformation caused by the spread of the rubber industry in the region. More importantly, however, I argue that ayahuasca shamanism is deeply embedded in the contemporary structure of social and economic relations in the region. This shamanic tradition can only be understood in the context of Amazonian social classification, the ideology of *raza*, "race," which defines positions within class hierarchy and their relations to commercial production and circulation. In particular, ayahuasca shamanism cannot be abstracted from the meanings Amazonian people attach to the "mixed blood" status of mestizos and to the spatial axis that runs from the city to the forest.

My argument has its roots in a number of problems raised in the analysis of the social system of the Bajo Urubamba River (Gow 1991). Like most ethnographers of western Amazonian peoples, I could easily accept that the native Piro and Campa people of this area associate their bosses, manufactured goods, school education, and state power with downriver cities like Pucallpa and Iquitos. But it was much harder to understand their assertions that shamanic knowledge comes from downriver and from these same cities, even when they traced out the lines of teaching and apprenticeship leading from there to the Bajo Urubamba. After all, ayahuasca shamanism seemed to me to be one of the most traditional and forest-oriented parts of their lives. It was not obvious to me what sets of values such claims could refer to, because it would have made more sense, at least to me, if they attributed the origins of shamanic knowledge to their own ancestors, or to even more remote forest-dwelling peoples.

This problem is caused by a failure to distinguish two distinct analytical levels, that of the spatiotemporal processes entailed in specific Amazonian cultural practices and that of the historical evolution of those practices. The ayahuasca curing ritual engages a set of images of time and space that are coherently related to the spatiotemporal symbolism of other domains, such as the extractive industry, subsistence economy, and class relations. Thus, the forest functions in the curing ritual as the original source of life, much as it does in economic activity as the source of value, and in class relations as the source of the autochthonous poor people. The complex sources of shamanic knowledge become clearer when placed within the spatiotemporal processes engaged by these practices.

But contemporary Amazonian practices, with their entailed spatiotemporal dimensions, also have a history. The ayahuasca curing ritual, and the network of meanings in which it operates, shows the signs of its own evolution over the past three centuries in Amazonia. Within it can be found evidence of its origin in a specific social milieu, the early Jesuit and Franciscan missions of the region, and in the specific context of the massive disruption caused by epidemic illness to certain indigenous populations. I argue that while the ayahuasca curing ritual evolved in this specific milieu, it was able, because of its very form, to expand to the region as a whole as the mission system was transformed by the rubber industry, which formed the basis of the contemporary socioeconomic system of the region.

My analysis is somewhat speculative and suffers from a lack of hard data to back it up. The literature on ayahuasca shamanism is quite rich, but much less is published on the western Amazonian social system, and still less on its historical development. At best, my analysis seeks to provide a solution that makes sense of the data from the Bajo Urubamba, and my discussion of commercial exchange and subsistence economy, of class and *raza*, and of Amazonian history is largely an extrapolation from the analysis presented in Gow (1991). I present it more as a hypothesis to be confirmed than as an asserted fact. My argument will undoubtedly require modification as more data becomes available on the areas I discuss, but at the very least, I hope to show that these areas are systematically related to each other.

Ayahuasca Shamanism in Western Amazonia

For the purposes of this chapter, I define western Amazonia as the whole rain forest area drained by tributaries of the Amazon above the mouth of the Javarí, that is, most of the eastern lowlands of Peru and Ecuador. The region has historically formed a unit based on riverine transport, bounded by Brazil to the east and by the foothills of the Andes to the west. The population is relatively small and mainly concentrated in the major cities of Iquitos and Pucallpa. Throughout the region, the nonurban population is dominated by native Amazonian peoples, speaking about eighty different languages, and by *ribereños* or mestizos. I exclude from the analysis southeastern Colombia, the site of Taussig's account of ayahuasca or *yajé* shamanism (Taussig 1987). The conditions of mass colonization from the Andes create a very different situation along the upper Putumayo River to the one I am describing here, and I know too little about curing practices in the lower Putumayo and Leticia to say anything definite. I likewise exclude reference to those areas within eastern Peru and Ecuador that have seen mass Andean colonization of the lowlands.

Despite the size of western Amazonia and the apparent cultural heterogeneity of its population, there is a remarkable uniformity of shamanic practice. Throughout the whole region, one finds shamanic curing through the use of the hallucinogen ayahuasca (known in the north as *yajé*). The uniformity of these practices goes well beyond the use of ayahuasca and includes techniques of training, curing, and a particular cosmology of supernatural agents. There are important exceptions to this uniformity, notably among certain remote indigenous peoples.

Ayahuasca shamanism centers on the use by a trained shaman of the hallucinogen ayahuasca to diagnose and then cure illness. The shaman, who is usually but not always a man, trains for many years with an older shaman, taking ayahuasca and other plant drugs frequently, and learning the *icaros*, the curing songs. A fully trained shaman has a wide repertoire of such songs, each with its particular efficacity. A shaman also has a magical phlegm called *yachay*, lodged in his stomach, which gives him the ability to blow away evil and to suck out the sorcery objects (*virote*) that cause certain forms of illness. The illnesses diagnosed by these shamans are relatively few.

Cutipa is the revenge of natural species or objects on people who use them (for example, as food, or in the clearing of forest). *Manchari* is the fright caused by proximity to demons. Both these sets of illness regularly afflict young children, but healthy adults are relatively immune to them. Much more serious for adults are the linked categories of *mal de gente,* "the evil of people," and *mal de diablo,* "the evil of demons." Both the latter categories are forms of sorcery, where *virote* are blown into the victim's body. In the first case, the source is a malevolent human shaman; in the second case, the source is a demon. There are other minor categories of illness, but in all cases, the curing ritual is both diagnostic and therapeutic: the shaman identifies and cures the illness at the same time.

Associated with ayahuasca shamanism is a particular cosmology of supernatural agency. Of supreme power are the "owner" and "mother" spirits of the river and forest. *Sacha runa* is the owner of the forest, and *sachamama* is the mother of the forest. *Yacu runa* is the owner of the river, and *yacumama* is the mother of the river. In both cases, the mother is the origin, or creator, of the ecological domain, and the owner is the guardian of the domain. *Sachamama* and *yacumama* are described as giant anacondas of the forest and river respectively. *Yacuruna* and *sacharuna* are usually described as having the physical appearance of white men. Below them in the hierarchy come other supernatural agents, like the manatee and dolphin, and in the forest, the powerful tree and vine species. All these supernatural agents are characterized by their powerful knowledge and their control over their physical form. Unlike humans, who are victimized by their bodies, these spirits control their corporeal forms, which they generate from their knowledge. Using ayahuasca, shamans may travel to remote countries and may even use the inhabitants of these places for curing, but with rare exceptions, they neither travel to or have contact with celestial or subterranean regions. The absence of a vertical axis to this cosmology of supernatural agency contrasts markedly with other western Amazonian systems, such as the Ene and Tambo river Campa described by Weiss (1975), where there is a complex classification of celestial and subterranean agents and locii. In the social milieu of ayahuasca shamanism, there a powerful vertical axis is present, but it is occupied by Christian eschatology.

The supernatural agents of the river and the forest are the primary sources of disease and of curing power. These major spirits are immortal and self-generating, and they are not dependent on humans for their survival. They avoid humans because they abhor human sexuality and its odors. They afflict only out of revenge for the invasion of their domains and for damage caused to the animal and plant species under their control. Equally, they have the power to remove illness from the afflicted person and to restore health. Despite their ability to afflict humans with illness, these spirits are not attributed strong moral qualities. Unlike human shamans or the dead, these spirits are not considered evil. They are morally neutral donors of illness and health.

To cure illness, a shaman must contact these spirits, and so he must overcome their dislike of humans. Shamans are aided in this by their helper spirits, the *arcana* or *incanto*, spirits that have become attached to the shaman, and whom he looks after.[1] The shaman is also helped by the ingestion of certain plant drugs, like tobacco, ayahuasca, and *toé* (*Datura spp.*) These plants are themselves spirits, and by ingesting them, the shaman achieves mastery over his own body and becomes like a spirit. When he drinks ayahuasca, he becomes partly a spirit, and the spirits reveal themselves to him. This revelation has two conditions. The first is that the shaman must refrain from sexual intercourse and eating foods offensive to the spirits. The second condition is his use of *ícaros*, curing songs. These songs are said to *amansar*, "tame" or "calm down," the spirits, and to enlist their aid in revealing the sources of a patient's affliction and removing it. It is important to stress that the idiom of this contact is taming or calming down, because the shaman does not order or subdue the spirits. The spirits are attracted by the compulsive beauty of the curing songs and by the fragrance of the shaman's body. The spirits are seduced by the shaman and respond by helping him.

The curing power of shamans depends not only on their contacts with the mother spirits of drugs and on their helper spirits but on their training. Though shamans claim that knowledge can be acquired directly from plant spirits, knowledge is mainly acquired through training with another shaman. The apprentice shaman learns through attending the curing sessions of his teacher and takes ayahuasca with

---

1. I was never told about *arcana* on the Bajo Urubamba, although Luna (1986:90–94) and Chaumeil (1988) record them in northern areas. Judging from Chaumeil's account, *incanto* are less important in the north than in the Bajo Urubamba, where their functions are performed by *arcana*.

him to learn the curing songs. The teacher also engages in more formal training and gives the apprentice his *yachay*, magical phlegm, and his helper spirits.

The Sources of Shamanic Knowledge

In urban contexts, shamans stress that their knowledge comes from forest Indians. The most famous of ayahuasca shamans, Manoel Córdova-Rios of Iquitos, claimed to have acquired his knowledge during his captivity among a band of jungle Panoan people on the Rio de las Piedras and subsequently with Lamista Quechua and Capanahua curers (Lamb 1971, 1985). Shamans I talked to in Pucallpa mentioned sojourns among the Campa, the Huitoto, the "Jivaro," and other native peoples noted for their remoteness from cities. Even where a shaman has not learned from such a source, there is the strong ideological assumption that forest Indians are the ultimate source of shamanic knowledge, and that any powers acquired directly from them are of particular value. This stress on the magical knowledge of forest Indians would tend to confirm the dominant view among anthropologists that ayahuasca shamanism is an autochtonous tradition, maintained in its purest form among the least acculturated tribal peoples of western Amazonia.

This position becomes complicated, however, if we turn to these tribal peoples. Contrary to expectations, the "forest Indians" have little respect for their own shamanic powers. My fieldwork was among the Piro and Campa people of the Bajo Urubamba area, relatively remote from urban Amazonia. These people do not think that local shamans are particularly powerful. Nor do they see any continuity of knowledge between contemporary practice and their ancestral traditions. Instead, they look downriver for the source of shamanic power, to the cities of Pucallpa and Iquitos, and to the powerful ayahuasca shamans of the lower Ucayali and Amazon mainstream. The native people of the Bajo Urubamba have little respect for their own shamans and even less for the shamanic powers of the "forest Indians" with whom they are in contact. No one on the Bajo Urubamba, except for passing gringo travelers, had any interest in the shamanism of the forest-oriented Amahuaca, Yaminahua, Machiguenga, or Pajonal Campa, and no one would have gone to such a shaman to be cured. Bajo Urubamba people fear these forest people for their capricious violence, but not for their shamanic knowledge.

This inversion of the gradient of shamanic power between urban and indigenous areas is not unique to the Bajo Urubamba but is found throughout western Amazonia. There are many cases reported where remote traditional indigenous peoples fear and respect the shamanic powers of more urban and acculturated peoples. Thus, the Achuar and Shiwiar of the Corrientes River fear mestizo shamans, the Rio Mayo Aguaruna fear Chayahuita shamans, and the Capanahua of the Trapiche River fear Cocama shamans from the Ucayali mainstream.[2] The best-known example of this inversion is the trade in shamanic knowledge between the Shuar and the Canelos Quichua, described by Harner. The Shuar, known better as the "head-shrinking Jivaro," are quintessential forest Indians, terrifying to outsiders. The Canelos are quintessential acculturated people and were dismissed by most anthropologists as of no real interest until Whitten's remarkable studies rescued them from oblivion. Yet the Shuar, whose fierce resistance to colonial penetration should have left their cultural traditions intact, trade their shamanic knowledge from the Canelos, whose long experience of missionization should have destroyed their cultural continuity.[3]

Thus, though a single tradition of shamanic curing is shared by the culturally heterogeneous peoples of western Amazonia, urban shamans attribute supreme authority to forest Indian sources, and tribal people locate that authority among urban practitioners. We could perhaps get around this paradox by invoking the principle that people always attribute greater shamanic power to other people, especially distant others. Apart from being very bland, this formulation would not explain a crucial fact. I can find no cases where white people, in the sense of actual immigrants from outside Amazonia, are categorically attributed shamanic power. Particular white people may train as shamans with local teachers, but white people as a category are never attributed shamanic curing power. This fact is more surprising than it appears, because white people are attributed remarkable powers by Amazonian people. The more remote the white

---

2. Seymour-Smith 1988, Uriarte 1982, Brown 1984, 1986, Fuentes 1988, and Loos, Davis, and Wise 1979. Cf. Taussig 1987:172 on the bemused response of Cofan shamans to Andean immigrants' categories of misfortune.

3. Harner 1972, Taylor 1981, and Whitten 1976, 1985.

people are, the more bizarre and awesome are the powers attributed them. But nobody in Amazonia attributes them with knowledge of ayahuasca shamanism.

The inversion in gradient of shamanic power becomes less of a problem if we ask about the ultimate sources of all illness and cures. Everyone in western Amazonia agrees that the source of illness and curing, like the source of ayahuasca, is the forest, *el monte* (in Quechua, *sacha*). All the problems an ayahuasca shaman cures derive ultimately from the forest, and his powers have the same source. How particular shamans acquire these powers and become the human agents of the transmission of such knowledge from the forest is a different matter. To understand this, we must explore how city-dwellers and forest Indians are not mutually separate populations but mutually defining parts of a wider social system. The problem of the sources of shamanic knowledge is really not about the identification of specific forms of knowledge with particular real populations. It is about how specific people live in Amazonia and the meanings of ways of living in the region. Essentially, ayahuasca shamanism is about relationships to the forest and how one lives in relation to the forest.

The Forest and the City

In this chapter, I have been using terms like *mestizos, forest Indians,* and *white people* as if these were self-evident sociological categories. Most writers on western Amazonia use such terms in a schema that can crudely be summarized as follows: Indians are those people who are indigenous to the area, bearers of an authentic indigenous culture until the forces of acculturation sweep over them. White people are the dominating and exploitative immigrants from Europe, bearers of an alien imperialist culture. Mestizos are a problematic category, a mishmash of poor immigrants and deculturated Indians. They live like Indians, look like Indians, but speak Spanish and thus cannot be bearers of an authentic indigenous culture.

The huge literature on the cultural classification of western Amazonian peoples, largely concerned with the cultural authenticity of particular communities, has ignored a simple fact. Amazonian people continuously use terms like *white people, mestizos,* and *Indians* as part of ongoing social practice. These terms are used not to define people in abstract cultural terms but to locate them in specific social relationships. They are used to locate people in particular positions in the hierarchy of socioeconomic power in the region and to contest such placements. These classifications locate people in a particular vision of history, which is closely related to the particular system of commercial exchange that dominates the economy of western Amazonia. These are in turn related to a specific symbolism of space, with the forest at the center of the region and the industrialized Western nations on the outside.

For Amazonian people, *mestizos* are the descendants of marriages between immigrant white men and local Indian women. The term means, quite literally, "mixed blood people." These people have their origin in the primordial moment of Amazonian folk history, the contact between civilized white immigrants and the autochthonous forest Indians. This folk history is very similar to that of other areas of Latin America (and to American folk imagery of that history). But Amazonian folk history has a very important difference to many other regions in Latin America, notably to the Andes: there is no notion of conquest in Amazonia. For Amazonian people, the civilizing whites did not violently conquer the forest Indians but tamed them. This is a crucial point. The forest Indians were *gente brava*, "wild people," and the whites tamed them through the addictive power of their manufactured goods. The word used here is *amansar*, "to tame, to calm down." The forest Indians were ignorant of the fine things of white people and succumbed to their desire for them. Equally, white people were ignorant of the potent love magic of these forest people and were seduced by Indian women. From this mutual seduction came the mestizos, the mixed blood people. This folk history thus describes three categories of contemporary Amazonian people: mestizo people, descended from the primordial mutual seduction of whites and Indians; white people, whether recent immigrants from outside or descendants of pure sexual relations among immigrants; and Indians or native people, descended from pure marriages among Indians.

This system of social classification is closely linked to *habilitación,* the system of credit and debt that structures virtually all commercial relations in western Amazonia. Habilitación has been translated as extractive merchantilism and is deeply embedded in the economic history of Amazonia. The Amazonian economy has always been characterized by very low capital investment and the extraction of primary products for external industries. The classic case is rubber, but there are many others, such as lumber, jute, barbasco, and coca. Capital investment takes the form of loans to primary producers, and production is a form of debt cancellation. Class position in Amazonia is determined by position in the flow of credit and debt: the Amazonian bourgeoisie are the primary debtors to external industry and the primary creditors of other local people; the direct producers of the goods for export are the major debtors in the system. Lowest of all in the hierarchy of habilitación, and hence of class, are the indigenous tribal people, who are often so indebted that they do not see money and are directly indebted in goods.

The economy of habilitación is characterized by the exportation of primary products and by the massive importation of manufactured goods. In particular, the Amazonian economy lacks a developed internal market in food. This is not because little food is produced in the area but because there is little commercialization of agricultural products. Most of the people low in the hierarchy of habilitación are subsistence producers, clearing the forest for gardens and fishing to provide food. Even in cities like Pucallpa, poor people migrate continuously between an urban residence and an outlying garden house, endlessly balancing subsistence and commercial production. For all Amazonian people, the forest is seen as a limitlessly fecund resource. For the bourgeoisie, the realization of this fertility is restricted only by the availability of external credit and the backwardness of the workers. For the workers, this realization is restricted only by the limitations of their own labor power and by the capriciousness of the *patrones,* the bosses.

Amazonian folk history and racial classification is the social armature of this economy. To be white in Amazonia is to claim recent immigration or pure descent from immigrants from outside. To be white is to be closely connected by family ties to the sources of credit, high up the chain of habilitación. To be Indian or native is to be at the bottom of this chain, furthest from the external sources of credit. But equally, to be native or Indian locates a person close to the forest and to the subsistence economy. To be native in this sense is to be linked by dense kinship ties to other subsistence producers, and so to bask in the secure knowledge that one will never go hungry. To be mestizo is to be in between. Mestizos are potentially connected to the network of white kinship that secures credit in habilitación and are simultaneously potentially connected to the network of native kinship that secures subsistence security. To be mestizo is to be equally remote from both, to risk rejection as too Indian to be trusted with a loan by a white boss or as too white to deserve feeding by native people. In this system, it is impossible to be white and Indian simultaneously, but the category of mestizo provides a continuous field in which Amazonian people can operate, reaching up for credit or down for food, and is a means for rejecting the inconvenient claims of others.

This socioeconomic system is woven into the physical landscape of western Amazonia. The cities of the region, like Pucallpa and Iquitos, are the points of contact between Amazonia and the exterior. They are the places where credit enters the economy, and the city centers are dominated by the commercial buildings and houses of the rich whites. The city center is the most civilized place, where knowledgeable whites manipulate the economy and the state for their own benefit. In the remote forest, the source of potential commodities, live the Indians. The Indians are the least civilized people, ignorant of civilized values, but rich in knowledge of the forest. In between live the mestizos, in the smaller communities along the rivers and in the slums on the outskirts of the big cities. As one would expect, mestizos are a shadowy and ambiguous population, continually moving in and out of the forest and the city in response to the flow of credit in habilitación. They are also at the middle point of knowledge, neither particularly civilized nor particularly associated with the forest. They are a potential switchpoint for knowledge from both domains.

The Economy of Ayahuasca Curing

Viewed from this perspective, urban ayahuasca shamanism ceases to be a mere survival of indigenous tribal cultures in the rootless misery of Amazonian city slums. It can be placed coherently within the symbolism of the Amazonian social order. The people of the slum barrios of Iquitos and Pucallpa are by definition ambiguously poised between the city and the forest and between the white people and the Indians. The worlds of white people and of Indians are enclosed worlds of kinship. For whites, descent and family ties structure business opportunity. For the Indians, kinship constitutes the community of food-sharing. As descendants of whites and Indians, mestizos are in theory linked by kinship to both, but as "mixed blood" people, they are formally excluded from both. This position in the middle has made them the most powerful ayahuasca shamans, masters of taming the curing power of the forest spirits.

The socioeconomic system of western Amazonia associates the forest with the autochthonous wild Indians and with the creation of wealth. The wealth of the forest is liberated for exchange through the availability of external credit. The forest is seen as a limitless fund of such wealth, which is endlessly and spontaneously regenerated. The limiting factor on local commerce is not the recalcitrance of the forest in providing wealth but the vagaries of external demand and hence the flow of credit. For instance, today the forest is full of rubber, and people will say, "This used to be worth money, but now no one wants it." For Amazonian people, the region's poverty is directly related to the capriciousness of foreign capital, not to the recalcitrance of the forest. There is an important contrast here to the Andes. Unlike the soils and mines of the highlands, the forest requires no sacrifice of human substance to survive and reproduce. The forest is not a benign provider, but neither is it bloodthirsty.

The forest is the potential or actual source of valuable commodities, but it is also present as constantly regenerating gardening land and hunting territory. As the economy of habilitación cycles in boom and bust phases, poor people cycle in and out of subsistence production. The forest is always available then as a source of life, albeit life without money. This same duality is found in the cosmology of ayahuasca shamanism. The forest spirits afflict people with illness in revenge for damage caused to their domain, but they also, through the curing session, cure illness. As Chevalier has noted (1982:347), this curing tradition works by identifying the patient with plants that are self-generating. But he does not stress sufficiently that curing identifies the patient with the supreme domain of plant self-regeneration, the forest itself, the limitless extension of trees and vines.

I have not yet referred to a very important feature of ayahuasca shamanism in the region under discussion. Ayahuasca shamans only cure illness or inflict it. I have heard of no cases in which an ayahuasca shaman gives a person luck in business or takes it away.[4] A shaman

---

4. Contrast to the cases in Taussig 1987.

may be contracted to inflict illness on a business associate who has reneged on a debt, but a shaman has no power to call in credit or to make money or other capital grow. The mother spirit of ayahuasca will show shamans everything in the world but offers only the powers of magical curing and killing. In this sense, the powers of the aya-huasca shaman are the powers of the forest, and he can only give the patient the gift of the forest, which is life or death. Ayahuasca shamans and their patients become like the forest—primordially healthful and alive, with potential for creation but with nothing accumulated. They are like the forest Indians, vital and potent, but without the accumulated possessions of civilization.

The idioms of ayahuasca curing are the idioms of the subsistence economy and result from and contribute to the intimate kinship that characterizes the social world of the forest Indians. The spirits cure illness that they themselves have afflicted because they want to, and they do so for no return other than the identification of shaman and patient with them. Chevalier has argued that the spirits are paid in goods and faith, as in habilitación (1982:371-76). I have never heard of spirits receiving goods from either shaman or patient, and I can-not imagine how such a transaction could take place, given the repugnance spirits show for human things. As to faith, I think that Chevalier has mistranslated the term. The spirits do not demand faith in the Christian sense, acceptance of the truth of the unknowable, but belief in the efficacity of the shaman as one who can contact the spirits and enlist their aid. Shamans tell their patients, "*Tu no me crees, pero vas a ver lo que puedo yo*" (You don't believe me, but you're going to see what I can do). Through the agency of his curing songs, the shaman seduces the spirits into revealing themselves as people, and hence into helping the shaman cure the afflicted patient. The idiom here is of "help" and is drawn from subsistence economy, where people help each other because they recognize their funda-mental identity. Here again, ayahuasca curing remakes people in the image of forest Indians.

Though the logic of relations in the curing session is one of identification and help, the relationship between shaman and patient is characterized initially by aggressive demands for money. Ayahuasca shamans must be paid, and their fees are often exhorbitant. They frequently demand full payment in cash and in advance. Such demands are a parody of habilitación, where credit is extended from a rich boss to a supplicant worker. In the economy of habilitación, the debt is repaid by a quantity of valuables extracted from the forest. In ayahuasca shamanism, the cash payment is validated by the patient's life. The shaman parodies habilitación by demanding the instant and prior cancellation of a debt, to stress the importance of the aid he will give. But if the patient cannot pay, the shaman will often simply forego payment in cash for lifelong "help" from the patient. Given life by the shaman, the patient is drawn into his personal network of "helping" kin. Many shamans I talked to seemed to prefer such helping relationships to straight monetary transactions, finding them more in accord with their own relations to the spirits.

My analysis here explains why Amazonian people should particularly associate ayahuasca shamanism with forest Indians. Curing through ayahuasca restores people to the primordial condition of identification with the forest and locates them in the life-sustaining network of relations that governs the subsistence economy. Ayahuasca shamans and their patients thus take on the primordial condition of forest Indians, who life in the forest and whose lives are an extension of it. But my analysis also points toward an explanation of why ayahuasca shamans are particularly associated with mestizos. Ayahuasca curing power is acquired through a process of training with other shamans. It is a technique of taming, *amansando*, the forest spirits into restoring the primordial condition of health to the patient. As such, ayahuasca shamanism is a form of "historical sorcery" (to borrow Taussig's phrase [1987]), which allows a return to the beginning of history. Only mestizos can effect such a return to the beginning, for they are the only category of people in Amazonian imagery whose origin lies in history. Mestizos, the "mixed-blood people" descended from whites and Indians, living between the cities and the forest, become the masters of the paths between them.

The historical sorcery of ayahuasca shamanism is centered on that spatial category that connects the forest and the city: the river. In Amazonian popular imagery, the forest lies upriver from the city, and the city lies downriver from the forest. The river provides the communication between them, and along it extends the chain of habilitación. Mestizos are frequently, and with justice, called *ribereños*, "people of the river banks." On the Bajo Urubama, I was told in awe of the maximally powerful ayahuasca shamans, the *muraya*. These shamans, I was told, can enter the river and visit the villages of the river spirit people. Such shamans are no longer human, because in their continuous contact with spirits, they have been taken over by them. They are *banco muraya*, "stool shamans," whose bodies are seats of the spirits. They are described as little old mestizo men, whose rustic houses and shabby dress disguise their terrible powers. The awe-inspiring muraya shamans are at the summit of the historical sorcery of ayahuasca shamanism. They are the supreme source of curing knowledge.

The imagery of the muraya shaman finds its counterpart in the imagery of ayahuasca. The vine is both a cultigen and a wild form: it may be planted or found in the forest. The best ayahuasca, I was told, is found in very old gardens, where it has matured with forest regeneration. Thus, ayahuasca belongs to the process of transition from domesticated space to full forest. Further, though ayahuasca is a forest plant, its winding habit is seen by Amazonian people as iconic of the winding paths of rivers. Similarly, the opacity and clarity of water is iconic of different states of ayahuasca visions, and hallucinatory vision is often likened to seeing underwater. The hallucinatory experiences of ayahuasca unite all spatial and temporal extensions in the curing ritual, as the takers of the drug see distant times and places revealed to them in the local time and place of the session. Like its counterpart the muraya, ayahuasca is a potent icon of curing as historical sorcery.

Ayahuasca Shamanism in History

Most histories of ayahuasca shamanism see it as indigenous to the pre-Columbian cultures of the area and as a recent import into urban mestizo contexts. This seems highly unlikely, given the pervasive association of ayahuasca shamanism with mestizo people and the actual flow of shamanic knowledge from the cities to the forest. Against this approach, I suggest that the origins of ayahuasca shamanism should be sought in the origins of mestizo as a social category and in the origins of Amazonian cities. Given the relative lack of historical analyses of western Amazonia,[5] the following account is sketchy and tentative. A fuller account of these historical developments, concentrating on the Ucayali area, is presented in Gow (1991).

---

5. Cf. Santos 1988.

The term *mestizo*, as it is used today in western Amazonia, is part of a tripartite hierarchy of "white," "mixed-blood people," and "Indians" (or "native people"). Many anthropologists have taken this classification literally and have searched for the origins of mestizo people in actual intermarriage between white colonizers and indigenous peoples. But the tripartite "racial" hierarchy of contemporary Amazonia is a transformation of a prior tripartite heirarchy of the early nineteenth century and before. This is the heirarchy of *wiracochas, indios cristianos,* and *indios infieles,* that is, "white people," "Christian Indians," and "pagan Indians."[6] This hierarchy was the social classification of the Jesuit and later Franciscan missions of Maynas. Maynas is the old name for the northern Amazonian area in Peru and Ecuador.

The missions of Maynas transformed the large riverine settlements of indigenous Amazonian people into the first "cities." They introduced the spatial heirarchy that still characterizes the region, with the center controlled by the religious authorities of the mission order and by the much less prominent white civil authorities. Around the mission were the barrios of the Indian converts, and beyond them, in the forest, were the pagan Indians who refused mission life. These Jesuit and Franciscan missions were important in western Amazonia from the early seventeenth century until the mid-nineteenth century, but they were never particularly powerful. Their power base came from their control over the trade routes between the northern Andes and Amazonia, and their fortunes waxed and waned with the local demand for such goods. Many tribal peoples moved in and out of this mission system at will, frequently killing the missionaries and burning the towns as they moved out.[7]

The only solid support for the missions, and the only long-term "Christian Indians," were those tribal people who had been so badly affected by depopulation that they were unable to sustain themselves against the military threats of their neighbors. These people moved onto missions for the admittedly slight protection they afforded, converted to Catholicism, and took up dialects of Quechua, the regional trade language of the area, as a main language. A good example of

6. Cf. San Roman 1975, Stocks 1981 and 1984, and Gow 1991 for accounts of western Amazonian history.

7. Cf. Stocks 1981 for the mission history of the Cocama and Cocamilla.

such peoples are the Omagua and the Cocama of the Amazon main-stream and lower Ucayali. These peoples remained hostile to missions, frequently attacking them, until a combination of epidemic illness and intensified slave raiding from Central Amazonia drove them to seek the protection of mission life.

I suggest that these are the conditions in which contemporary ayahuasca shamanism evolved out of older shamanic practices. Space does not allow for a detailed analysis here, but this early mission context explains many features of ayahuasca shamanism. The main language of this tradition is northern Amazonian Quechua, the mission lingua franca, with some contribution from Cocama, the language of one of the most important mission peoples. The cosmology of ayahuasca shamanism dovetails beautifully with the reduced Catholicism of the missions: the priestly "fathers" and celestial Deity of Catholicism are the other side of the "mother" and "demon" (*supay*) spirits of the forest and river. This cosmology is inscribed in Amazonian social space, with the center of the city a civilized Christian domain, surrounded by the river and the forest. Further, the vertical axis of the cosmos, which is apparently absent from ayahuasca curing, is present: it is the axis of Christian eschatology. The sky and underworld, in Amazonian cosmology, are occupied by the Christian heaven and hell. Ayahuasca shamans deal with the restoration of life and claim no power over the destinations of those they fail to cure.

One of the most remarkable aspects of the ayahuasca curing session is the way it implicitly parodies the Catholic Mass. This is most dramatically evident in the way in which the shaman blows tobacco smoke over each little cup of ayahuasca before it is given to the drinkers. The ayahuasca brew is explicitly said to be the body of *ayahuascamama*, such that in curing, the body of a powerful forest mother spirit is physically ingested in the pursuit not of salvation but of earthly life. Though the similarity between the two ritual activities was never pointed out to me by any informant, and I never voiced my impressions to anyone, the following story makes the connection rather more clearly. Early in this century, the missionary Espinosa asked a Cocama shaman the reason for his ritual actions of curing. The shaman replied: "Well, you priests, when you baptize people, don't you blow, spit, pour over salt and oil, and do lots of other stupid things? Well, we do the same" (Espinosa 1935:146). This

Cocama shaman's statement was not, I suspect, a piece of cultural relativism, but a revelation of the inner logic of ayahuasca shamanic practice.

A crucial factor in the development of ayahuasca curing and its relationship to Catholicism must have been the mission people's experience of epidemic illness. The writings of missionaries show they had no means to combat these deaths. Writing on the missions in western Amazonia in 1661, the Jesuit priest Figueroa noted:

> The baptisms which we have done in the time since these holy missions started number more than six thousand, eight hundred and eighty. Of these around three thousand are children of seven years or less. And many more than half of these have died before arriving at the adult age in which they might have lost the grace of baptism. Just for them, even had they been fewer, one must admit to the good use of the time and work necessary, for they have with certainty flown to heaven, and almost all, or most of them, would have died without baptism if the Fathers had not walked these forests. (Figueroa et. al. 1986:239)

The peoples most seriously affected by such epidemics were those who became Christian Indians. The failure of missionaries to deal with such illnesses, and their complacency in the face of them, would have provided a major impetus to the development of alternative modes of power. In particular, the split between curing power and eschatology in western Amazonian popular religion fits well with such a situation.

We should look for the evolution of ayahuasca shamanism in western Amazonia in the historical context of such missions, not in the contemporary cultures of traditional indigenous peoples. Much more historical research needs to be done, including a far more meticulous and sensitive reading of the documentary evidence than that I have presented here. The ayahuasca shamanism of these mission peoples presumably developed out of the transformation of preexisting shamanic systems, which may have been of a very different order. For example, the transformation of the vertical cosmic axis into a Christian eschatological axis must have displaced and transformed prior vertical cosmologies. As Hugh-Jones has shown for the northwest Amazon (this volume), particular kinds of shaman are differentially affected by historical changes, as they transform, decline, or burgeon into messianic cults. Most suggestively for the present analysis, he suggests that foreign missionaries can come to occupy the places of certain kinds of shamans in historical change. Such research into western Amazonian ayahuasca shamanism remains to be done and would undoubtedly reveal a much more complex historical evolution than the crude outline presented here. At the very least, by challenging the survival and importation model of urban ayahuasca shamanism, this chapter shows the necessity of such research.

Even if the basic pattern of ayahuasca shamanism evolved on these early missions, its history does not stop there. In the late eighteenth century and early nineteenth century, the Franciscan mission system came into conflict with the developing trade along the Amazon with Brazil. The traders and missionaries vied for control of the Christian Indians, whom the traders wanted as boatmen for their trading voyages. The traders extended goods in credit to these people and persuaded many to move into the new trading towns like Nauta and Pevas. This process intensified dramatically with the expansion of the rubber industry from Brazil into western Amazonia in the later nineteenth century. The missions collapsed, and with them the social heirarchy of European missionaries, Christian Indians, and pagans. It was transformed into the social hierarchy of habilitación. The Christian Indians became *mozos,* "workers," or mestizos to distinguish them from the "real Indians," the violent and recalcitrant forest peoples who had to be tamed by the rubber industry bosses.

I suggest that as rubber production and debt relations expanded into the world of the forest Indians, so did ayahuasca shamanism. The mestizos, who were the workers of the rubber industry bosses, brought with them a readymade technique for curing the massive rupture caused for these tribal people by the extremeties of violence and exploitation in the rubber industry. My data for the Bajo Urubamba Piro suggests that prior to the rubber industry period, shamanism was rather different from its current form, involving possession by forest animal spirits. It seems to have been less exclusively focused on curing illness: shamans apparently dealt in the magical control of game animals as well. A number of messianic-type movements accompanied the transformation of the Piro from a politically independent people into debt slaves.[8] In this century, shamanic knowledge was imported by the Piro form mestizo people from the Ucayali, who first arrived in the area during the rubber industry period, and it continues to be imported. Today, ayahuasca shamanism is the dominant curing tradition, far eclipsing what little remains of old-style Piro or Campa shamanism. I suggest that *ayahuasca* shamanism continues to grow and evolve in the Bajo Urubamba and in other similar areas of western Amazonia, because the same relations that governed the rubber industry govern the region today.

Tentative as my historical analysis is here, it explains why ayahuasca shamanism is found where it is today. It is found among all those people who were linked into the economy of rubber in western Amazonia and is absent among those who were not. It is absent among the Perené Campa and Amuesha, who do not use ayahuasca for curing purposes. These people worked rubber, but in social relations focused on the Andes. Ayahuasca shamanism is not found among the Sharanahua, Cashinahua, and Culina of the Purus River, who worked rubber for Brazilian bosses, or among the Harakmbút of Madre de Dios, who violently repelled rubber workers.[9] All these peoples use ayahuasca, but in very different contexts to that of ayahuasca shamanism. Most significant of all, given their location next to such classic systems of ayahuasca shamanism as those of the Canelos and Napo Quichua and the Achuar, it is not found among the Waorani of Ecuador, who, according to Laura Rival, have violently repelled all contact with their neighbors (Laura Rival pers. comm.). Rival reports that Waorani shamans use ayahuasca, but not in the curing ritual.[10] This is also true of the Perené Campa and the Purús peoples, where ayahuasca is the focus of collective ritual but is not used in the curing session. The integration of ayahuasca use into the very heart of curing ritual, and the attendant conflation of the meanings of the drug and of the shamanic act, is the distinctive hallmark of ayahuasca shamanism.

This historical exposition has been brief and tentative and requires much more historical research. But it at least questions the

---

8. Cf. Gow 1990.

9. Weiss 1975; Santos, letter to the author, (1985); Siskind, 1973a, 1973b; and McCallum, letter to the author, (1984).

10. Rival, letter to the author, (1990).

plausibility of the dominant view of ayahuasca shamanism among the mestizo people of western Amazonian cities as an ad hoc import from "authentic" indigenous cultures and a fundamentally pathetic response to their historical conditions. Chevalier writes that ayahuasca shamanism lends itself to "the degrading treatment of lower-class subjects as the living images of an undomesticated and quasi-infantile [Indian] humanity" (1982:423). We might ask here, "Degrading treatment by whom?" The only other people in Amazonia who I have heard talk about ayahuasca in this way are certain Catholic priests influenced by the Marxism of Althusser. The Amazonian bourgeoisie despises the mestizos and native peoples for their poverty and ignorance, but not for their curing powers. We anthropologists should not turn on our informants and blame them for the failure of our own search for authentic knowledge.

Ayahuasca shamanism responds directly to the lived experience of illness among mestizo and native people in western Amazonia and to the historical circumstances of their affliction. That, I have argued, is what ayahuasca shamanism evolved to do. My interpretation, I hope, also goes some way toward explaining new contexts of ayahuasca shamanism, such as those along the colonization frontiers between the Andes and Amazonia in southeastern Colombia, described by Taussig, and in the cult of Santo Daime in the State of Acre in western Brazil. Ayahuasca shamanism, evolved to cure the disease of western Amazonian colonial experience, is available to respond to the new ills afflicting those who are coming into the region from the Andes and southern Brazil.

REFERENCES

Brown, Michael F.
1984 *Una Paz Incierta: Historia y cultura de las comunidades Aguarunas frente al impacto de las Carreterra Marginal.* Lima.
1986 *Tsewa's gift: Magic and meaning in an Amazonian society.* Washington and London.

Chaumeil, Jean Pierre
1983 *Voir, Savoir, Pouvoir: Le chamanisme chez les Yagua du nord-est Peru.* Paris.
1988 Le Huambisa défenseur: La figure de l'Indien dans la chamanisme popularie (région d'Iquitos, Pérou). *Recherches Amérindiennes au Québec,* 18, nos. 2–3:115–26.

Chevalier, Jacques M.
1982 *Civilization and the stolen gift: Capital, kin, and cult in eastern Peru.* Toronto.

Dobkin de Rios, Marlene
1972 *Visionary vine: Psychedelic healing in the Peruvian Amazon.* San Francisco.

Espinosa, P. Lucas
1935 *Los Tupí del Oriente Peruano: Estudio lingüístico y etnográfico.* Madrid.

Figueroa, Francisco de, Cristobal de Acuña, et al.
1986 *Informes de Jesuitas en el Amazonas, 1660–1684.* Iquitos.

Fuentes, Aldo
1988 *Porque las piedras no mueren: História, sociedad y ritos de los Chayahuita de Alto Amazonas.* Lima.

Gow, Peter
1990 Could Sangama read?: The origin of writing among the Piro of eastern Peru. *History and Anthropology* 5:87–103.
1991 *Of mixed blood: Kinship and history in Peruvian Amazonia.* Oxford and London.

Harner, Michael
1972 *The Jívaro: People of the Sacred Waterfalls.* Garden City, N.Y.

Lamb, F. Bruce
1971 *Wizard of the Upper Amazon: The story of Manoel Córdova-Rios,* Berkeley, Calif.
1985 *Rio Tigre and beyond: The Amazon jungle medicine of Manuel Córdova-Rios.* Berkeley, Calif.

Loos, Eugene, Patricia M. Davis, and Mary Ruth Wise
1979 El cambio cultural y el desarollo integral de la persona. In M. L. Larson, P. M. Davis, and M. Ballena Dávila, eds., *Educación Bilingue: Una Experiencia en la Amazonia Peruana.*

Luna, Luis Eduardo
1986 *Vegetalismo: Shamanism among the Mestizo population of the Peruvian Amazon.* Stockholm.

San Ramon, Jesus V.
1975 *Perfiles históricos de la Amazonia Peruana.* Iquitos.

Santos, Fernando
1988 Avances y limitaciones de la historiografía Amazónica: 1950–1988. In F. Santos, ed., *Primer seminario de investigaciones sociales en la Amazonía.* Iquitos.

Seymour-Smith, Charlotte
1988 *Shiwiar: Identidad étnica y cambio en el río Corrientes.* Quito and Lima.

Siskind, Janet
1973a *To hunt in the morning.* Oxford and New York.

1973b   Visions and Cures among the Sharanahua. In Michael Harner, ed., *Hallucinogens and shamanism*. Garden City, N.Y.

Stocks, Anthony W.
1981   *Los nativos invisibles: Notas sobre la história y realidad social de los Cocamilla del Río Huallaga*. Lima.
1984   Indian Policy in Eastern Peru. In M. Schmink and C. H. Wood, eds., *Frontier expansion in Amazonia*. Gainesville, Fla.

Taussig, Michael
1987   *Shamanism, colonialism and the wild man: Healing, terror and the space of death*. Chicago.

Taylor, Anne-Christine
1981   God-Wealth: the Achuar and the Missions. In N. Whitten, ed., *Cultural transformations and ethnicity in modern Ecuador*. Urbana, Ill.

Uriarte, Luis M.
1982   Reductores reducidos? Petróleo, Protocolo y Tsantsa: Fronteras etnicas de los Jívaro Achuara. Manuscript. Paper presented at the 44th International Congress of Americanists, Manchester.

Weiss, Gerald
1975   *Campa Cosmology: The world of a forest tribe in South America*. Anthropological papers of the American Museum of Natural History. 52/5. New York.

Whitten, Norman
1976   *Sacha runa: Ethnicity and adaptation of Ecuadorian jungle quichua*. Urbana, Ill.
1985   *Sicuanga runa: The other side of development in Amazonian Ecuador*. Urbana, Ill.

Part 2. Shamanism and the State

Saints' Cults and Warrior Kingdoms in South India

Susan Bayly

Precolonial south India is a tantalizing venue for the exploration of ecstatic or inspirational religion and its interaction with the power of kings, chiefs, and warrior elites. At first glance, the region might seem to be a domain of clear and unexciting oppositions. The southern Tamil- and Telugu-speaking country (which became the Madras presidency of British India after the colonial conquest of the early nineteenth century) has often been thought of as a homogenous society. It is supposed to have an all-pervading tradition of high Brahmanical orthodoxy that was shaped over many centuries by the interaction of the region's great Hindu temples and its dynasties of pious Hindu kings. It would therefore follow that something resembling shamanism would belong to the fringes of this supposedly caste-bound Hindu world; one would look for cult worship, possession, and mediumship among marginalized forest tribal peoples or an agrestic "underclass." Furthermore, there ought to be a clear-cut opposition between the values and institutions of so-called traditional south Indian kingship and the dangerous powers accruing to charismatic cult saints, healers, and those in touch with destructive or demonic spirits.

However, even in the late eighteenth century, in the period immediately preceding the onset of formal colonial rule, south India was anything but an established or static Hindu society. Just beyond the rich rice-growing river valleys where the region's Brahmans and ancient dynastic centers were concentrated was an arid hinterland terrain full of warriors and brigands and recently sedentarized cattle-keepers and predator groups. These people included Tamil-speaking plains-dwellers like the Maravas and Kallars, as well as their arms-bearing Telugu neighbors, descendants of immigrant peasant warriors from modern Andhra Pradesh, who were commonly known as "Vadugas" or "northerners." The domains of these fierce martial plains-dwellers did not conform to the well-known stereotype of river valley high culture, Brahmanical caste ranking schemes, and purified temple worship. The importance of this other south India is now being widely recognized, especially in the work of such ethnohistorians as Nicholas Dirks (1987).

In the seventeenth and eighteenth centuries, these hinterland territories were galvanized and transformed by a series of new developments, only some of which derived from the expansion of European commercial and military power. These new developments included a very rapid commercialization of agriculture and commodity production, and the creation of a multitude of new kingdoms and warrior-ruled chiefdoms. Some of these realms were founded by rulers whom we would now regard as Hindus, and some, crucially, were built up by avowedly Muslim dynasts. Throughout the subcontinent, this was a time of massive expansion in the scope and effectiveness of state power. Well before the establishment of British colonial rule, in both north and south India the growth of a dynamic maritime trading economy accelerated the pace of commercialization in the agrarian hinterland and provided the wherewithal for assertions of power by aspiring sovereigns and dominion-builders. Among the most dynamic of these new would-be rulers in south India were the Kallar, Marava, and Vaduga clansmen, who were continually competing with one another to consolidate new resources and to establish themselves as chiefs of the small, volatile warrior domains, which became known as *poligar* [*pāḷaiyakkārar*] kingdoms.[1]

This was also a period of rapid change in south India's religious landscape. Among these martial predator groups and their competing new kingdoms, the shrines and devotional traditions that are now thought of as those of traditional Hinduism were only just coming to be recognized in the seventeenth and eighteenth centuries. Almost everywhere in the Tamil and Telugu country, the worship of the so-called pure gods of theistic high Hinduism overlapped and inter-

---

1. On south India see Stein 1980; Ludden 1985; Washbrook, forthcoming; Dirks 1982, 1987; Subrahmanyam 1990; S. Bayly 1989:19–27. For north India in this period see, e.g., Barnett 1980; C. A. Bayly 1988:7–44; Perlin 1983.

penetrated with the worship of fierce male power divinities and blood-taking goddesses, forever locked in combat with fearful demonic enemies (*asuras*). With their clubs and boomerangs and their taste for blood sacrifice, these divinities were conceived of as bringers as well as healers of disease and affliction. Most had the power to possess human sufferers and to speak and act through the possession of trance dancers and inspired adepts. This world of dark powers and demonic cult traditions would therefore seem to fit into the category of inspirational or noninstitutionalized religion.

The most distinctive feature of the region is that this same period of seventeenth and eighteenth century dominion building was also a time when its hinterland populations, devotees of such warrior divinities as Karuppan, the club-bearing Marava hero god, and Aiyanar, the conquering horseman, were also taking a leading role in creating dynamic local manifestations of Islam and Christianity.[2] A century or more later, under the influence of European missionaries and the British colonial authorities, there was at least a partial separation into formal confessional groupings, with an emphasis on scripture and doctrine. This involved an attempt to identify clear-cut constituencies and a tendency toward the formation of distinct communities of those who would now be thought of as Hindus, Muslims, or Christians in the modern sense.

In this fluid and violent world of competitive kingdom building, Islam and Christianity were being received in the south Indian hinterland in the form of individualized saint cults. The devotees of these cults placed themselves under the sovereign power of living gurus and deified warrior heroes who were perceived in the same terms as the region's power divinities, that is, as kings, avengers, and conquerors, and as leaders of demonic armies with the double-edged capacity to heal and inflict disease and destruction. Even though their distinguishing Muslim or Christian origins were acknowledged by their devotees, these cult divinities partook of the same supernatural energy, or *sakti*, that empowered the fearful warriors and power divinities of the "Hindu" pantheon. (The term *Hindu* is used here to denote deities who would now be classed as part of traditional south Indian Hinduism.)

These pervasive forms of cult worship lacked priestly hierarchies

---

2. For an extended treatment of this see S. Bayly 1989.

and formal structures of authority. Their appeal was charismatic and inspirational and was therefore not a force that could easily be subordinated or institutionalized. Even so, the rulers of the region's dynamic new warrior chiefdoms were among the most ardent devotees of Muslim and Christian heroes and cult saints. These kings and chiefs viewed Christian and Muslim cults and shrines as indispensable resources; the cults' predominant themes of supernatural conquest, power, and sovereignty were seen as crucial adjuncts in the generation of political power. Thus, through their acts of pious patronage, the poligar rulers (who are now routinely described as professing Hindus) became key agents in the transmission of Islam and Christianity across hinterland south India.[3]

How did this come about? Looking first at the expansion of cult-centered Christianity in the warrior kingdoms, it is known that such cults as those of St. Thomas the apostle and of the Tamil Lord Yagappan, St. James of Compostella, were spreading in the poligar country from the early seventeenth century. In the Ramnad Marava domains, Yagappan/St. James was (and still is) portrayed as a hero on a white horse meting out destruction to a demonic enemy. Like St. Thomas, he inflicts and cures diseases, and he is an embodiment of sakti like the region's warrior divinities and Muslim cult saints. Also, like so many of these entities, he is a being of the wilderness and forest fringes, and in this he becomes a supernatural counterpart of the Maravas and other warrior predator groups for whom he became a special focus and tutelary.[4]

Shrines to "indigenized" Christian figures like Yagappan, St. Thomas, and the Virgin Mary were being built and patronized in the south Indian poligar country at a time when organized missionary endeavors were still confined to the remote coastal trading stations of the Portuguese *Estado da India*.[5] Those who disseminated these cults were not western priests or missionaries but inspired individuals, south Indians who may have had some contact with the missionary churches, but who then built up personalized followings on their

---

3. The Kallar rulers of Pudukkottai were typical patrons of these shrines (S. Bayly 1989:205); inscriptions recording such benefactions can still be seen in the former poligar domains, and early Jesuit letters describe acts of kingly patronage at Christian sites (*Travels of the Jesuits* 1762, 1:452–75).

4. Durairaj, Kaithanal, and Jeyabalan, 1973:6; Mosse 1986:57–59, 454–62.

5. The *Estado* comprised the regions of Asia over which Portugal claimed ecclesiastical and imperial authority in the sixteenth and seventeenth centuries.

own, in the tradition of the gurus of devotional Hindu bhakti worship. These gurus are the spiritual masters whose devotees cultivate ecstatic union with the divine, through submission to the guru's god-given kingship, and through veneration of his supernatural attainments.

The region's Christian gurus are widely remembered as builders of early cult shrines to such beings as St. Peter and Yagappan/St. James, and as supernaturally endowed founder figures in vernacular local histories that chronicle the origins of south India's early Christian communities.[6] The guru preceptors were revered by their followers as sovereign lords whose command of an esoteric teaching (the Christian "way," or *margam*) endowed them with miraculous healing skills. Although most of them were local Tamils and Telugus, a number of European missionaries also came to be revered in the same way. Such individuals were not honored as representatives of an overarching church authority, but again, as holy men and cult saints who were readily absorbed into these traditions of spontaneous, informal cult building, with their associated notions of miraculous preceptorship and demonic antagonists. In oral histories that grew up around the medieval fortress and temple town of Madurai, for example, the Jesuit missionaries of the seventeenth century were described as summoning up demonic beings to engage in cosmic warfare on their behalf. In one such legend, the Jesuits try to overcome the Hindu god Siva by conjuring up a demon *asura* in the shape of a cow. The cow dies of love when confronted by Siva's champion, the divine bull Nandi. The smitten cow is then turned into a hill, the Pasumalai, which stands just south of the city.[7]

Similarly, the canonized sixteenth century Jesuit missionary Francis Xavier was (and still is) revered by his south Indian devotees as a bringer of the Christian margam to the Tamil country. The vernacular hagiographical traditions portray him as a king in majesty, and also as a fierce healer and disease bearer with the power to cure the sick and reanimate the dead. Even the official Jesuit histories incorporated this tradition of the guru preceptor and saint as king and healer of kings. In one of many such accounts, a Christian guru is credited with the miraculous healing of a local poligar chief who

---

6. French Jesuit missionaries collected five hundred such Tamil manuscripts (*ōlais*); extracts are cited in Caussanel ca. 1925.

7. Baliga 1960:403.

has been afflicted with an ulcerous skin disease.[8] In such accounts, whether the divinely endowed preceptor or adept is a Christian saint or guru or a Muslim *pir* (an unaffiliated Sufi mystic or adept of the type discussed below), these awesome and painful displays of supernatural power usually lead on to an account of the afflicted earthly king or chief offering up his ecstatic submission to the saint (or the guru, in this case). So what really was the relationship of these Christian cult saints and the region's warrior chiefs?

In the seventeenth and eighteenth centuries (and to a considerable extent today), the divine domains of the sakti goddesses and warrior hero gods overlapped and intersected with the domains of Siva, Vishnu, and the other pure vegetarian Hindu high gods. The blood sacrifice that was demanded by gods like Karuppan or the region's fearsome smallpox goddesses involved the offering of a sacrificial goat or buffalo. The animal's death and dismemberment can be seen as recreating an act of triumph, the beating back of the demonic forces that are always on the verge of overwhelming the created universe. These forces manifest themselves in the form of the feverish and eruptive diseases with which these deities are so closely associated.

The values and imagery of kingship lie at the heart of this religious tradition, and so it is not surprising that this worship was such a vigorous force in the poligar realms. The divine victory is an assertion of dominion; it affirms the supernatural kingdom that is preserved and ruled over by the triumphant god or goddess, whose subjects are the suppliant worshipers who revere the deity as grateful subject-devotees. These traditions were closely connected with the acts of conquest and usurpation by which all the region's aspiring warrior chiefs sought to establish and perpetuate their rule in the seventeenth and eighteenth centuries. The milieu was one of perpetual conflict. Every would-be dynast was seeking to expand his domain, to incorporate new men of power into his networks of alliance and affiliation. But at any moment these tribute-paying lesser chiefs might seek to annihilate the bigger lords to whom they were affiliated.

Throughout the chronicles that recount the founding and history of the south Indian poligar kingdoms, local bards and chroniclers recount the rise to power of a new warrior dynasty as an act of grisly blood sacrifice.[9] This constantly repeated metaphor exactly mirrors

8. Durairaj, Kaithanal, and Jeyabalan 1973:7.

9. Many such chronicles have been preserved in the compilations made by the

the dismemberment of the sakti deity's demon-enemy. The aspiring lord turns on his overlord's enemy, dispatches him, and severs his head from his torso. This creates a new tie of blood and kinship with the greater dynast until, inevitably, the lesser lord elects to turn on his patron and dispatch him in exactly the same way. Thus, these accounts of dismemberment and blood sacrifices are a wholly accurate reflection of the volatility of the region's precolonial political landscape. Hierarchies of power and affiliation really were continually created and reformulated in this period. The shedding of blood was seen as a means by which to transfer or assert the warrior dynast's claims of dominion and to associate the power of the aspiring king with the supernatural domain of the region's warrior gods and power divinities.[10]

These same themes of dominion and disease bearing came to permeate the language and worship of the newly constituted hinterland Christian cult traditions. As in the case of the Muslim saint martyrs, or *shahids,* who were also a dynamic force in indigenous south Indian religion, themes of dismemberment and sacrifice also predominated in the autonomous Christian cult traditions, not only in religious imagery, but in the generation of political power. By the late seventeenth century, Jesuit chroniclers were reporting tens of thousands of so-called Christian converts in the poligar country.[11]

But while the Jesuits were beginning to tour and to carry out mass baptisms among these warriors and recently sedentarized ex-pastoralists, powerful Marava and Kallar poligar rulers were now making lavish acts of patronage to the autonomous shrines and cult centers associated with figures like Yagappan/St. James. At one level, these links can be viewed in purely strategic terms. Some poligar chiefs created ties of allegiance and affiliation with independent Christian cult groups, at the point when such rulers began to assert claims of sovereignty against the demands of overlordship imposed by their more powerful warrior suzerains. In this sense, the followers of Christian saints and gurus were no different from any other recipients of an aspiring ruler's pious patronage. South India's would-be dynasts supported an impressively eclectic array of Muslim saint cult shrines,

---

nineteenth-century ethnographer Colin Mackenzie, now in the Mackenzie Collection—General, India Office Library, London.

    10. E.g., Mackenzie Collection—General, 9:61–62, India Office Library, London.

    11. *Travels of the Jesuits* 1762, 1:452–53; Strickland and Marshall 1865:42.

Hindu temples, and sakti, or power-divinity, cults. This was all consistent with the loose and assimilative character of south Indian kingship, and with the ruler's capacity to incorporate almost any new
affiliates within their political networks, without regard for formal
boundaries of community or confessional adherence. In supporting
Christian shrines, such a ruler was simply asserting dominion, incor-
porating one more locus of power, so as to proclaim that he was
lord of an active and expanding sacred network.

But if all saints, shrines, and gurus could be of such value to
an aspiring warrior dynast, why did south India's most powerful
warrior king subject one of the best known Jesuit missionary heroes
to a particularly grisly martyrdom? Do we have here a case of the
uncontrolled guru and cult divinity as an enemy of established political order? I think not.

The victim in question was the celebrated seventeenth-century
European Jesuit John de Britto. Like the earlier Jesuit Francis Xavier,
de Britto's travels in south India in the 1680s endowed him with the
stature and reputation of an autonomous guru or holy man, a spiritual
exemplar and master of the power-giving Christian path, or margam.
Under his influence, large numbers of Marava clansmen around the
domains of the powerful Marava poligar ruler of Ramnad accepted
baptism, particularly retainers and close kin of this lord's chief rival,
who was another aspiring Marava king, the raja of Siruvalli.[12] The
Ramnad ruler viewed these cult adhesions as a direct challenge to
his expansion in the poligar country. By attaching themselves to
de Britto and to de Britto's Christian margam, these warriors were
enhancing this other kingdom-builder's power and marking themselves off as affiliates of a rival realm. De Britto's power as a holy
man was now being deployed against the Ramnad ruler, and so he
had no choice but to neutralize the missionary's dangerous powers.
When de Britto refused to leave the region and continued to attract
Marava adherents, the Ramnad ruler had the missionary carried off
to a remote forest hiding place, where he was tortured, beheaded,
and impaled on a wooden stake.[13]

As in the case of south India's shahids, or martyred warriors,
and its many deified cult heroes, this act ensured that de Britto was
perceived forever after as a being of supernatural attributes who had

12. Kadhirvel 1977:9, 40–42; Mosse 1986:39.
13. Bertrand 1850–54, 3:447; Neill 1984:307; Mosse 1986:428–33.

been bloodily martyred and dismembered. His execution site has become a famous south Indian cult shrine revered for its powers of miraculous healing and fertility. This part of the story stands out particularly in relation to the political aspect of the de Britto cult. According to the legends, de Britto's executioners beheaded the saint, cut off the hands and feet of the corpse, and tied them to the execution post "because they feared his power."[14] Whether or not all these gory events really took place, such details suggest that the cult tradition reflected the real political conflicts of the poligar country. What is implied is that when the Siruvalli ruler launched his challenge to the Ramnad king, de Britto became a focus, a source of power and dynamism, for this other ruler's expansive new regime.

This is why it was not enough to kill the missionary. He had to be offered up as a dismembered sacrifice, like the sacrificial victims of the poligar kings' state-building chronicles. Some accounts say that de Britto's limbs had to be nailed down "so as to immobilize his vengeful spirit."[15] Even in death, he would otherwise possess the capacity to build up a perpetually expanding supernatural domain, and the saint's patron would still be able to latch on to his expansive divine power.

Similarly, among the hundreds of pirs or Muslim cult saints who had come to be venerated in south India by the end of the eighteenth century, one in particular, a being known as Khan Sahib, functioned in precisely this way. The full name of this pir and martial hero was Muhammad Yusuf Khan. Like many such cult figures in India and beyond, Khan was a real historical personality, and much is known about his career as the romantic eighteenth-century "rebel comman-dant" of Madurai.[16] He was one of the period's typical would-be conquerors and state-builders, and in 1764 he was executed by the ruling *nawah* of south India's Arcot domain, whose power Khan had been trying to usurp with an army of Kallars and other local warriors. After the death of this rebel general, the aspiring usurper's severed limbs were transferred to a series of shrines that were revered as repositories of power by large numbers of subject-devotees. To this

---

14. Versions of this tradition are still recounted today. See also Neill 1984:307; Ramaswami 1972:90.

15. Ramaswami 1972:90.

16. Orme 1803–62, 2:251, 398–459; Burhan Ibn Hasan 1934–39, 2:152, 215–38, 274–80.

day Khan is honored as a deified cult hero in the southern Tamil country, and he is a special focus of worship among members of the martial Kallar clans whose ancestors had fought in Khan's armies.[17] In the case of de Britto, however, the Ramnad Marava ruler made sure that such a transformation could not take place. *His* enemy's supernatural champion was neutralized as a source of danger to the realm: when the missionary's body was "immobilized," his executioners deactivated his power as a rival dominion-builder.

This does not seem to indicate opposition between kingship and the representatives of inspirational cult religion. In the volatile world of the south Indian chiefdoms, the expansion of cults and the creation of new political realms were expressions of almost indistinguishable forms of power and authority. They employed the same idiom of blood sacrifice and dismemberment; they were mutually intertwined, mutually indispensable, however contentious their relationship might be in the real world of competitive statecraft.

How then do south India's distinctive manifestations of Islam fit into this picture of autonomous cult worship and political conflict? Here it is useful to look again at the eighteenth-century nawab of Arcot, the south Indian Muslim ruler who executed the martyr-general Khan Sahib. This aspiring dynast, Muhammad Ali Walahjah (1722–95), was the son of a north Indian soldier-adventurer. From his installation as British-backed ruler of the Arcot realm in 1749, Muhammad Ali fought to establish himself as an embodiment of pious Islamic kingship, according to conventions of sovereignty and princely conduct that had become standardized across most of the Asian lands in which Islam had been implanted.[18]

Here one might expect to encounter a clear-cut opposition between ungovernable cult worship and the demands of an insecure but self-consciously Islamic political tradition. But there were relatively few long-standing Muslims among the people whom Muhammad Ali was seeking to rule. The great majority of those who could be classed as professing Muslims were linked with a much larger constituency of believers who possessed extremely ambiguous com-

---

17. For more details see S. Bayly 1989:193–215. A key source for the Khan tradition in the Kallar and Marava country is the Tamil narrative ballad *Kān Sāhibu Saṇḍai* ("Khan Sahib's War"), which portrays the hero as a deified embodiment of indigenous poligar kingship (Vanamamalai 1972).

18. See Burhan Ibn Hasan 1934–39.

munal affiliations. For these people, the key institutions of worship were the shrines of pirs. As can be seen from the case of Khan Sahib, in south India such beings comprised a large array of miraculously endowed cult saints and warrior heroes who shared all the distinctive features of the south Indian sakti deities and Christian cult divinities, but who were still recognized as personages with distinctively Islamic origins. Apart from Khan, there were (and still are) as many as five or six hundred pirs in the Tamil and southern Telugu country. These include avengers and disease bringers like the mythical forest-dweller Kat Bava, the blinder of malefactors, and the terrible Nathar Wali of Trichy, who fights a cosmic war with demonic antagonists and visits his opponents with hideous ailments and afflictions.[19]

By the time Muhammad Ali came to power, the Arcot realm contained hundreds of the characteristic domed tomb shrines (dargahs) at which devotees of pirs congregate to make contact with the activated energy, or *barakat*, of the saint, and to cultivate the skills that bring the inner initiates of such cults into a state of ecstatic communion with the divine. In many parts of the Muslim world, the representatives of formal or scriptural or mosque-centered Islam maintain an ambiguous or openly hostile relationship with this tradition of autonomous cults. This is because their practices bring devotees very close to the worship of non-Islamic peoples (Hindu-Buddhists in Java, for example, or the followers of Christian and autonomous Hindu cult divinities in India).

Muhammad Ali Walahjah, however, was an assertively Islamic ruler who managed to identify himself as a mosque-builder and a patron of correct Islamic scripturalism, while simultaneously supporting the region's rich networks of pir cult devotion so as to nourish his new claims of kingship. Here, too, there was indispensable sovereign power embedded in the sacred authority of the unaffiliated cult divinities. The greatest of them, the pirs with the most awesome reputations and the most popular pilgrimage centers, were cult saints who ought to have been particularly unappetizing to a pious Muslim king. The forest-dwelling Kat Bava and the disease-bearing Nathar Wali were explicitly endowed with the attributes of Hindu divinity. Their activated sacred energy was described in their legends and

---

19. Information on the region's *pirs* and shrine networks can be derived from, e.g., Sali 1981; Suharwardy, n.d.; Ghulam Abdul Qadir Nazir 1950; and Turnbull, ca. 1823.

hagiographical texts as sakti, the power of the goddess and demon-slayer.[20] Their shrines were centers of trance dancing, exorcism, and miraculous healing. And in praise poems and chronicles, the pirs' miraculous feats took place in a sacred landscape full of unmistakably Hindu features: the saints journey to Kasi (Benares) on the sacred Ganges and interact with such divine beings as Nandi, the companion of the god Siva.[21] But however apparently heterodox or "unIslamic," these pirs were repositories of the activated supernatural energy from which any would-be ruler would have to derive his earthly power and legitimacy.

Every pir was identified as a sovereign lord and ruler of an invisible supernatural domain, a *vilayat*.[22] And because Muhammad Ali's kingdom was so lacking in strong historical antecedents, he had no choice but to claim as many pirs as he could as his supernatural predecessors and sponsors. The shrines of saints like Kat Bava and Nathar Wali received lavish benefactions from this Arcot ruler. Key rituals of the new Muslim state were designed to map Muhammad Ali's temporal realm onto the sacred landscape that his court chroniclers said had been marked out and occupied for him by the great south Indian pirs in their personifications as warrior conquerors and martyred sovereign lords.[23]

Throughout his reign and that of his successors (right up to the time when the nawabs were reduced to the status of privileged British pensioners in 1851), there was no attempt by the Arcot court to diminish these cult traditions or to forge them into some new form of Islamic conformity. On the contrary, through the great state pilgrimages during which the rulers beat out the boundaries of their domain and exchanged symbolic kingly offerings with the cult saints' representatives, the Arcot rulers attempted to match themselves to

---

20. *Tōḷḷayiram Vitaikaḷ* 1976:39.

21. Janab Gulam Kadhiru Navalar 1979:81; Ghulam Abdul Qadir Nazir 1950:63; Shaik Hasan Sahib 1980:30, 32; Persian hagiography of the Penukonda Saint Baba Fakiruddin in Unbound Translations, class 1—Persian 18, India Office Library, London. (Again, the term *Hindu* is used here to refer to traditions of worship that would be classed today as part of formal theistic Hinduism.)

22. Cf. Eaton 1984:348.

23. One of the most elaborate of these ceremonies was recorded in Ghulam Abdul Qadir Nazir's account of the great Arcot state pilgrimage to the *dargah* at Nagore, 200 km. south of Madras. The pilgrimage was undertaken in 1823 and described in Ghulam's *Bahar-i-Azam Jahi* (translation published in 1950).

the sovereign status of these reigning supernatural lords.[24] The nawabs' official dynastic literature acknowledged that the unaffiliated cult saints commanded powers that were unpredictable, even menacing, to the conventional pious Muslim. Many pirs were identified with drug taking, transvestism, and other wild and unconventional behavior. But it was accepted that the wilder they were, the truer their powers and the more effective their ecstatic and self-generating communion with the divine would be.[25]

Again, this made the pirs indispensable to any ruler who had hopes of attaining legitimacy in a society where such cult beings were figures of paramount importance. The result was that the petty poligar chiefs (now identified as Hindus), and the builders of this much larger and more elaborate Muslim-ruled dominion, devised traditions of kingship that identified the aspiring ruler as a co-equal sovereign and a subject-devotee of the region's untamable and awesome cult divinities.

Colonial rule altered some of these relationships. The long-term impact of British rule was to bring about an artificial turning toward more formal, more scriptural, and more hierarchical forms of religion. With the suppression of the poligar chiefs at the beginning of the nineteenth century, the balance between temple-centered high Hinduism and the religion of the blood-taking cult divinities shifted in favor of an artificially Brahmanized religious culture. Missionary churches absorbed many of the autonomous Christian cult traditions. And the British dismemberment of the Arcot nawabi realm, and the colonial authorities' fear of uncontrolled pir cult traditions as bearers of potential subversion and rebellion among their soldiery, gave new prominence to the Islam of learned jurists and formal Sufi mystical orders.[26]

In this sense, then, south India acquired a new definition of state power that seems to have been the enemy of at least some forms of ecstatic or noninstitutional religion. Even the looser and more all-embracing forms of kingship that prevailed in the seventeenth and eighteenth centuries were sometimes in violent opposition to the cult domains of figures like Khan Sahib or de Britto, at times when their power was connected with dangerous new forms of affiliation and

---

24. Ghulam Abdul Qadir Nazir 1950:27–32.
25. Ghulam Abdul Qadir Nazir 1950:116.
26. This shift can bee seen, for example, in Kokan 1974. See also Chinian 1982:4, 15–24.

alliance-building. It may be, then, that we should look at different stages in the emergence of states and kingdoms. It would seem that inspirational or cult-centered religions can reach a more comfortable accommodation with young, vigorous, and expansive kingships, and that there may be a crisis in these relationships when new and more ambitious forms of state power come into being.

REFERENCES

Baliga, B. S.
1960 *Madurai district gazetteer*. Madras.

Barnett, Richard
1980 *North India between Empires: Awadh, the Mughals, and the British 1720–1801*. Berkeley.

Bayly, C. A.
1988 *The new Cambridge history of India*. Vol. 2, pt. 1 *Indian society and the making of the British Empire*. Cambridge.

Bayly, Susan
1989 *Saints, goddesses, and kings: Muslims and Christians in south Indian society, 1700–1900*. Cambridge.

Bertrand, J.
1850–54 *La Mission du Maduré*. 4 vols. Paris.

Burhan Ibn Hasan
1934–39 *Tuzak-i-Walajahi*. Trans. S. Muhammad Husayn Nainar. 2 vols. Madras.

Caussanel, Fr. A., S. J.
ca. 1925 Historical notes—Tinnevelly district. MS. Madura Mission archives of the Society of Jesus, Madras.

Chinian, P.
1982 *The Vellore Mutiny—1806*. Madras.

Dirks, Nicholas B.
1982 The pasts of a *Palaiyakarar:* The ethnohistory of a south Indian little king. *Journal of Asian Studies* 41 (4): 655–83.
1987 *The hollow crown: Ethnohistory of an Indian kingdom*. Cambridge.

Durairaj, A. S., Kaithanal, P., and Jeyabalan, S.
1973 *Directory of the diocese of Palaiyamkottai for the year of our Lord 1973*. Palaiyamkottai.

Eaton, Richard Maxwell
1984 The political and religious authority of the shrine of Baba Farid in Pakpattan, Punjab. In B. Metcalf, ed., *Moral conduct and authority: The place of Adab in south Asian Islam*. Berkeley and Los Angeles.

Ghulam Abdul Qadir Nazir
1950   Bahār-ī-A'Zam Jāhī of Ghulam 'Abdu'l-Qadir Nāzir. Trans. S. Muhammad
      Husayn Nainar. Sources of the history of the Nawwabs of the Carnatic.
      Madras University Islamic Series no. 11. Madras.

Janab Gulam Kadhiru Navalar
1979   Karuṇaik-k Kaṭal: Nākūr Āṇṭavaravarkaḷin Punita Vāzhkkai Varalāṟu.
      (Ocean of grace. The holy biography of the Nagore lord). Nagore. 2d ed.

Kadhirvel, S.
1977   A history of the Maravas, 1700–1802. Madurai.

Kokan, Muhammad Yousuf
1974   Arabic and Persian in Carnatic. Madras.

Ludden, David
1985   Peasant history in south India. Princeton.

Mosse, C. D. F.
1986   Caste, Christianity, and Hinduism: A study of social organization and
      religion in rural Ramnad. D.Phil. diss., Oxford University.

Neill, Stephen
1984   The beginnings to A.D. 1707. Vol. 1 of A history of Christianity in India.
      Cambridge.

Orme, Robert
1803–62.   A history of the military transactions of the British nation in Indostan.
      3 vols. Madras.

Perlin, Frank
1983   Proto-industrialization and pre-colonial south Asia. Past and Present
      98:30–95.

Ramaswami, A.
1972   Tamil Nadu district gazetteers: Ramanathapuram. Madras.

Sali, J. M.
1981   Tamiḻakattu Tarkākkaḷ (Tamil dargahs.) Madras.

Shaik Hasan Sahib, S. A.
1980   The divine light of Nagore. Nagore.

Stein, Burton
1980   Peasant state and society in medieval south India. Delhi.

Strickland, W., and Marshall, T. W. M.
1865   Catholic missions in southern India to 1865. London.

Subrahmanyam, Sanjay.
1990   The political economy of commerce: Southern India 1500–1650.
      Cambridge.

Suharwardy, H.
N.d.   The life and works of the past Muslim sufis of Tamilnad with special
      reference to Urdu literature. Typescript.

Tōḷḷāyiram (900) Vitaikaḷ kōṇda orē oru mātuḷampazham (Nine hundred seeds,
    one pomegranate).
1976   Trichinopoly (Tiruccirapalli).

Travels of the Jesuits into various parts of the world.
1762   2 vols. 2d ed. London.

Turnbull, Thomas.
ca. 1823   Geographical and statistical memoir of Tirunelveli and its Zemindaries.
    Revenue Department Sundries, no. 38. Tamilnadu archives, Madras.

Vanamamalai, N., ed.
1972   *Kān Sāhibu Saṇdai* (Khan Sahib's war). Madurai.

Washbrook, David
Forthcoming   South India. Vol. 2, pt. 7 of *The new Cambridge history of India.*
    Cambridge.

The Slaves, the King, and Mary in the Slums of Antananarivo

Maurice Bloch

This chapter deals with phenomena that are characteristic of modern Antananarivo, the capital of Madagascar, and to a lesser extent, of other large towns in that country.[1] These are possession cults of a kind that seems quite different from those we know from the past and from contemporary rural Madagascar, although they are not unrelated.

In particular, I am concerned with a possession cult of a mythical queen called Ranoro and of her son Rakotomanditra, which has reached a high degree of organization and was, for a while, a regular tourist attraction. Although my knowledge of what goes on in this cult in detail is sketchy, it has been described a number of times by different writers (Cabanes 1972). It is similar to certain other Malagasy possession cults where the spirit is often a dead Merina ruler or member of the royal family (Baré 1977). The cult of Ranoro and her son is by far the most important of such urban cults. Because of the royal status of the spirits, these cults can be seen as a celebration or continuation of the Merina state. The Merina kings and queens dominated Madagascar during the nineteenth century, but their gov-

---

I would like to thank Fenella Cannell for help in the preparation of this manuscript and Professor Franciose Raison-Jourde for useful comments on an earlier draft.

1. This chapter is not based on systematic field research, although it relies for background on my intermittent research on the rural Merina from 1964 to 1976, on my long-standing closeness to a number of families involved in urban Merina christianity, and on my lifelong knowledge of Catholicism. Because of this rather ad hoc basis, this chapter should be seen as merely theoretically suggestive for further research.

ernment completely disappeared as a result of the imposition of direct rule by the French shortly after the invasion of the island in 1895.

I shall concentrate on two features of the cult of Ranoro and her son. First, most adherents are of slave descent, which is also true of all similar royal cults. The demography of the adepts of the cults has been noted by Raison-Jourde (1983:59–61), among others. The cult mediums, the shrine keepers, and the congregations are almost exclusively descendants of Merina slaves, whose ancestors were for the most part brought to Imerina as captives of Merina troops during the latter half of the eighteenth century and the first part of the nineteenth century. Most of these slaves were taken from other peoples in Madagascar and come from ethnic groups quite different from the Merina. In many cases the slaves and their present day descendants are physically distinct from the free Merina and their descendants, because marriage with descendants of slaves is strongly disapproved for descendants of freemen and therefore very rarely occurs. Second, there has, of late, been a symbolical rapprochement made by the adepts between Ranoro and the Virgin Mary, which is partly explained by the fact that most cultists are Roman Catholics.

The fact that most of the participants in these cults are of slave descent at first seems odd and counterintuitive. One would think that these people could find little to celebrate in a state that treated their ancestors so badly and that created a society where most of them remain second-class citizens, often living in the worst slums of the capital. In fact, possession of slaves by royal ancestors is not entirely new.

In 1863, after the traditionalist queen Ranavalona was succeeded by her bizarre son, Radama the second, who was in large part the puppet of the Europeans, a great and spontaneous revolt arose in indignation against the innovations that were being introduced and against the fact that the country was being handed over to foreigners. One aspect of this revolt was described by the missionaries of the time, such as Davidson, as "a dancing mania" (Davidson 1867, Raison-Jourde, 1976). Large numbers of people in trance, possessed by the spirit of the dead Ranavalona and by the spirits of anonymous members of her court, especially the carriers of the royal impedimenta, who accompanied her everywhere, formed a gigantic procession, marching, or rather dancing, toward the capital to restore the dead queen and her reign. All the eyewitness accounts of this awesome, but by no means unique, event noted that most of the possessed were slaves. We may ask why the slaves were so keen to restore a ruler who, together with her father, had personally been the cause of their unfortunate social situation (Raison-Jourde 1976).

The reason the slaves or their descendants were so keen to re-create in imagination the Merina kingdom at its apogee is found when we look at Merina notions of descent and of the state, as well as at Malagasy-wide ideas concerning slavery. When people are taken as slaves, their ties to their ancestors are broken, because they no longer receive blessing from their ancestors at the various familial rituals. As a result, not only are the people taken in slavery lost to their families and forebears, but they also lose their ancestors in an irrevocable way. To understand the catastrophic nature of the rupture, one has to know that Malagasy descent is never simply a matter of folk biology, of the transfer of "blood," "genes," or other substances held to create continuity from parents to children. Instead, it has to be created and maintained by blessing from ancestors. The slave, severed from this blessing and hence from the control of his ancestors, comes to be seen as a danger to other people, and for the same reason, he also becomes a problem for his former kinsmen.

The consequences of this conception of descent are shown by a number of reports concerning what happened to slaves after they were officially freed by the French. To the surprise of the French administrators, very few of the freed slaves went back to the areas where they and their ancestors had originated (André 1899:189–91). We also know that those who did were often not well received and, most significantly, that their free countrymen were unwilling to inter-marry with them,[2] although they found marriage with freemen from other descent groups or even other ethnic groups acceptable. Only the former slaves had been placed, we might say, outside potential kinship and almost outside humanity. It was as if the interruption in blessing had simply been too long.

In contrast to what seems frequently to happen in Africa, the slaves that were not free did not become absorbed into the families of their owners. The slave-owners were very careful to ensure that the slaves did not receive the blessing of *their* ancestors either (Bloch 1980). To explain this phenomenon, I shall summarize some points

2. This was made clear to me during brief fieldwork near Fandriana in 1964, when I tried to trace relatives of Merina slaves then living in northern Imerina.

concerning Merina blessing that are discussed in previous publications (Bloch 1986).

All Merina rituals are rituals of blessing and involve the blesser getting into contact with the ancestors—that is, with the physical remains of the ancestors—by obtaining water, which is the symbol of vitality (but in this case a vitality controlled by the power of the ancestors), and then blowing it onto the blessed. In the past, the blessers were very careful to ensure that not a single drop of the water of blessing reached the slaves during such rituals, because if it did, they would become descendants of the ancestors and thus cease to be slaves. Contact with the water of blessing, or with the ancestral remains, makes you a descendant of the ancestors. This is often understood in a very material way—it makes a dry, "ancestral" element grow inside the body of the blessed. Little by little, the ancestral element will completely take over, until finally, after death, nothing will be left but ancestral remains, which can in turn become a source of blessing. The transmission of bodily substance in Merina descent is therefore achieved not by biological means but by ritual means, which explains why slaves, excluded from full participation in the rituals of their own group and in those of the masters', are so quickly cut off from the ancestors.

Another way to think of the taking over of the body of descendants by the ancestors, a way implied by Merina descent, is as a form of possession, which is how I have often described it. Descent is logically a kind of possession, because through it the ancestors enter your body and make it act according to their will. The process of embodying descent also takes forms familiar from other types of behavior that are more readily recognized by anthropologists as types of possession. When Merina elders, people whose bodies have already been largely taken over by the ancestral, speak in the form of oratory appropriate to elders, they are behaving and speaking in a way empirically identical to the way they behave when possessed for other reasons. Moreover, when speaking in this way, they say that they allow the ancestors to "speak through them."

If descent can be understood as a form of transmission through gradual possession, one feature of this transmission is central. It is a highly policed and restricted form of transmission, and the policemen are the elders, whose task is to ensure that the transmission of the ancestral goes to the right people and not to the wrong people.

Denying slaves access to the water of blessing is one way they do this in Merina society.

This discussion of the blessing of descent also has a more general relevance for understanding the ideology of the Merina state as it existed until the coming of the French. The Merina state often represented itself in ritual as if it were one big descent group. The king (or queen) dispensed the blessing of their ancestors onto free subjects, represented as children, through a nationwide ritual of annual blessing, the ritual of the royal bath (Bloch 1987). This ritual also symbolically transformed the recipients of the blessing into permanent "descendants" of the monarch—that is, into subjects. This blessing was most carefully policed. The monarch blessed the various segments of the population in strict rank order and took great care not to let any slave receive the water of the blessing of the royal bath, because if they did, the slaves would be automatically freed. That this apparently did occasionally happen is another indication of the seriousness of the right to inclusion in the blessing.

I have now assembled, I believe, the elements of Merina ritual that enable us to understand why the slaves, at least before the French conquest, were attracted to possession by spirits of Merina royalty and their entourage. Violently cut off from their original source of blessing in the villages of their own ancestors, the slaves had been made hungry for blessing, so that they might be reconstituted as full moral beings. However, under normal circumstances, access to the blessing of the ancestors whose tombs occupied the areas where the slave-owners had brought them was also impossible, because of the strict policing of the flow of blessing. Slaves were thus rigorously excluded from blessing in all formal Merina ritual contexts.

This policing, however, could not extend to the instances of direct possession by Merina ancestors that occurred during the dancing mania in the nineteenth century. It is always a possibility within the Merina system that ancestors, especially remote ancestors—ancestors who have loosened the ties to their descendants and are on the way to becoming local ancestors rather than descent ancestors—will bypass the proper channels and seize and possess a passing living body at random, any living body, who is thereby directly and violently made a descendant. Such an event, although fairly common, is always problematic, because it bypasses the proper authorities, who will, in normal circumstances, try in various ways to neutralize the threat to their power.[3] But, when for political or economic reasons, everything is in chaos, as was the case in Imerina in 1865, and when furthermore, as was also the case then, the proper channels of authority are discredited (because they had sold out to foreigners), random possession is likely to well up in the bodies of those hungry for ancestral blessing, and the manifestation of this possession will go unchecked by the normal gate-keepers of ancestral contact. When we understand the nature of other Merina forms of contact with the supernatural, it is possible to see why possession epidemics should have occurred in 1863 and why they should mainly have affected those of slave descent.

This explanation of possession of slaves by royal spirits in the nineteenth century does not, however, account for why this sort of thing is happening nowadays, when the Merina state has long been considered dead, or why it is occurring in the part of Imerina that one might think most distant from the past: the slums and suburbs of Antananarivo.[4] But a similar phenomena is occurring nowadays because the Merina state is not completely dead. The constituent descent groups of freemen of the old kingdom, which I called "demes" in *Placing the Dead* (Bloch 1971), still live on, in part by means of Christian churches, mainly Protestant churches, which in that same book I called "ancestral churches."

These churches have congregations that are usually closely linked by kinship ties, that have a strong tendency toward endogamy,[5] and that consist not so much of locals as of people who consider the territory in which the church is found "land of the ancestors," that is, people who have tombs in the area and will be buried there.[6] As a result, these congregations are one of the ways the demes continue to exist. On Sundays, whenever possible, these congregations meet for services that always last several hours and that are led by pastors

---

3. This may be done through exorcism, or the possessed person may be made to undergo various ordeals to prove the genuineness of their possession, and these ordeals were usually fatal.

4. Although the area where the cult of Ranoro prevails is an area where many Protestants of free descent live, it is generally acknowledged that the Catholic descendants of slave descent are her devotees.

5. Because I have not done systematic fieldwork in Antananarivo, I cannot quantify the actual degree of endogamy. I feel confident in making the statement from what I know of a few families.

6. The Malagasy term used by the churches to refer to the people is *zanaka ampielezana* literally, "the dispersed children."

of their choosing. A great deal of the time of these interminable services is taken up with notices concerning the various members of the congregation and their activities, religious and otherwise. Another feature of these churches is the extremely large numbers of members of the congregation who hold, or have held, some office on the multitude of committees that are formed for the upkeep of the church, celebrating this or that anniversary, organizing youth groups, and so on. The result of these intensely demanding and often expensive activities is that these congregations are as corporate "corporate groups" as Fortes could have ever dreamed of.

The churches thus succeed in reconstituting the Free Merina society of precolonial times, and like the demes of old, they too channel blessing to the younger generations who will be their successors.[7] Though this blessing is mainly Christian blessing, it is also a blessing coming from the ancestors of the deme, that is, from the previous members of the congregation. This ancestral blessing is not distinguished from blessing obtained from ancestors by more typically Malagasy rituals dispensed at such occasions as circumcisions or secondary funerals. Furthermore, because such blessing can be seen to originate with the deme, which itself was a constituent part of the precolonial kingdom, the blessing obtained in church is also a continuation of the blessing that emanated, and emanates, from Merina royalty.

The significance of these congregations is not merely mystical, however. At the same time as blessing, membership of the congregation of ancestral churches passes on less spiritual advantages, such as membership of tight networks of connections and relationships that are highly relevant for life in modern Madagascar and that give critical advantages for the members of such congregations in business or when dealing with all aspects of the administration, whether this be ministries, schools and universities, or doctors and hospitals. Belonging to an ancestral church gives you practical advantages and an apparently privileged access to the blessings of the various Christian supernaturals and the blessings flowing from the ancestors of the deme and the ancient kingdom.

This transfer of blessing and social advantage is, or at least is experienced by outsiders and insiders alike as being, tightly policed,

7. The word used for blessing, *Tsodrano*, can apply both to Christian and ancestral blessing.

like the traditional transfer of the blessing of the ancestors. Insiders know that they must participate completely in the all-absorbing activities of the church and must obey the senior members of the church if they want access to the essential spiritual and material continuity that these congregations canalize. Outsiders, especially descendants of slaves, experience the policing of blessing within congregations as a systematic exclusion, which it is in part intended to be. This policing, above all, takes the form of ensuring that no descendant of free Merina marries a descendant of slaves.[8]

One of the more admissible reasons for not intermarrying with descendants of slaves is that these are often Catholics. Although there are a number of Merina of free descent who are Catholic (and who therefore try to form similar Catholic ancestral congregations), on the whole, and especially to the north of Antananarivo, where the shrine to Ranoro is situated, the Catholics tend to be of slave descent, and they do not form the same kind of ancestral congregations.[9] They do not have any "land of the ancestors" to refer to, and because Catholicism is not Merinized like Protestantism, it does not lend itself so well to the maintenance of quasi-demes in a Christian form. The Protestant churches are therefore seen as devices that cut off the descendants of slaves from the flow of blessing from the ancestors, and thus the present-day descendants of slaves find themselves in a position quite similar to that of their forebears.

It is not surprising that they, rather like their ancestors, are hungry to establish a direct connection with sources of blessing that bypass the policed transfers from which they have been excluded. In the past, Catholicism filled this need to some extent, and now some of the independent churches, such as the Adventists and some recently formed syncretic churches, seem able to do so better. However, given the continuing central importance of ancestors for all Malagasy, Christian or not, such churches can supply only a partial sort of blessing.

To gain ancestral blessing, the descendants of slaves, who are

---

8. Many pastors and members of these congregations feel that an inconsistency exists between such practices and the liberal Christian doctrines to which they adhere in other contexts, so there is much heart searching.

9. There are, I believe, one or two exceptions to this generalization. These concern ex-slave groups that had special privileged status in the kingdom and that were and have remained endogamous.

in an analogous position to their forebears, must turn to possession by Merina royals or to participation in cults focused on their mediums. In the terms in which it is seen by the participants of the cults, they welcome the autonomous predations of the old kings and ancestors into their bodies, or the bodies of people like them, because these give them a place in the religious and social configuration that normally distributes its blessing in a way that excludes them. Possession by royal Merina ancestors makes the descendants of slaves suddenly, unexpectedly, and directly the blessed recipients of the power of their ancient oppressors, which the descendants of freemen carefully and exclusively cultivate for themselves. As was the case for the nineteenth century, the reason that the descendants of slaves are possessed by Merina royals is found by looking not only at slave practices but at other practices focused on the descendants of their masters.

What I have said so far applies to all the royal cults in Antananarivo and its suburbs, but in the final part of this chapter, I want to consider aspects that are more specific to the cult of Ranoro. These are, firstly, that Ranoro is believed to have been a Vazimba and, secondly, that she is being merged with Mary.[10]

The shrine at Ranoro is situated where it is because this is where, at her death, the queen entered a lake, now a prime object of the cult, and because she made this lake her tomb. This action marks her out, probably more than anything else, as a Vazimba,[11] one of those aboriginal peoples who the ancestors of the Merina are believed to have driven out but who nonetheless remain closely associated with the fertility of the land and of those who live on it (Bloch 1986: chap. 6).

The break between the Merina and the Vazimba is not believed to have been total. The most important way in which continuity with the Vazimbas has been maintained is that Vazimba queens are believed to have married the invaders and thereby to have become the mothers of subsequent Merina royals. Chief among such Vazimba queens is Ranoro.

---

10. I am told by Professor Franciose Raison-Jourde that the association of Ranoro and Mary had not yet occurred in the 1960s.

11. The prime symbol of Merina tombs is stone, and water is seen as its opposite. This matter is discussed throughout Bloch 1986.

At the shrine we find not only a cult of the mother Ranoro but one of her royal son Rakotomaditra, who is a part, though not in a way about which I am all that clear, of the main royal genealogies. Although the shrine is always referred to as the shrine of Ranoro, her son presently possesses the resident medium and gives advice to suppliants and public predictions at rituals held at the shrine.

The combination of a Vazimba mother and a Merina royal son seems to me a particularly suitable cult object for the descendants of slaves who are attaching themselves directly to ancestors in a way that bypasses the policed descent of the state and the Protestant church. The Vazimba are often associated, although loosely, with the slaves by the idea that they are stereotypically black, so a black woman who is conquered by a Merina king and produces a Merina king from her womb seems a particularly appropriate object of worship for the descendants of slaves. Possession is often thought of in Madagascar as elsewhere in sexual terms, so the black medium possessed by a Merina king seems to reecho Rakotomaditra's conception. Also, the products of this union are seen as those who receive the blessing of the spirit, and by participating in the cult of Ranoro, the descendants of slaves place themselves both at the beginning and at the end of the line of legitimate descent.

Recently, however, Ranoro has become more than a Vazimba; she has become associated with Mary. The association of Ranoro with Mary is not mine and is quite explicit, perhaps nowhere more so than in the fact that in the holy of holies of the shrine of Ranoro, at the place where the most important offerings are made, there stands in the middle a very French plaster statuette of the virgin. I was told by the keeper of the shrine that this statuette had been brought by a devotee of Ranoro who had a dream in which Ranoro had told her that she and Mary were one. The shrine keeper then went on to explain to me at great length that this was highly appropriate, because "both were holy, both could cure, and both were mothers of holy beings." His explanation in terms of "elective affinities" seems to me totally satisfactory, and I want to expand on his suggestion. In doing so, I have to admit that I have not done systematic research on the cult of Mary.

What has always seemed to me to be exaggerated in modern anthropological and other discussions of Mary, and here I am thinking of such writers as Leach (1967) and Warner (1976), is their emphasis on the sexual aspect of her virginity. I think it is fair to say that the semantic field evoked by the word virgin in Romance languages has as much to do with purity in general as with the absence of sex in particular. The central Catholic image of Mary, the image of the annunciation, is, as far as I know, hardly mentioned in the anthropological literature. By far the most important act of the Marian cult is the recitation of the *Ave Maria*, which are the words the archangel Gabriel addressed to Mary at that key moment.

Most often stressed about Mary in folk Catholicism is the stereotyped story of the poor, ordinary girl who finds herself, much to her surprise, being chosen by God from among "all other women" to be the vessel of the highest honor possible. It is often suggested that Mary was chosen precisely because of her meekness. This story finds parallels at every level of popular culture, from womens' magazines to film plots in which the ugly duckling of the typing pool is suddenly scooped up by the tall Texan oil millionaire and transformed into a creature of beauty, wealth, and social honor. Mary's election having been "chosen" irrespective of her status—that is, her sex or her descent—for direct bodily unification with God is what I believe makes her so attractive to her followers, who like all worshipers identify with the object of their worship.

The cult of Mary, at its most intense, is very close to the experience of spirit possession. It is the experience of being chosen and penetrated "out of the blue." To fully understand this experience, it is necessary for us to look at the Marian cult in the same way as I have just done in the discussion of the cult of Merina royals, that is, in terms of what it stands in contrast to.

The Marian cult, as Andrea Dahlberg stresses in her thesis on Lourdes, stands in contrast to the cult of God and Christ (Dahlberg 1987). Christ, by contrast to Mary, is holy, not because of being chosen "out of the blue," but because of descent. Not only is he the son of God, but he is also, as the Gospel according to St. Matthew says at its outset, the son of Abraham, David, Isaac, Jacob, Jehosaphat, Joram, Azariah, and many others who are all men. This policed transmission is furthermore reflected in the way the blessing of God through Christ is received by Catholics. It is passed on by priests, who obtain their positions through carefully controlled transmission/descent channels, this time those of the church, with its apostolic succession. It reaches the layperson in the form of communion under very strict conditions. First, the communicant must have been baptized, that is made a spiritual descendant in the Christian genealogy. Second, he must have confessed his sins. Then, after a good deal of bargaining in confession, in which the priests require the acknowledgement of their authority as traffic police between God and man, and only then, can the worshiper enter into contact with the divine body. Could we have a greater contrast with Mary, who was filled by God without the authority of any institution, was caught by surprise by an angel without being asked for any proof of being particularly deserving, and like most of her devotees, was of the wrong sex to be included in the genealogy except at the lowest rung. It is surely this experience in which her devotees seek to participate.

Mary's situation is like that of the Merina slave who lacks the proper descent credentials for contact with the ancestors and, furthermore, is excluded by the traffic policemen called elders from ever being included in the line of blessing, but who is suddenly and "out of the blue" possessed by the greatest of all ancestors. And again, it is this experience in which the devotees of the royal spirit mediums seek to participate. The similarity between Mary and Ranoro and the attraction of their cults is therefore perhaps even stronger than was seen by the woman who brought the statue or by the shrine keeper who explained the matter to me. Or perhaps they, also brought up in the French variant of Catholicism, were somehow aware of what I am saying, but because they had not been invited to participate in an academic seminar, they did not feel the need to go on about it at such length.

REFERENCES

André, E-C.
1899   De l'esclavage a Madagascar. Paris: Rousseau.
Baré, J-F.
1977   Pouvoir des vivants, langage des morts. Paris: Maspéro.
Bloch, M.
1971   Placing the dead: Tombs, ancestral villages, and kinship organization in
        Madagascar. London: Seminar Press.
1980   Modes of production and slavery in Madagascar: Two case studies. In
        J. Watson, ed., Asian and African studies of slavery. Oxford: Blackwell.
1986   From blessing to violence: History and ideology in the circumcision ritual
        of the Merina of Madagascar. Cambridge: Cambridge University Press.

1987   The ritual of the royal bath in Madagascar: The dissolution of death, birth, fertility into authority. In D. Cannadine and R. Price, eds., *Rituals of royalty: Power and ceremonial in traditional societies.* Cambridge: Cambridge University Press.

Cabanes, R.
1972   Cultes de possession dans la plaine de Tananarive. Cahiers du centre d'Etudes des costumes. Faculte de Droit 9. Tananarive, Universite de Madagascar.

Dahlberg, A.
1987   *Transendence of bodily suffering: An anthropological study of English Catholics at Lourdes.* Ph.D. diss. University of London.

Davidson, J.
1867   *Choreomania: A historical sketch with some account of an epidemic observed in Madagascar.* Edinburgh: Oliver and Boyd.

Leach, E. R.
1967   Virgin Birth. *Proceedings of the Royal Anthropological Institute, 1966.*

Raison-Jourde, F.
1975   Les Ramamenjana: Une mise en cause populaire du Christianisme en Imerina, 1863. *ASEMI* 7 (2–3): 271–93.
1983   Introduction to F. Raison-Jourde, ed., *Les souverains à Madagascar.* Paris: Karthala.

Warner, M.
1976   *Alone of all her sex: The myth and culture of the Virgin Mary.* London: Weidenfeld and Nicholson.

Astrology and the State in Imperial Rome

Tamsyn Barton

Astrologers, who for most of their history have denied or minimized their links with religion, do not fit easily within even the loosest definition of shamanism. Study of astrologers in Imperial Rome does, however, reveal a struggle over access to knowledge of destiny with varying political ramifications in a complex precapitalist society.[1] Astrology, the art of discovering the future by studying the movements of the stars, first emerged in Mesopotamia in the first half of the second millennium B.C., where it was in the overwhelming majority of cases concerned with questions of state. The first horoscope of a private individual to be found dates from 410 B.C.[2] However, the rudiments of the present system do not emerge until around the second century B.C., as a result of a dialogue with the rest of Greek science. I shall only be concerned here with individual astrology, rather than other parts of the discipline—such as astrological meteorology or astrological ethnology, the study of the effect of the stars on racial characteristics—because the domain of individual astrology is the locus of conflict.

---

1. To facilitate cross-disciplinary dialogue, I am also deliberately offering a highly schematized historical depiction that avoids reference to the scholarly controversies in the secondary sources as much as possible, with the aim of minimizing detail that might prove tedious for the nonspecialist. Most glaringly absent from my schematization is the question of regional variation throughout the empire, but I am not convinced this would be a fruitful line of investigation, given the biases of our evidence.

2. For Mesopotamian astrology see Bottéro 1974. It was relatively simple in method; a typical prediction runs as follows: "If in a (certain) month Mercury is visible in the East and then in the West, there will be a battle."

It seems from our evidence that this kind of astrology takes off in the era when Greece was falling under Roman domination. The old adage that dates back at least to the Augustan period (end of the first century B.C.) onward, was that though the Romans proved victorious in war, the Greeks ended up the cultural imperialists.[3] There was a long period of adoption and adaptation of Greek learning, initially through the educational role taken by Greeks who came to Rome, whether as delegates, as refugees in search of patrons, or as slaves captured in war. The stereotypical astrologer is one such Greek—the "founder of astrology in Rome" is described by a much later source as a Greek slave.[4] They were nicknamed "Chaldaeans" because of the Mesopotamian origin of their art. He—the stereotype is certainly male—is likely to be learned in other disciplines, such as grammar and philosophy. As other Greek scholars, he was always in the ambiguous position of possessing highly valued intellectual skills or cultural resources while being socially marginal, though there were some opportunities for social mobility, more as time went on. Here I am speaking of the high-profile astrologer who would be consulted by wealthy Romans, not the dubious type who hung around the Circus Maximus to be consulted by the poor. This latter figure is mentioned in passing with scorn by our elite sources.[5]

Astrology and the Fall of the Republic

Before the Late Republic (the first century B.C.), astrology does not figure in elite politics. The new form of divination is mentioned rarely, and then solely as appealing to lower social strata. The elite only appear as attempting to prevent this. For instance, Valerius Maximus, a historian who writes under the second emperor Tiberius, reports that in 139 B.C., astrologers were officially expelled from Italy on the

---

3. "Greece, the captive, made her savage victor captive, and brought the arts to rustic Latium" (Horace *Epistles* 2.1.156).

4. Manilius Antiochus, cousin of a famous mime writer, a slave who came to Rome "perhaps during the Mithridatic Wars of the second century B.C.," as Rawson 1985 suggests. Pliny *Natural History* 35.199.

5. Cicero *On Divination* 1.132 ("*de circo astrologos*"). Juvenal *Satires* 6.582, 588, says that the plebeians go to the Circus Maximus to find out their fates; the rich call in foreign experts.

grounds that theirs was a fallacious means of divination that exploited the gullible.[6]

Astrologers as a category of persons can only be defined in relation to the state diviners who played so prominent a role in Republican political life.[7] Our sources tell us little of private divination, though it certainly existed.[8] Our main source for public divinatory activity is the historian Livy, who wrote under the first emperor Augustus. He records the prodigies,[9] omens, and divine signs of all sorts, and the consultations and rituals that followed year by year, material probably derived ultimately from senatorial records.[10] There are three groups of diviners. First are the augurs, who were originally concerned with interpreting the movements and cries of birds, but by the first century B.C. at least, they generally took the auspices by feeding the sacred fowl.[11] Refusal to eat was seen as a sign of disfavor. The second group is that of the Fifteen Men, the keepers of the Sibylline books, a collection of oracles in Greek supposedly bought from a prophetess by the last king of Rome (traditionally dated in the sixth century B.C.). They were consulted more rarely, about prodigies or new religious cults. When asked, they could recommend the necessary ritual after referring to the Sybilline books. The evidence about the third group is more confusing. The name *haruspices* (traditionally from Etruria, modern Tuscany) is used of both interpreters of prodigies and readers of the entrails of sacrificial animals. There may be two groups here. The entrail-readers may have been originally distinct from the officials responsible for deciding whether a sacrifice was accepted in Roman divination, but there was

---

6. Valerius Maximus *Anecdotes* 1.3.3. This is the apparently superior reading of one manuscript. Another version merely reports that "Cornelius," without mentioning his full name or office as praetor, expelled the "Chaldaeans and ordered them to leave Italy within ten days." For elite attempts to prevent the rest from having access to such diviners, see the elder Cato's *On Agriculture* 1.3.4, where he prohibits his bailiff from having dealings with them.

7. The most helpful work on Republican divination has been done by John North (1986 and 1990). I am much indebted to it in this chapter.

8. Cicero's *On Divination* of 45 B.C., which is concerned with philosophical questions regarding the validity of divination, hardly mentions it.

9. Unusual events, such as eclipses, the birth of monsters, lightning striking prominent buildings or statues, or rains of blood, stones, or milk, were reported from around Italy as prodigies. The Senate retained ultimate control over whether they were to be dealt with as such or not.

10. The surviving books are concerned with the years 219–167 B.C.

11. Cicero *On Divination* 70–74.

probably a gradual fusion of the two techniques throughout the Republic (Schilling 1979).

The keynote of Roman divination is the establishment and maintenance of the *pax deorum*, the right relationship between the city and its gods. Divination, like other religious activity, is closely implicated in political activity; it is an integral part of it. For instance, the auspices had to be taken by a holder of political office at prescribed times during the exercise of this office.[12] This power of *auspicium* was the religious counterpart of his constitutional power or *imperium*. The ritual had to be carried out properly to guarantee his activity as an officeholder.

In Livy's portrayal of divinatory activity, expiation takes precedence over interpretation. It is more important to prevent the impending disaster than to be precise about its nature. Thus, in the case of sacrifice in the traditional Roman ceremony, if the entrails are "abnormal," the victim is taken to be rejected by the gods, and more are taken till one is accepted, though naturally a run of rejections is a bad omen. Such sacrifices were performed to ensure the favor of the gods on particular occasions, like the auspices. The Etruscan tradition brought in a degree of interpretation. The disaster portended, as in the case of prodigies generally, might be narrowed down to defeat in battle, fire, or civil discord.[13]

Raymond Bloch (1963) has argued that the ancient Roman conception of the prodigy as an inevitably dire sign of rupture of the pax deorum began to change under the pressures of the Second Punic War in the late third century, through the influence of Greece, into a conception of a prodigy as a presage for the future. Others look to Etruscan influence (Schilling 1979). The timing and, correspondingly, the causes of this shift are difficult to establish. Records of public prodigies dramatically diminish in number after the Social War, at the beginning of the first century B.C.,[14] and are replaced by private omens relating to the personal fortunes of the great military commanders who dominate the history of the Late Republic.

We may expect political shifts to be mirrored in religious shifts

---

12. The auspices had to be taken before the Senate met, before electoral or legislative assemblies, or before the officeholder crossed the sacred boundary of the city.

13. See MacBain 1982:122–25 for lists of prodigies and interpretations.

14. Livy 43.13.1. See MacBain 1982.

here, because religious activity is so much a part of the political process in Rome. Religious authority to divine is diffused in the classical Republic, in the same way as political authority. The Senate as a group retained ultimate control. The groups of diviners mentioned above did not function exclusively as diviners, nor were they the only ones responsible for divination. Office holders, who were members of the Senate, were mainly responsible for the taking of the auspices and for the public sacrifices necessary for divination from entrails. Further lower-class specialists were involved.[15]

In the classical Republic, these groups of diviners remain unnamed. Celebrated individuals are rare until the Late Republic, though they are, interestingly, found in myths of the regal period (North 1990:69). This change, I think, relates to the shift from expiation to more complex interpretation. The celebration of individuals is linked to their possession of specialized, complex skills, of which the most highly valued is specific prophetic utterance. Cicero's *On Divination* (2.70–74) reveals the scorn in which some held the technique of feeding the sacred fowl by the first century B.C. This system provided only negative or positive answers to questions of a ritual nature. Something more sophisticated, more in tune with the new Greek learning, was required. Further, the records of divinatory activity in the Republic do not seem to suggest that its role in political decision making was important.[16] Something that promised more precise guidance was likely to appeal to the powerful individuals emerging. The keeping of a personal diviner serves as a sign of the appropriation of power.

In the Late Republic, the old system of checks and balances that distributed political power among the elite began to break down, as the great generals, Marius and Sulla, Pompey and Caesar, and finally Mark Antony and Octavian, the future emperor Augustus, fought their civil wars. The impressive, individual diviner began to emerge in tandem with the new political giants. C. Gracchus has his diviner Herennius Siculus, Sulla his C. Postumus and Caesar his Spurinna.[17]

---

15. *Victimarii* and *popae* were expert in techniques of sacrifice, *pullarii* in reading the auspices (North 1990:53). North thinks that the haruspices who read the entrails were of similar social origin.

16. Divinatory institutions did not function as the Zande poison-oracle in Evans-Pritchard's account, where controversial decisions could be made by an apparently impartial system.

17. On Siculus see Valerius Maximus 9.12.5; cf. Velleius Paterculus 2.7.2. On

These diviners are haruspices, but they are not the anonymous members of an official group established for consultation by the Senate.[18] There had always been haruspices for private divination, but they did not show up much in the records we have. Their reappearance in this semipublic capacity makes it seem as if they have come loose from their official political moorings in the same way as their patrons. These diviners, above all, found themselves facing astrologers, from outside the official religion altogether, as rivals. Plutarch presents Sulla as lending an ear to both types.[19]

The first Roman aristocrat associated in our sources with natal astrology was the consul Octavius, killed when Cinna and Marius took Rome in 86 B.C. According to Plutarch, writing in the first to second century A.D., the astrological diagram that lured him to his death was found on his corpse.[20] By the time of Pompey, Crassus, and Julius Caesar, contemporary comments of Cicero reveal astrologers attempting to play a political role in encouraging their ambitions.[21] Later sources attribute astrological predictions of imperial power in 44 B.C. to Octavian, and in 42 to Tiberius.[22] Important, regardless of whether the cases are well-founded or not, is the stereotypical role of astrology here. Crucially, natal astrology is associated with the struggles of individuals for sole power. It is, above all, an individualized art.

But in the rivalry with the haruspices, there were advantages on both sides. The haruspices had tradition and the state religion on theirs. Astrologers had novelty, a novelty associated with the new Greek learning—learning of a most impressive sort, with its complex

Postumus see Plutarch *Life of Sulla* 9.3. On Spurinna see Cicero *Letters to his Friends* 9.24, *On Divination* 1.119; Suetonius *Life of Julius Caesar* 81; Valerius Maximus 8.11.2. See Rawson 1978.

18. There is some controversy as to whether the haruspices were ever formally constituted as a group on the model of the other priestly colleges in Rome. See Bouché-Leclercq 1900, Torelli 1975, Rawson 1978, and MacBain 1982.

19. For Sulla and haruspices see n. 18 above; for Sulla and astrologers see *Life of Sulla* 37.1. Possibly Sulla has an earlier claim to association than Octavius, though the reference is to the end of his life in 78.

20. *Life of Marius* 42.1–5. Was this just an embellishment to add dramatic irony? Was it, anyway, appropriate only to a later age?

21. In the second part of his dialogue *On Divination*, at 47.99, Cicero makes cynical comments on the flattering predictions of astrologers that failed to come true.

22. Suetonius, writing at the beginning of the second century, attributes astrological predictions of imperial power to almost all the emperors who were the subjects of his *Lives*.

mathematical calculations—and with the proven success of astro-
nomical predictions. (Not that the astrologers represented themselves
as novel; on the contrary, they emphasized the enormous length of
time during which empirical evidence had been amassed.) Against
this, the haruspices were specialists in prodigies. Again though, astrologers could provide answers to immediate questions ("catarchic"
astrology) as well as information about the whole of life. Several
figures in the Late Republic seem to have been learned in both arts.[23]
Certain common domains of interest emerged: the interpretation of
celestial phenomena and the examination of astral influence on the
viscera. The evidence discussed by Bouché-Leclercq (1900), who
remains an important authority on divination, suggests that the
haruspices were modernizing their art under astrological influence (cf.
Weinstock 1951). Though haruspices continue to figure sporadically
in our evidence until the Christian Empire, signs in the Late Republic
indicate that they were losing their grip on political life and were
being forced to move with the times.

A critical point in the rivalry of these two divinatory styles came
with the appearance of the comet shortly after the death of Julius
Caesar, on the first days of some games that Octavian was sponsoring
for the people. The haruspices were in a position to attach the appearance of comets to ready-made theory. Comets were for them a species
of lightning bolt, inflamed torches hurled by thundering deities. The
official interpretation was that the comet presaged a new *saeculum*,
or era, a suitably ambiguous prediction, but one with negative connotations, because this was traditionally the last of the *saecula*. We
hear that the haruspex Vulcatius went before the popular assembly
to announce this but collapsed and died on the spot, which underlined
the sinister connotations of the omen.[24] There was some disagreement
as to the meaning of the comet. Cassius Dio, a third-century historian
who is a key source for the period, says that some called it a comet
and associated it with the usual (negative) consequences, but the
majority ascribed it to Caesar, interpreting it to mean that he had
become immortal and translated to the skies.[25] This was an inter-

23. Strabo 16.1.6.739C calls the haruspex Sudines a *mathematicus*, the usual
name for an astrologer; cf. Polyaenus 4.20. See Cramer 1956:77. Also Tarutius of
Firmum (Cicero *On Divination* 2.47, 98); see Bouché-Leclercq 1900.

24. Servius *Commentary on Virgil's Eclogue* 9.47 cites Baebius Macer. Vulcatius
was said to have prophesied his own death.

25. Dio 45.7.1.

pretation accepted, perhaps even encouraged, by Octavian.[26] The notion of *catasterism*, translation to the stars, was associated with astrology in its most popular form. Interestingly, the Elder Pliny suggests that Octavian secretly considered the comet to be the star of his own new birth as the adopted son of Caesar, an interpretation that has been ascribed by one scholar to one Theogenes, an astrologer who had already advised Octavian of his imperial destiny.[27] This must remain speculation, but more than one level of astrological interpretation was possible, and at least popular astrology had triumphed over the haruspices.

Astrology was a flexible art, and it offered a particularly appropriate type of legitimation in its more complex form, with its more sophisticated development of the familiar beliefs in the signifying power of the heavens. It was a new, designer version of the old omen-lore, for the individuals who had ousted the chorus as protagonists on the political stage. Following traditional divination, it was a learning dependent on books, but as a development of tradition, it promised to answer better the new demands made of divination, demands for subtlety and precise information for help in decision making. It was finally set up as a legitimator in its complex form when Augustus established the principate. This was a form of sole power based on developments of Republican precedents, which thus never became definitely hereditary. The comet might offer the possibility of interpretation as a traditional omen, but Augustus's official publication of his horoscope in A.D. 11—in an edict, Dio tells us[28]—accorded horoscopal astrology a new superior status, leaving the haruspices behind. Suetonius adds that he had his birth sign stamped on coins to be seen everywhere in the empire.[29] Here was proof that his rule was decreed by destiny. It seems likely that he published his horoscope—despite the risks that became evident later—to quell rumors of his impending death, which were probably encouraged by another comet (Cramer 1956).

Augustan literature furnishes ample evidence of the way in which

---

26. Servius *Commentary on the Aeneid* 6.81.

27. Pliny (mid-first century) *Natural History* 2.23. Suetonius *Life of Augustus* 94. Cramer 1956.

28. Dio 56.25.5.

29. Suetonius *Life of Augustus* 94 mentions Capricorn.

astrology suddenly became fashionable. An amusing consequence of this is the fact that traditional seers in Augustan poetry are suddenly obliged to be endowed with astrological knowledge to retain their credibility.[30] The first Latin astrological work appears at this time, from the pen of a poet who obviously got his knowledge secondhand. Not just poets with their heads in the skies but practical men like Vitruvius, engineer and architect, accepted the truth of astrology in a matter-of-fact way.[31] Some knowledge of the discipline became part of the educational curriculum.[32]

Astrology under the Empire

Thus, as Constantine later took the Christian God as his ally, Augustus took the macrocosm, in a very public way. But it was not such a neat solution to the problem of legitimating his rule as it might first appear. Astral legitimation was no imperial monopoly. Though the carefully balanced Republican system always retained the possibility of being vulnerable to disturbance, it was hardly so pregnant with the seeds of dissension as the new astrological dispensation. The historian Tacitus, who aligned himself with the believers in astrology, summed up the art's double-edged nature pithily: " . . . astrologers, a breed of men whom the powerful cannot trust and who mislead the ambitious, practicing a profession that in our country will always be outlawed and always maintained."[33] Augustus had to try and limit access to this reservoir of power. In A.D. 11 he issued an edict prohibiting consultations either about death or without witnesses.[34] He was chiefly concerned about predictions of his own death (in the same year, he released his horoscope) or of imperial destinies for others. This was not an isolated move; he had large numbers of the Sibylline Books burned and the rest put under strict control.[35]

---

30. E.g., Virgil *Aeneid* 3.360, Propertius 4.1.109; cf. Statius *Thebaid* 3.558. See Cramer 1956.

31. Manilius *Astronomica*, Vitruvius *On Architecture* 9.6.2.

32. That is not to say that Roman schoolboys were taught to cast horoscopes, but they gathered a smattering of star-lore, enough to inculcate some degree of respect for astrology.

33. *Histories* 1.22 (" . . . *genus hominum potentibus infidum, sperantibus fallax quod in civitate nostra et vetabitur sempur et retinebitur").*

34. Dio 56.25.5.

35. Tacitus *Annals* 6.12.

In the reign of the next princeps, Tiberius, the tensions that characterize the use of astrology under the empire emerge from our sources. Tiberius kept a retinue of astrologers, most famously the man who taught him something of astrology, the polymathic Thrasyllus,[36] whom he elevated to such a level that he founded an illustrious dynasty studded with royal connections. The emperor is depicted as shut up in Capri with a sort of "occult cabinet," whose chief job was to locate those marked out for great destinies by the stars, so that they could be destroyed.[37] The theme of power exercized from behind closed doors recurs in the accounts of the stereotypically bad emperors.[38] The involvement of imperial women is seen as a stage further away from Republican precedent and a step toward the usurpation of power by the unworthy. Nero's wife Poppaea, perhaps a precursor of Nancy Reagan in this respect, kept her own retinue of astrologers for her secret councils, "the vilest tools in the employ of the imperial household," according to Tacitus (*Histories* 1.22). Though the emperor could justify his consultations of astrologers on all important issues on the grounds that it was the best method of ascertaining the future, he could not allow others access to this knowledge without fear of subversion. There are several reports of trials from Tiberius's reign onward where consultation of astrologers was regarded as tantamount to conspiracy.[39] Also, Tiberius included haruspices when he reenforced the Augustan law of A.D. 11.[40]

There are numerous anecdotes about astrologers encouraging the ambition of would-be emperors, spurring them on to revolt at crucial moments, or ensuring their delay until the most propitious time. The nonhereditary character of the principate encouraged would-be emperors to consult astrologers. Naturally, it was all the more important that an emperor who was not an obvious successor should be seen to have astral backing, but almost every emperor is equipped with a prediction of future greatness in our sources.

Astrologers are also credited with having predicted the death-

---

36. The archetypal learned astrologer, Thrasyllus, was an Alexandrian grammarian who copublished what became the standard edition of Plato.

37. Juvenal *Satires* 10.94, Dio 57.19.3–4.

38. Cf. Domitian; see Dio 67.15.76, Suetonius *Life of Domitian* 10.3.

39. See Cramer 1956:251–76. It was, however, rarely the sole charge. Others, like magic, adultery, and poisoning, were also recurrent extras in treason charges.

40. Tacitus *Annals* 2.32, Suetonius *Life of Tiberius* 36, Ulpian *On the Office of Proconsul* 15.2.1, Dio 57.15.8–9.

dates of emperors. In a typical anecdote, an astrologer called Ascletarion, who had predicted the death of the stereotypically bad emperor Domitian, was called before him. Domitian asked him what he saw in store for himself. The man shuddered and said that he would shortly be torn apart by dogs. The emperor then gave orders that the astrologer should be burned at the stake to prove him wrong. However, just as the fire got going, a sudden shower sent the men in charge scurrying for shelter. Immediately, a pack of dogs fell on Ascletarion and tore him to pieces. Domitian happened to get wind of this and was seized by terror that the astrologer had been right in his case, too, and so it proved.[41]

Considerations of narrative power are important in cases like these. It makes a better story if the astrologer is proved right against all the odds, and often one can see the process of exaggeration in this direction taking place in successive accounts. But the hold such stories had on the imagination could only reinforce the high opinion held of astrology's potential. Apocryphal as these anecdotes must usually have been, that they were common currency is the really significant fact.

Astrology's access to the truth was taken extremely seriously by emperors and their rivals. This concern is abundantly clear in the anecdotes and is behind the measures taken against astrology. We should view these measures not as signs of the contempt in which astrology was held but as indications of respect for its potential. Dio tells us that in the unstable period when conflict was building up between Mark Antony and Octavian, in 33 B.C., astrologers and magicians were expelled.[42] In the following century up to 93 A.D., at least a further ten expulsion decrees were passed involving astrologers, sometimes magicians, and once philosophers, because street philosophers had subversive potential too. Once, other diviners apart from astrologers were expelled by Tiberius.[43] All the decrees can be associated with political instability; they are often a response to it. There are also no less than 11 cases of trials of high-ranking Romans involving treason (*maiestas*) and the use of astrology in the first century. We hear less of the prosecution of astrologers themselves

---

41. Dio 67.16.3. Suetonius's earlier version only has the shower put out the funeral pyre (*Life of Domitian* 15.3).

42. Dio 49.43.5.

43. See n. 41 above.

under the Augustan law of A.D. 11—only seven cases to A.D. 371—because they are less interesting to our sources.[44] Spectacular executions could follow: one of those involved in the Libo conspiracy under Tiberius was thrown off a rock; another was conducted outside the Esquiline Gate and beaten to death with rods "in the ancient manner," to the sound of bugles.[45]

The repressive laws could not have been expected to have any permanent effect, and, although almost every emperor reimposed them according to the early third-century lawyer Ulpian,[46] it was not anticipated that in every case the law would be applied in all its rigor. Normally, the study of astrology was allowed. Only the sorts of professional uses outlined above were outlawed as subversive.

In the fourth century, all forms of divination that were not public were prohibited on pain of death.[47] The presumption was that the sorts of inquiry astrology had led the way to, inquiry about death or about imperial destinies, was likely to have taken place. Only public divination, as part of the old religion, was allowed. Denise Grodzynski (1974:286) argues that unstable political circumstances are not sufficient to explain the increase in severity of punishment of diviners in the late empire, and that the blanket explanation of this change as being part of the struggle of the newly Christian state against paganism is incomplete. The laws, especially after Constantine, stress the reprehensible character of the curiosity involved in divination. This curiosity to know what is forbidden is more subject to penalty than is divination per se. Such audacity could only come from the devil, and thus deserved the strictest punishment.

The Christian context has changed the meaning of the repressive measures, but the continuities with the pagan state are also striking. Before, only the emperor was allowed to know, and curiosity on the part of others was reprehensible. Now it looked as if the Christian emperors' right to know was under threat: only God retained the privilege in the writings of the Church Fathers. But there are indications that at least in the Eastern empire and for some time in the Western, emperors were not cut off from astrologers.[48] There is still

---

44. For fullest discussion of the legal evidence, see Cramer 1956:251–76.
45. Tacitus *Annals* 2.32.
46. Ulpian *On the Office of Proconsul* 15.2.2–4.
47. *The Theodosian Code* 9.16.
48. We hear of an attempted coup in 371 involving the astrologer Heliodorus.

evidence in the late fifth century that astrologers were involved in coups.[49] In 334 Firmicus Maternus, a senator from the West, was still able to dedicate his astrological treatise to an official high up in the government and to address prayers to the stars on behalf of the Christian emperor. Firmicus was also following a trend set in the first century by the Augustan Manilius when he set the emperor above the influence of the stars, though he takes it a stage further by saying that it is useless to inquire about the emperor at all.[50] There remains in both astrological authors the desire to present the emperor's rule as destined, so this move by no means renders astrology harmless.

Despite the risks for those who claimed it for their side, astrology retained such a high status as an art, and was so well qualified for its role, that one can understand Tacitus's belief that it could never be abandoned. Astrologers saw in the movements of the stars reflections of relations between earthly potentates, as certain terminology makes clear,[51] a trend that becomes more obvious in the late empire. This not only reflects an anthropomorphizing tendency but shows the desire to inscribe the temporal order in the eternal. The successive attempts of emperors and their supporters to bind the former intimately to the serene, unchanging world beyond the moon often appear rather wistful in retrospect. The emperors' relation to astrology was one of dependence as much as exploitation; this is why they were led, as much by belief in its power as by realization of the political implications, to crush those who found backing in the stars that was similar to their own.

Astrology and the Church

The conflict between the Christian church and astrology brings out the discipline's religious side more clearly. The cult of solar mono-

---

The Christian emperor Valens seems to have made the offender his court astrologer (Ammianus Marcellinus 29.1–2). This emperor is also reported to have executed a man found with a horoscope labeled "Valens."

49. The evidence for this period is patchy, and much of it also suffers from the inevitable biases of orthodox Christianity, which would tend to suppress stories of prominent astrologers. But see Pingree 1976, who has edited and commented on a series of horoscopes that illustrate the involvement of astrologers in coups and counter-coups in the fifth century.

50. Firmicus *Mathesis* 2.32.4, Manilius *Astronomica* 1.384f.

51. Examples are the use of the terms *kathuperteresis, epidekateuein,* and *doryphoria,* with connotations of tithing and retinue, describing certain relations of planets to other planets or stars. See Bouché-Leclercq 1963.

theism immediately preceded Christianity as the state religion, and Christian authors are preoccupied with the threat of star-worship. But the fundamental issues are similar to those present in the case of pagan authorities. Astrology was subversive because it offered unmediated access to knowledge of the future.

As long as Christianity remained an illegal religion, long treatises on astrology were rare (Laistner 1941), but once Christianity was established, astrology presented a threat, particularly as it is frequently associated with heretical sects.[52] Reading the hostile writings of the Church Fathers, one receives a strong impression of the power struggle between the stars and God, astrologers and the Church. Though they reuse the arguments made by pagan philosophers of the second century B.C. (Amand 1945), these are not germane to their real concerns. The issue is almost invariably the question of free will versus determinism, but the Church's espousal of free will to sin or not to sin, in the face of its doctrines of original sin and God's omniscience, looks more and more like an effort to eliminate logical contradictions and moral qualms with the iron fist of dogma, as its rule becomes established and its attitude hardens. This culminates with Augustine, who argues for God's predestination and attacks astrology on behalf of free will. Arguments that seem paradoxical to secular reasoning abound in the writings of the Fathers of the Church. God is allowed to combine knowledge of the future with human free will, but this is quite impossible for astral divinities. God is presented as trumping the astrologers with the star of Bethlehem; they had indeed offered knowledge of the future, but only until then. Alternatively, astral powers can only be allowed to control pagans; Christ emancipates the faithful by baptism (Riedinger 1956, Gundel and Gundel 1966). Whichever argument astrologers might choose to pursue, the Church could change the rules. The only insight into the future was to be through prophecy authorized by the Church. And the Church moved to crush its rival. In the "Constitutions of the Apostles," astrologers are refused baptism or damned.[53] And at numerous successive Church councils, the anathema was pronounced against them.[54]

---

52. Gundel and Gundel 1966 set out briefly what is known of the astrological beliefs of various Gnostic sects, of the Manichaeans and the Priscillianists, followers of the late fourth-century bishop of Avila.

53. 8.32.11. Probably fourth-century; see Tester 1987.

54. This was sparked off particularly by the Priscillianists in 447, 561, and 572

Astrology seems to have become marginalized in the Western empire. Astrological manuscripts only reappear in any number in library lists of the twelfth century. But astrology appears to have continued to retain a high intellectual profile and some political importance in the Byzantine Empire. It looks as if there was a lean period for astrology in the East between the fifth and the eighth centuries, but it did not die out completely.[55] Why did the Western Church succeed where the Eastern failed? Laistner's argument, on the basis of library lists, was that "not persecution or prosecution, but the lack of manuals caused the disappearance of 'scientific' astrology in the West for four or five centuries after Firmicus composed his handbook." This approach counterposes two different sorts of causal factors. One might ask why the production of manuals stopped. Presumably Laistner would have to argue for lack of interest. It seems hard to justify dissociating this issue entirely from the attitude of Church and state. It must remain matter for speculation, but one possible answer would be that the different heritages from pagan religion exerted their influence on the Christian era.

Arthur Darby Nock, a very eminent scholar of ancient religion, pointed to the crucial difference between Greek and Roman religion, when commenting on the attitude to prodigies (Nock 1972). Greeks and Romans alike regarded prodigies as indication that all was not well with the gods' relation with the city and took some action to propitiate the supernatural, but only the Romans had this formalized as a proceeding regularly organized by the Senate. Similarly, there

---

(See Chadwick 1976). On the councils and papal condemnation, see Bouché-Leclercq 1963, Gundel and Gundel 1966, and Laistner 1941.

55. So much seems to be agreed on by Cumont 1903:436, Laistner 1941 (who concentrates on the West) and Dagron 1984a, 1984b. The evidence for the continued flourishing of astrology in the East is not plentiful until the high Byzantine period, except for the existence of a continuous Greek tradition in the *Catalogus Codicorum Astrologorum Graecorum* and of a continuous tradition of attacks on astrology by Church Fathers (see Reidinger 1956). See n. 49 on Pingree 1976 for an exception. Dagron (1984a:119) considers that the tradition of learned astrology is dramatically reinforced in the eighth century and cites stories of astrological prophecy made to emperors and of emperors who became learned in astrology in an attempt to control fate rather than leaving it in the hands of others. Gundel and Gundel (1966) are impressed that the council held at Constantinople in 553 under Justinian was effective in removing astrology from its privileged position, and they are only surprised that it did not succeed completely. Whatever happened in the intervening centuries, one Stephanus the Philosopher claims to reintroduce astrology to "Rome" (Constantinople) in the eighth century.

is nothing corresponding to *auspicia* as the concomitant of *imperium*. The control of religion had been centralized in Rome to a degree unknown in Greece, and those who controlled it claimed their decrees were valid in heaven as on earth. On the consul's speech about the Bacchanalian rites of 186 B.C., Nock observes that "the control is legal in form, it accepts and defines the situation, and its definition is explicit rather than implicit." He goes on to connect this with the Christian era, where he claims to detect a specific inheritance of the precise tendency to define, not only de facto, but also de jure, what is permissible. The Roman Church early claimed the right to determine whether an offense was a mortal sin and to give absolution. Here, then, is one possible explanation for the different fates of astrology in East and West. In the East, astrology was subject to sporadic attack in particular circumstances. The Roman Church, however, inherited a concern for precise, legalistic definition of good and evil, and the desire and political means to take for itself the power to impose that knowledge. Astrology was evil, so it was crushed.

REFERENCES

Amand (de Mendieta), E. A.
1945   *Fatalisme et liberté dans l'antiquité grecque.* Louvain: Université de Louvain.

Bloch, R.
1963   *Les Prodiges dans l'antiquité grecque.* Paris: Presses Universitaires de France.

Bottéro, J.
1974   Symptômes, signes, écritures. In Vernant 1974.

Bouché-Leclercq. A.
1900   Haruspices. In C. Daremberg and E. Saglio, eds., *Dictionnaire des antiquités grecques et romaines,* vol. 3. Paris: Librairie Hachette.
1963   *L'Astrologie grecque.* Bruxelles. (Originally published in Paris, 1899.)

Chadwick, H.
1976   *Priscillian of Avila: The occult and the charismatic in the early Church.* Oxford: Clarendon Press.

Cramer, F.
1956   *Astrology in Roman law and politics.* Philadelphia: American Philosophical Society.

Cumont, F.
1903   La polémique de l'Ambrosiaster contre les païens. *Revue d'histoire et de la littérature religieuse* 8:417–40.

Dagron, G.
1984a Constantinople imaginaire: Études sur la recueil des "Patria." Paris: Presses Universitaires de France.
1984b Le saint, le savant, l'astrologue. In La Romanité chrétienne en orient: Héritages et mutations. London: Variorum Reprints.

Grodzynski, D.
1974 Par la bouche de l'empereur. In Vernant 1974.

Gundel, W., and H. G. Gundel
1966 Astrologumena: Die astrologische Literatur in der Antike und ihre Geschichte. Sudhoffs Archiv, Beihefte 6. Wiesbaden.

Laistner, M. L. W.
1941 The Western Church and astrology in the early Middle Ages. Harvard Theological Review 34:251–75.

MacBain, B.
1982 Prodigy and expiation: A study of religion and politics in Republican Rome. Bruxelles: Latomus.

Nock, A. D.
1972 A feature of Roman religion. In Essays on religion and the ancient world, vol. 1. Oxford: Clarendon Press.

North, J. A.
1986 Religion and politics, from republic to principate. Journal of Roman Studies 76:255–57.
1990 Diviners and divination in Rome. In M. Beard and J. A. North, eds., Pagan priests: Religion and power in the ancient world. London: Duckworth.

Pingree, D.
1976 Political horoscopes from the reign of Zeno. Dumbarton Oaks Papers 30:133–50.

Rawson, E.
1978 Caesar, Etruria, and the Disciplina Etrusca. Journal of Roman Studies 68:132–52.
1985 Intellectual life in the Late Republic. London: Duckworth.

Riedinger, U.
1956 Die heilige Schrift im Kampf der griechischen Kirche gegen die Astrologie von Origenes bis Johannes von Damaskos. Innsbruck: Universitätsverlag Wagner.

Schilling, R.
1979 À propos des exta: L'extispicine étrusque et la litatio Romaine. In Rites, cultes, dieux de Rome. Paris: Klincksieck.

Tester, S. J.
1987 A history of Western astrology. Woodbridge: Boydell.

Torelli, M.
1975 Elogia Tarquiniensia. Firenze: Istituto di Etruscologia e Antichità Italiche.

Vernant, J.-P.
1974 *Divination et rationalité.* Paris: Éditions du Seuil.
Weinstock, S.
1951 *Libri Fulgurales. Papers of the British School at Rome,* n. s., 6:422–53.

The Roman and the Foreign:
The Cult of the "Great Mother"
in Imperial Rome

Mary Beard

Look, in come the devotees of frenzied Bellona and of the Mother
of the Gods. And in comes the huge eunuch—the one that the rest
of the obscene crowd must honour. Long ago he grabbed a bit of
broken pot and sliced through his soft genitals, and now before
him the howling crowd, with their tambourines, give way. His
vulgar cheeks are covered by a Phrygian bonnet.
　　　　　—Juvenal, *Satires* 6.511–16 (written A.D. ca. 115)

The eunuch priests of the goddess Magna Mater (the Great Mother
or Cybele) were a flamboyantly foreign, sometimes unsettling presence in the city of imperial Rome. With their flowing hair, extravagant
jewelry, and long yellow silken robes, they offered an image of mad

This chapter is a much amended version of the paper delivered at the colloquium.
In its revised form, it owes much to the comments of those present at the colloquium
(especially Michael Taussig) and to subsequent discussion with Keith Hopkins and
Caroline Humphrey. As always, Robin Cormack has patiently improved both the
English and the argument.

I have assumed only a minimal knowledge of the ancient world and have tried
to avoid the arcane language of professional classicists. Any remaining technical
terms can be decoded with the help of the *Oxford Classical Dictionary* (2d ed.,
1970). Translations of all classical texts cited are available (except where stated) in
the Loeb Classical Library series (Harvard University Press and Heinemann).

The epigraph is part of a long verse satire "On Women." Juvenal goes on to
pillory the influence of such religious figures over the women of Rome. For the complex
literary and cultural context of this poem, see Henderson 1987. The "Phrygian bonnet"
refers to the distinctive eastern headdress of the eunuch priests of Magna Mater, with
flaps covering the cheeks.

religious frenzy involving not only ecstatic dancing but frenetic self-flagellation and (the essential marker, so it was believed, of their religious status) the act of self-castration performed in a divine trance.[1] Commonly of Eastern origin (from the cult centers of the Great Mother in Asia Minor), they made a striking contrast with the priests of the traditional state cults of the city.[2] These religious officials were drawn almost exclusively from the Roman governing elite, and they dealt with the affairs of the gods in much the same way as they dealt with the affairs of men.[3] They normally undertook their priestly duties in the plain traditional dress (the toga) of a Roman citizen or magistrate.[4] Frenzy, bright colors, and dancing were carefully controlled.[5] In most cases, bodily "wholeness" was a prerequisite for Roman religious office.[6]

1. For a full discussion of these priests (the *galli*), see Graillot 1912:287–319; more briefly, Vermaseren 1977:96–101.

2. I use the words "traditional state" (rather than "official") advisedly. As I will make clear, the cult of Cybele was imported into the city *officially*, at the instigation of the Roman authorities; but it remained distinct from those cults whose history was believed to go back to the earliest phases of Rome and whose organization was closely bound up with the political institutions of the city.

3. Note, for example, the remarks of Cicero (first century B.C.), addressing one of the colleges of priests in his speech *On his House:* "Gentleman of the pontifical college, among the many divinely-inspired expedients of government established by our ancestors, there is none more striking than that whereby they expressed their intention that the worship of the gods and the vital interests of the state should be entrusted to the direction of the same individuals, to the end that the citizens of the highest distinction and the brightest fame might achieve the welfare of religion by wise adminstration of the state, and of the state by a sage interpretation of religion." These priesthoods (normally held alongside other political office) are fully discussed in Beard 1990. For the close interconnection of religion and politics at Rome, see Beard and Crawford 1985:25–39; Beard, North, and Price forthcoming.

4. The civic character of major Roman rituals (particularly sacrifice) is clear from numerous surviving relief sculptures. See, conveniently, Scott Ryberg 1955. Some priests did, however, have a distinctive costume: the priest of Jupiter (*flamen Dialis*) wore a particular form of pointed headdress; the *salii* (whose rituals included a twice-yearly series of dances through the streets of Rome at the beginning and end of the traditional warring season) carried a figure of eight shield and wore a military cloak, brightly colored tunic, and breastplate.

5. We tend to underestimate the more picturesque side of Roman rituals—the dancing, singing, and elaborate feasting—in our efforts to make the Romans conform to their rather staid image in our contemporary stereotypes. Nevertheless, the broad point holds: traditional Roman religion was not "ecstatic."

6. Aulus Gellius (*Attic Nights* 1, 12, 3) documents this requirement for Vestal Virgins; and Plutarch (*Roman Questions* 73) states that augurs were not permitted to watch for omens if they had a "sore." See also Morgan 1974 (who queries the existence of a general rule that priests should have no bodily defect).

This chapter explores the contrast between these two different types of religious practitioner in the city of Rome during the first three centuries of our era and examines the relationship of the cult of Magna Mater with the Roman state. I argue that throughout this period there was a constant tension between, on the one hand, Roman rejection of the cult of Magna Mater as something dangerously foreign and, on the other, the incorporation of the cult in the symbolic forms of state power. This tension can, in my view, be seen as part of a wider debate in the culture of imperial Rome, a debate on the nature of "Romanness"—on what it was to be Roman and on what could count as Roman religious experience—in the context of a huge and ethnically diverse empire that had dramatically transcended any definition of Rome as a single, homogeneous city-state.[7] By emphasizing the unresolved tension between the incorporation of the cult and its rejection, I am distancing myself from the conventional scholarly approach to this material—which either stresses the flagrant incompatibility of the Eastern rituals of Magna Mater with Roman tradition or constructs a linear narrative history in which a "tamed" version of the cult is gradually incorporated into the mainstream of Roman state religion.

This chapter is not about shamanic activity or inspirational religion in the Roman Empire as a whole. It focuses on one cult—the cult of Magna Mater—in one place—the city of Rome. The reason for this focus is partly the sheer wealth of evidence for religious experience that is available from the capital and its relative paucity elsewhere in the empire.[8] But underlying the decision to concentrate on one urban cult is my sense that generalizations about the religion of the Roman Empire as a whole (as if it were the politico-religious unity that Romans often wanted to claim it was) obscure more than they illuminate. The empire covered an enormous expanse of territory—stretching from Britain to the African desert in the south and to the borders of modern Afghanistan in the east; and it included a vast variety of very different native religions. Not only did these react in quite diverse ways to the conquering, or ruling, power of Rome, but the symbolic

---

7. This imperial expansion is discussed in greater detail on pp.185–86.

8. At stake here is not just sheer bulk but variety and range. For example, considerable evidence for religious life exists in the papyri of Roman Egypt, which survive in their thousands. But only in relation to the city of Rome can we assemble the evidence of a wide spectrum of literary texts (historical narratives, satirical poetry, philosophical treatises, drama, antiquarian speculation); and only there can literary evidence be brought together easily with various types of archaeological data (remains of temples, inscriptions recording the careers of priests, images in sculpture, and so forth).

forms of that ruling power varied according to place, time, the nature of the process of conquest, and Roman perceptions of the various native traditions.[9] Roman religion in the cities of Greece was very different from Roman religion in the "barbarian" tribal societies of Northern Gaul. A deity might be known by the same name across the empire, but there can be no reason to suppose that its associations, political context, forms of worship, and meaning would be consistent from one part of the Roman world to another. The Roman empire had no single religious system, but a set of sometimes interlocking, sometimes flagrantly inconsistent, sometimes openly hostile systems.[10]

I hope that my analysis of the cult of Magna Mater at Rome suggests new ways of understanding other ancient inspirational cults. Part of the justification for taking a close look at one cult must obviously lie in the implications of that study for our understanding of other areas of ancient religion. But no analysis of this type can act as a simple paradigm for Roman shamanic activity in general.[11]

The Cult of Magna Mater: Its History and Character

The Introduction of the Cult to Rome

The goddess Magna Mater was formally introduced into Rome in 204 B.C.[12] In the previous year, in the middle of their great war against

---

9. Different Roman reactions to "native" religious traditions are explored in Gordon 1990a:240–45.

10. For this reason, most histories of Roman imperial religion are unsatisfactory: they purport to make a single (narrative) subject from what is not a single subject at all. As Gordon rightly observes (1990b:201), "To construct a history of religion in the Roman Empire is a well-nigh impossible task: there are topics but no subject, quantities of information but little sense to be made of it"; see also, with a similar warning, Scheid 1985:117.

11. Roman history offers many fruitful areas for exploring the relationship between inspirational religion and political authority. For example, the leaders of rebellious Sicilian slaves (in the second-century B.C. "slave-wars") paraded direct divine inspiration from Eastern deities. (See, conveniently, Wiedmann 1981:199–207, for translations of the main ancient accounts.) On several occasions, the Roman authorities acted to expel from the city priests of foreign (often inspirational) cults. (See, for a brief account, Wardman 1982:113–15.) I have not touched on these incidents in this chapter.

For various aspects of shamanic activity and mythology among the Greeks, see (for example) Dodds 1951:135–78; Metzler 1983; Ginzburg 1990 (with full references to earlier studies).

12. The main ancient narrative account is in Livy Histories 29.10.4–11; 8;

Hannibal, after a series of religious portents, the Romans had consulted the so-called Sibylline books[13] and the famous oracle at Delphi. Both had recommended that Magna Mater, the patron deity of Pessinus in Asia Minor (in modern Turkey) should be brought to Rome. Roman religious traditions regularly incorporated new deities, and the Sibylline books had been responsible for the introduction of a series of gods and goddesses from the Greek world and the East— Asklepios, Dis and Proserpina, Hebe, Aphrodite of Eryx, and several others.[14] But Magna Mater was unusual in this series for two (apparently conflicting) reasons. First, she could be thought of as a genuine ancestral Roman deity, because she had close connections with the city of Troy, which was (according to well-known legend) the ultimate origin of the Roman race.[15] Second, she was associated with a far more radical form of ecstatic worship than any other of the series of imports. Although it is hard to be certain of the precise character of the goddess in her native Pessinus and in other areas of the Greek East (she seems variously to be associated with fertility, with mountains, and with the wild), ritual eunuchism and frenetic singing and dancing were recognized features of her cult.[16]

In response to the Sibylline books, the Romans dispatched an embassy[17] to the king of Pergamum (in whose territory the ancient city of Troy lay). The king gave permission for the goddess to be

---

29.14.5–14. What follows is an oversimplifying account of the history and main characteristics of the cult of Magna Mater and is in some ways quite misleading; but it provides the essential background for the arguments presented in the later parts of this chapter. Readers already familiar with this material are advised to skip directly to the next section. Further information on all aspects of the cult (of greater or lesser degrees of reliability) is available in Graillot 1912, Vermaseren 1977, G. Thomas 1984, and Turcan 1989:35–75. I have only cited these standard works in my notes where they offer a particularly useful discussion of the points raised.

13. A collection of oracular texts in the charge of one of the traditional priestly colleges—the "decemviri sacris faciundis" ("The Ten men for the Performance of Ritual," later increased to "Fifteen"); they were consulted on the instruction of the Roman Senate (the council of magistrates and ex-magistrates). For their important role in Roman religious innovation, see North 1976:9.

14. For the significance of these imports, see North 1976: esp. 8–12.

15. The Trojan identity of the goddess is discussed in Wiseman 1984.

16. For evidence for the cult of Cybele in the Greek east, see Vermaseren 1977:13–37; Turcan 1989:35–42.

17. On the way to Asia Minor, the embassy called in at the oracle at Delphi; see Livy *Histories* 29.11.5–6.

taken to Rome, and her renowned cult image (in the form of a black meteorite), together with a small group of priests, was dispatched to Italy. The cult was eventually installed in a temple on the Palatine Hill, in the very center of the city of Rome. The goddess had come to join the Trojan descendants in Italy: she had come back "home."[18]

Closely associated with Magna Mater, both in the East and in Rome, was the god Attis. There were various versions of the myth of Attis, various (ancient) interpretations of his role and importance in the cult of Magna Mater. But one central element is common to almost all these different traditions: as a young mortal boy, in a frenzy inspired by Magna Mater (who was jealous of his affections for another woman), Attis was driven to castrate himself; after his death, which followed his mad self-emasculation, he was brought back to eternal life through the intervention of Magna Mater herself.[19] These myths of Attis were closely related to various features of the cult and rituals of Magna Mater. His self-castration provided a model for the self-castration of the priests. The story of his resurrection offered an explanation of (or symbolic commentary on) one of the major ritual cycles of the cult that I shall describe below.

Attis is mentioned in none of the ancient accounts of the introduction of Magna Mater to Rome. In all these, the goddess arrives alone, a deity without a consort. On the basis of this silence, historians of the cult sometimes assumed that Attis (who is well attested in Rome at later periods) was a secondary import—a yet more

---

18. There are complications and inconsistencies in the accounts of Rome's acquisition of the goddess in Asia Minor. Pessinus was not in the territory of Pergamum, but Livy is explicit that King Attalus of Pergamum went to Pessinus (over 200 miles from his capital) with the Romans to remove the black stone. Other accounts (ancient and modern) suggest that the Romans actually took a cult image from a temple in Pergamum. For the controversy, see Hansen 1971:50–52 (see Welles 1934:241–53 for connections between the Attalid dynasty and Pessinus).

In addition to Livy, note also the account of the poet Ovid (*Fasti* 4.179–372, written in the late first century B.C.) which particularly stresses the links between Rome and Troy. Magna Mater, he says, had wished to come to Italy with Aeneas, "but she felt that fate did not yet call for the intervention of her divinity in Latium (central Italy), and she remained in her accustomed place." When the king of Pergamum at first demurred to the Romans' request to take Magna Mater to Italy, the goddess herself spoke, "Let me go; it is my wish"—and the king acceded, complimenting himself that "Rome traces its origins to Phrygian ancestors."

19. Vermaseren 1977:88–95. Note also, for example, Catullus *Poem* 63 (written in the first century B.C.) on the self-castration of Attis.

extremely oriental deity, who followed only when Magna Mater was well established.[20] Recent excavations on the site of Magna Mater's main temple on the Palatine have, however, proved this wrong. A large number of figurines of Attis have been discovered there, dating from the very earliest phases of the temple's occupation.[21] It now seems certain that when Magna Mater was introduced to Rome, she was introduced along with her castrated consort, Attis.

The Rituals of Magna Mater and Attis

The details of most Roman religious rituals are irretrievably lost. It is not that Roman sources are silent on their calendar of ceremonies: a good deal of debate on the meaning of particular festivals survives, as do numerous poetic recreations of individual rituals, and Christian deconstructions of and countless casual references to particular ceremonies. Not normally found is the kind of coherent account, aimed at elucidating the procedure of the ritual, that even the most partial participant observer might provide—who did what, in what order, and in what place?[22]

The ceremonies of Magna Mater are no exception. In this section, I delineate three rituals associated with her cult: the two major annual festivals explicitly in honor of the Great Mother and Attis, and a distinctive form of sacrifice that was a particular feature of the cult. In the case of each one, my brief account is largely an imaginative, simplified, reconstruction based on literary texts whose aim was not to provide a description of the rituals concerned.[23] Many important details remain completely unknown.

---

20. See, for example, the views of Lambrechts 1952a, 1952b.

21. Note the original publication, Romanelli 1963, with the now accepted date explained by Coarelli 1982:39-41.

22. The only significant exception to this are the surviving inscribed stone records of the priesthood of the Arval Brethren, which preserved a day by day detailed account of their ritual activity and administrative business. See Beard 1985.
The paucity of detail on Roman rituals of all types makes further analysis of the overall character of these rituals very difficult. So, for example, the attractive idea (suggested to me first by Caroline Humphrey) that traditional Roman state rituals might be seen as liturgy-centered, in contrast to the performer-centered rituals of Magna Mater and other "oriental" cults (see Atkinson 1989:14-16), is very hard to develop. It is intrinsically plausible and may well even be right; but there is almost no evidence that can be used in its support.

23. It is impossible to overemphasize the fragility of such a reconstruction. Many apparent "facts" are based on nothing more than casual, humorous, maybe quite tendentious allusions in satirical or comic poetry.

The anniversary of the introduction of the goddess to Rome was commemorated by an annual cycle of games and feasting, the so-called Megalesia[24] (4–10 April). These games included not only displays in the circus but theatrical performances that (at least originally) were presented directly in front of the Palatine temple of Magna Mater. Throughout this period, the temple was open to the Roman people, and the goddess was given offerings of *moretum*, a mixture of cheese and herbs, while her eunuch priests were free to range through the streets of the city and (on this one occasion) to beg for alms. At the same time the Roman elite held banquets together, inviting one another in turn, also apparently in honor of the goddess.[25]

The other major cycle of rituals took place in March. A Roman calendar from the middle of the fourth century A.D. records the whole series of festival days from 15 to 27 March:

15 March: Canna intrat (the reed enters)
22 March: Arbor intrat (the tree enters)
24 March: Sanguem (blood)
25 March: Hilaria (day of joy)
26 March: Requietio (rest)
27 March: Lavatio (bathing)

Many details of this ritual cycle remain obscure. We do not know, for example, at what date or in what circumstances each of the festivals was introduced into the Roman calendar; we do not know whether (as is often claimed) they were directly derived from Eastern cult; and we cannot even be certain whether they were introduced individually or en bloc, as a more or less complete series.[26] But most of the different elements were established by the end of the second century A.D., and the cycle as a whole related closely to the worship of Attis as well as Magna Mater.

The connection with Attis is seen most easily on the days between 22 and 25 March. On 22 March the priests and other cult officials

---

24. The title *Megalesia* (sometimes written *Megalensia*) is derived from the Greek title of Magna Mater—*Megele* Meter.

25. For a clear account, see Scullard 1981:97–100.

26. Different views of the development of the festival are offered by Carcopino 1942:49–171, Lambrechts 1952b; Fishwick 1966.

cut down a pine tree and carried it across the city to the Palatine temple in a mock funeral procession, beating their breasts in mourning. An image of Attis was fixed to the tree, which itself evoked the young god, because Attis was said to have died under a pine tree after his self-castration, and in some versions of the myth, he was eventually granted immortality in the form of a pine tree. The festival on 24 March (the day of blood) was marked, as its name suggests, by the shedding of human blood in the temple precinct. The priests and other worshipers tore their flesh with whips and pierced their breasts with the pine needles, sprinkling the blood on the tree and on the altars of the precinct. It may also have been on this day that the would-be priest castrated himself, becoming a "living Attis." At some point during these proceedings, the pine tree was buried. On the next day (the day of joy), the resurrection of the god was celebrated. Particularly striking in the city was a grand procession displaying an image of Magna Mater, precious works of art, silver, gold, and statues, to the accompaniment of music and dancing.

This whole cycle was concluded on 27 March with a ritual that focused specifically on Magna Mater. On the day of washing, the cult statue of the goddess (the famous black meteorite, now set into a silver anthropomorphic image) was taken in procession to the stream of the Almo, a small tributary of the Tiber. There the statue and many other of the cult objects were washed before being brought back to the city and scattered with flowers in a procession, once again, of singing and dancing.

A particular form of animal sacrifice was practiced during these March rituals and on other occasions connected with the worship of Magna Mater.[27] The *taurobolium*, "killing of the bull," seems to have involved the slaughter of an animal in such a way that the blood spattered the sacrificant—quite contrary to the practice of traditional civic sacrifice in Rome, in which the blood was carefully collected and the officiant never sullied.[28] The taurobolium is often represented by modern scholars as an elaborate ceremony in which the priest

---

27. These occasions included internal cult celebrations (on, for example, the inauguration of a new priest) and (see p. 181 below) the initiation of new devotees of Magna Mater and Attis.

28. For full discussion (and reference to earlier material), see Duthoy 1969 (though his view of the chronological development of the sacrifice is controversial and probably wrong). On the bloodless nature of traditional civic sacrifice, see Gordon 1990b:202–6.

stood in a deep pit covered by planks and the animal to be killed was placed on top, so that the blood flowed through, drenching the priest beneath. This may have been the normal arrangement. But almost all the details on which this reconstruction is based come from a Christian verse polemic in which the taurobolium is portrayed as a perverted form of baptism. The most that can be said with certainty is that the taurobolium repeated the visible spilling and spreading of blood found in other aspects of the cult and contrasted violently with the surprisingly bloodless nature of traditional Roman sacrifice.[29]

The Cult Officials of Magna Mater and Attis

The eunuch priests were not the only cult officials of Magna Mater and Attis in Rome. There was an elaborate cult organization and numerous small groups of officials—male and female, Roman and Eastern, of high and low social status. Three groups were specifically associated with the rituals of March: the *cannophoroi* ("reed-bearers," who took charge of the reeds for the ceremonies of the 15th); the *dendrophoroi* ("tree-bearers," responsible for the pine tree); and the *doryphoroi*, or *hastiferi* ("spear-bearers," probably involved in the procession of the 25th). Likewise, the *ballatores Cybelae* (the "dancers of Cybele") presumably played their part in accompanying processions of the goddess during the same spring cycle of rituals. Other officials had a wider range of responsibilities in the cult. Several "priests" and "priestesses" of Magna Mater (*sacerdotes*—not the eunuch priests, known in Latin as *galli*) are attested in Rome, who no doubt had a general oversight of the cult, its adherents, and its rituals.

However, in the Roman imagination, the eunuch priests (*gallus,* singular, *galli,* plural) represented the cult of Magna Mater. The galli (under their head *archigallus*) were the priestly symbol of the cult. Once again, we know very little in detail of their cultic role. It is even far from certain that all of them, literally, as was regularly claimed, castrated themselves with a stone or broken pot on entry to their priesthood. Although I have referred to them as eunuchs, it

---

29. Prudentius *Crowns of Martyrdom* 10:1006–50. This "description" is spoken by a Christian martyr, who (in a particularly gory scene) miraculously manages to deliver a speech even though his tongue has just been cut out!

is possible that we should imagine a normally lesser form of mutilation or scarification, legitimated by the figure of Attis and by a very few, dramatic, paraded examples of actual castration performed by only the most exceptional religious enthusiasts. But whatever their precise physiological status, they stalk the pages of Roman literature as mad, frenzied, foreign eunuchs.[30]

Rejection and Incorporation

It is conventional (and convenient, as a first step) to describe the cult of Magna Mater as I have—to attempt to define the nature of its rituals and the obligations of its cult officials and to delineate its history. But to do only this misses the point. It inevitably leads to repeated statements of regret and disappointment about what the Romans fail to tell us. These disappointments are real: there is much that we would like to know about Roman religion and ritual that we never shall and never could. But to concentrate on the absences and regrets conceals from view what should be the center of investigation: the distinctive *Roman* ways of presenting and re-presenting religious practice—in poetry, in law, in the visual arts, in history, in humor, in all their cultural forms. If we are to understand Roman religion, we must enter, explore, even celebrate, that apparently frustrating gap between Roman preoccupations and our own, between what the Romans tell us and what we would like to know.

In this section, I consider more closely Roman representations of the cult and officials of Magna Mater and the patterns of contradiction and conflict in those representations. I am concerned here not with how the cult really worked, or with whether the galli were really castrated, but with the imaginative insistence on the cult in Roman poetry, legal regulation, and history. Part of that insistence concentrates on marking and remarking the opposition between the practices of the cult of Magna Mater and traditional Roman norms. It is an insistence on distance and difference, particularly focused on the eunuch galli.

The passage from Juvenal quoted at the beginning of this chapter

---

30. For an immensely learned discussion with full bibliography, see Sanders 1972. Castration was a risky business in the ancient world. The emperor Justinian (A.D. 527–65) noted in a legal ruling that on one occasion eighty-seven boys died out of a group of ninety who had undergone castration (*Novels* 142; no English translation).

is typical, highlighting, as it does, the foreignness, turbulence, and lack of (Roman) control in the eunuchs. This is a common theme in Roman literature,[31] and it is often combined with vilification of the sexual habits and preferences of the galli. Important here is not so much the simple claim that the eunuchs were sexually active[32] but the type of sexual activity involved, activity flagrantly transgressive of Roman norms. For example, in the following epigram of the poet Martial (ca. A.D. 40–100), the fondness of the galli for oral sex is the target of attack. Martial writes as if speaking to a priest called Baeticus.

To Baeticus, a eunuch priest (or gallus)

What, licking women down inside there, Gallus?
The thing you should be sucking is a phallus.
They cut your cock off, but not so to bed,
Cunt-lover: what needs doctoring now's your head.
For while your missing member can't but fail,
Your tongue still breaks Cybele's rule: it's male.[33]

The double edge of the transgression is clear. The galli are portrayed as breaking the laws of nature by becoming "women," or at least only "half-men" (castrated, dressed in women's clothes, long-haired—the apt sexual partner, as Martial has it, for a man). But they compound that crime by not obeying the rules of either their new or their old gender. Not only do they continue to play an active male sexual role, but by taking the male part, they (inevitably perhaps) pervert the norm of phallic penetration that was the only acceptable form of heterosexual activity for the Roman.[34] In the

---

31. See, for example, Lucretius *On the Nature of Things* 2.610–28; Ovid *Fasti* 4.179–88; Seneca *On the Happy Life* 26.8. Note also Richard 1966.

32. Intercourse is normally possible for those men (like the galli) who are castrated as adults—in contrast to those castrated before puberty. For further discussion of the physical effects of eunuchism, see Hopkins 1978:193–94.

33. Martial *Epigrams* 3.81: "Quid cum femineo tibi, Baetice Galle, barathro? / haec debet medios lambere lingua viros. / abscisa est quare Samia tibi mentula testa, / si tibi tam gratus, Baetice, cunnus erat? / castrandum caput est: nam sis licet inguine Gallus, / sacra tamen Cybeles decipis: ore vir es." I am grateful to Simon Pembroke for this (reluctant—he assures me) translation of the epigram.

34. For the awful appropriateness of this pun, and for the Roman version of "what a man's gotta do," see Henderson 1987.

Roman imagination, the eunuch gallus was both a non-man and a man who broke the rules of proper male behavior.

It was not only in poetry that this opposition was constructed between the activities of the galli and the accepted norms of "Romanness." In writing the history of Rome, in recording Roman legal decisions, ancient authors likewise paraded the "unacceptability" of the eunuch priests. For example, in *Roman Antiquities*, Dionysius of Halicarnassus (writing in the late first century B.C.) lists the "Phrygian" aspects of the cult of Magna Mater and records a "law and decree of the senate" forbidding any involvement in these by native Romans.

> The priest and priestess of the goddess are Phrygians, and it is they who carry her image in procession through the city, begging alms in her name according to their custom, and wearing figures upon their breasts and striking their timbrels while their followers play tunes upon their flutes in honour of the Mother of the Gods. But by a law and decree of the senate no native Roman walks in procession through the city arrayed in a multi-coloured robe, begging alms or escorted by flute-players, or worships the goddess with the Phrygian ceremonies.[35]

This passage not only repeats the now familiar association of the galli with frenzy and loss of control but adds a new element of contrast with "normal" religious or priestly behavior—begging and the collection of alms. In traditional Roman religion, the role of the priest was inextricably linked with the role of civic benefactor, and the offering of public sacrifice was one of the most visible symbols of the elite's "generosity" toward the Roman people.[36] The priests of Magna Mater flagrantly reversed that norm: they were the recipients not the providers of generosity—beggars not benefactors.

Other texts directly concern the castration of the galli. We have details of a legal ruling by Emperor Hadrian and others that explicitly forbade the (forced or voluntary) castration of any Roman, whether free or slave.[37] This general prohibition necessarily emphasized the cultural exclusion of the eunuch galli, putting him outside the bound-

---

35. Dionysius of Halicarnassus *Roman Antiquities* 2.19.
36. See, especially, Gordon 1990b:219-31.
37. For the precise terms of the prohibitions, see Justinian *Digest* 48.8.4-6 (trans. A. Watson, University of Pennsylvania Press).

aries of proper Roman society. But that exclusion could also be paraded in what might seem to us the minutiae of Roman legal decision making. Valerius Maximus (writing in the first century A.D.), records the case of a disputed inheritance. A gallus of Magna Mater, one Genucius, had received a legacy, which had been ratified by a Roman magistrate. On appeal, the consul (a higher magistrate) disallowed the inheritance on the grounds that Genucius was "neither man nor woman" and so was ineligible to inherit under Roman law. Genucius was not even allowed to plead his case in public, "for fear that the tribunal of the magistrates should be polluted by his obscene presence and corrupt voice."[38] The gallus is here seen as so alien that he cannot come within the terms of Roman law.

These strident expressions of Roman distaste for the galli have seemed relatively easy to reinterpret in modern scholarly terms. One common view among historians has seen the introduction of Magna Mater into Rome as a classic case of "biting off more than one can chew."

The Romans had brought their ancestral (i.e., Trojan) Goddess to the new country and provided her with proper accommodation, only then to discover how widely and profoundly their own attitude differed from the Asian mentality.[39]

Or, as another writer has it, "The Romans probably did not fully realize [the cult's] real nature when they admitted it to the city."[40] In these terms, the insistent vilification of the galli, or the stress on their legal disability, is the predictable Roman reaction to the true character of the cult. It was one way of handling a goddess and her priests who could not simply be sent away again, but who could never be comfortably incorporated into Roman religious practice and traditions.

At a more general level, the opposition paraded between the galli and the priests of the traditional civic cults could also be understood as a reflection of the opposition between two different and conflicting means of access to divine power at Rome. On the one

---

38. Valerius Maximus *Memorable Deeds and Sayings* 7.6 (no English translation).
39. Vermaseren 1977:96.
40. Scullard 1981:98–99.

hand was the routinized, formal approach of traditional priesthood, embedded in the political and social hierarchies of the city. On the other hand were the claims of the galli that they enjoyed direct inspiration from the gods—an inspiration that came with frenzy and trance, open to anyone, without consideration of political or social status. Seen in this way, the literary representation of the galli is partly a reflection of their own parade of that alternative route to divine power. It is also partly a reflection of Roman anxiety about what that alternative implied. By challenging the position of the Roman elite as the sole guardians of access to the gods, the eunuch priests were effectively challenging the wider authority of that elite and the social and cultural norms they have long guaranteed.

Something can be said in favor of these interpretations of Roman reactions to the cult of Magna Mater. No doubt some Romans were utterly horrified when they discovered that the "ancestral" goddess they had introduced came with priests and rituals that seemed so decidedly foreign. Some would have perceived the inspirational aspects of the cult as a direct threat to the carefully ordered relations with the gods, relations under the control of the Roman elite. The problem is that all interpretations of this kind explain only part of the story. They emphasize distance, difference, and hostility, while ignoring the equally insistent attempts at incorporation—attempts to portray the cult not as alien but as part of Roman religious practice. The jokes of Juvenal and Martial, the legal controls over the galli, and the repeated vilifications of the non-Roman aspects of Magna Mater and her priests must be set alongside another, very different type of literary representation.

The accounts (part history, part myth) of the introduction of Magna Mater to Rome provide a clear example of these literary attempts to Romanize the cult. For example, Livy (writing his *History of Rome* from ca. 30 B.C. to A.D. 17) describes in detail the story of the goddess's arrival at Rome—emphasizing her incorporation in the framework of traditional Roman religion, under the control of the social and political elite of the city. It is not just that her introduction was ordained by a collection of "official" oracles (the Sibylline books), interpreted by a group of high-ranking Roman priests. Livy lays even more stress on the arrangements concerning Magna Mater's first reception into the city of Rome. The oracle at Delphi, it was said, had instructed that the goddess should be welcomed to Rome by the "best man" in the city. The senate duly discussed the matter and agreed that this honor should be granted to the young Publicus Scipio Nasica, a member of one of Rome's most prestigious families, a man who was later to hold the highest offices of the Roman state. When the goddess's ship drew near the city, Scipio went to the port to meet her; and with him, so Livy claims, went all the married women of Rome, who passed her cult image (the black meteorite) from hand to hand until it reached the temple of Victory in the city, where it was to rest until a new shrine was ready.[41] The message is clear: the goddess was a guest of the traditional Roman governing class; she entered the city under their protection and (by implication) on their terms.

Other versions of the reception of Magna Mater have much more to say about the role of one Roman woman in particular. Livy mentions in his account a certain Claudia Quinta, whose prominent role in the ceremonies, he claims, ensured that her reputation, which was "previously not unquestioned," became most celebrated for its purity. But he does not discuss her in any detail or elaborate on her actions. In Herodian's version of the story, by contrast, written in the third century A.D., Claudia Quinta is precisely identified as a Vestal Virgin who is under suspicion of having broken the vow of chastity to which those priestesses were bound. When the ship transporting the cult image became grounded on a sandbank, Claudia Quinta "took off her belt and threw it onto the prow of the ship with a prayer that, if she were still an innocent virgin, the ship would follow her." The ship did follow. Claudia Quinta managed to draw it in to land with her belt, effectively establishing her innocence on all charges of inchastity. This story emphasizes yet more strongly the acceptability of Magna Mater in Roman terms. In making the goddess's successful entry into the city depend on the action of a vestal—a member of one of the most ancient Roman priesthoods and a guardian of the sacred hearth (the focus) of the city—Herodian is forcefully parading the Roman legitimacy of the cult.[42]

Some ancient descriptions of the rituals of Magna Mater likewise

---

41. Livy *Histories* 29.10.4–11, 8; 29.14.5–14.

42. Herodian *History* 1.11.4–5. A stone altar found in Rome appears to illustrate the scene (Vermaseren 1977: pl. 30.). For the role of the vestal virgins, their vow of chastity and the series of anecdotes on miracles they performed when under suspicion of having broken their vow, see Beard 1980.

imply her close interconnection with the traditional cults and priests of Rome and with the symbolic power of the state. The image of frenzy, dancing, and oriental ecstasy is only one side of the picture. The other side shows a cult whose ritual forms overlap with those of Roman civic religion, broadly encompassed in the framework of state control. Even the cycle of festivals in March, often assumed by modern scholars to be the most extremely Eastern aspect of the cult, can be shown to include a range of distinctively Roman elements. Particularly striking was the grand procession on the occasion of the Hilaria (day of joy, 25 March), with its display of an image of Magna Mater and other precious works of art. The most splendid of those precious objects were, according to Herodian, the treasures of the emperor's palace, carried through the streets of Rome in honor of the Great Mother—a public parade of the symbiosis between imperial power and the power of the goddess.[43] But on numerous other occasions throughout the fortnight's festivities, the "official" participation of the traditional Roman public priests is noted. For example, the so-called *Quindecimviri Sacris Faciundis* ("The Fifteen Men for the Performance of Ritual") were involved, alongside the galli and other functionaries of Magna Mater, at the ceremony of Lavatio (bathing);[44] and the springtime rituals of the Salian Priests (whose traditional Roman function was connected with the opening of the military campaigning season in March) came gradually to be seen as part of the cycle in honor of Magna Mater.[45] This reciprocity is in stark contrast to the sense of complete separation sometimes evoked between the wild excesses of the oriental cult and the sobriety of traditional Roman religion.

A similar overlap is sometimes paraded in records of the performance of taurobolia. It appears to have been common practice for the participants at such a sacrifice to commemorate the event with a carved stone inscription noting briefly the date of its occurrence, the circumstances, and the principal officiants. Over 120 of these inscriptions survive, from Rome and elsewhere, giving (admittedly at no

---

43. Herodian *History* 1.10.5.

44. See Lucan *Pharsalia* 1.599–600.

45. This is a rather stronger claim—but it is borne out by the fifth oration of the (fourth-century A.D.) emperor Julian (the *Hymn to the Mother of the Gods*), where (section 168C) the dance and trumpeting of the *salii* are treated as part of the March festival of Magna Mater.

great length) a rare, insider's view of the ritual.[46] A few of the texts seem to support the suggestion of some kind of mystical significance attaching to the sacrifice: one, for example, talks about "rebirth into eternity";[47] another seems to refer to "taking over the power" of the bull.[48] But others have a quite different focus; they were said to be performed, like many Roman public sacrifices, "for the safety of the emperor."[49] The significance is clear: even the taurobolium—a form of ritual that appears at first sight to pervert so flagrantly the symbolic code of civic sacrifice—could be portrayed as an integral element in the traditional structure of Roman religion and Roman political power.

Finally, the place of the galli in the symbolic geography of the city of Rome offers a particularly striking indication of their inseparability from the center of Roman political and religious life. It is true that part of the image of their marginality lies in their confinement to their temple precinct. Occasionally they were allowed to process through the streets or beg for alms, but normally (in contrast to traditional Roman priestly groups) they were visible only at their temple. But where was that temple? It was not safely hidden away, remote from the center of civic action. It was on the Palatine Hill, a stone's throw from the forum, at the very heart of the city—an area occupied at the time of the cult's introduction by the houses of the grandest of the Roman elite, and later by the imperial palace. It is hardly an exaggeration to claim that the galli were the Roman emperor's closest neighbors. Far from an image of separation, from

---

46. For a full catalog of these texts (without translations), see Duthoy 1969. No inscriptions recording taurobolia are found in Rome until the very end of the third century A.D., though earlier examples are found elsewhere. This absence of early texts in Rome may simply be an accident of survival.

47. Duthoy 1969: no. 23 (from Rome, 376 A.D.).

48. Duthoy 1969: no. 126. The precise sense is uncertain. The word *vires* (which I have translated here as "power") occurs in other inscriptions: in one (no. 83) the *vires* are said to be "hidden away"; in two others (nos. 120 and 123) they are "consecrated." It seems likely that *vires* refers both to a part of the animal (perhaps genitals or blood) and, metaphorically, to the "power" communicated by the sacrifice.

49. Duthoy 1969: nos. 35, 36, 38 and 40 (all from Ostia, the port of Rome)— normally adding a prayer for the safety of the Senate, "The Fifteen Men for the Performance of Ritual," and other official institutions); no. 52 (from Teate, modern Chieti); and twenty-six examples from the empire outside Italy. Note also that many of these inscriptions record the involvement of state priests in the sacrifice, either perhaps coincidentally (the officiant just happened to be a state priest) or with some specific role in the ceremony (for example, no. 21—suggesting a formal part for "The Fifteen Men").

the point of view of the Roman onlooker, the emperor and the eunuch priests were bound together in the same field of vision.[50]

How does this image of incorporation of the cult of Magna Mater relate to the other equally insistent image of its rejection and marginality? The inconsistency seems at first sight awkward, even nonsensical. There is an obvious temptation to try to rationalize—to construct a history of the cult that would (reassuringly) erode the apparent incompatibility between its two very different representations. Could there be, for example, a chronological dimension? Are we dealing with a situation in which the boundaries between the cult of Magna Mater and traditional Roman religion, at first rigidly guarded, gradually broke down, as emperors and the state authorities found it convenient, perhaps, to assimilate rather than reject the power of the goddess? Or should we imagine the cult divided throughout its history into two very different forms of worship: on the one hand, a "domesticated" version, easily incorporated into Roman practice; on the other, the wild extremes of the Phrygian version of the cult, offensive to Roman sensibilities, and constantly reviled in Roman literature?

Such historical reconstructions may provide part of the answer to the apparently conflicting images of the cult. It seems likely, for example, that the interconnections between the worship of Magna Mater and traditional state religion increased over time,[51] and that some of the initial shock at the apparent foreignness of the priests of the goddess wore off as they became a more familiar presence in the city. Also, different elements in the cult and its rituals had very different character, attracted different types of participants, and displayed different degrees of "Romanness." Most obviously the "Phrygian" festivals in March—though including, as I have shown, many more "Roman" elements than has often been supposed—still present

---

50. The proximity of the temple of Magna Mater and the residence of the first emperor Augustus is shown by Wiseman 1984:124 (plan of the southern end of the Palatine) and (including the later imperial palaces) by Wiseman 1981:191, fig. 1.

51. Some of the most extreme interconnections (for example, the incorporation of the rituals of the *salii*, are documented only in late imperial sources. This does not prove that they are a late development; the fragmentary nature of the surviving sources would not allow any such certain argument from silence. Nevertheless, a gradual increase in the overlaps and connections seems likely. See the remarks of Gordon 1990a:246—"('Oriental cults') were not immune to that widespread pattern whereby "ancestral tradition" gradually enlarged itself to include originally private cults."

a contrast with the Megalesia in April, which was almost entirely in the control of the Roman elite.[52]

No reconstruction can successfully turn the story of the cult of Magna Mater from a sometimes bewildering set of conflicting images into a neatly consistent narrative. There are always inconvenient "facts" that cannot magically be made to fit; the conjuring trick always fails. The intense and unresolved debates among modern scholars on apparently central issues of the cult (the significance of the taurobolium and whether or when Roman citizens were allowed to become galli or archigalli[53] are proof of that failure. These debates are not the consequence (as their protagonists often imagine) of inadequate information; they are the consequence of a rich variety of evidence, offering sometimes staggeringly different pictures of the subject at issue; they are the consequence of undeniable and important inconsistency in ancient representations of the cult. Rather than try to erode or abolish it, we should turn our attention much more closely to the nature of that inconsistency: what is at stake in the parading of two such different images of the cult of Magna Mater?

To answer this question, I shall start by briefly considering relations between state and cult at Rome from a historical, political point of view—before focusing again on those same issues in the domain of Roman representation and their "imaginative economy."

The Cult of Magna Mater and the State: Defining the Roman

Modern discussions of the relations between shamanism and the state tend to assume two clearly defined (or at least definable) subjects: ritual practices involving possession, ecstasy and inspiration; and that complex nexus of power, hierarchy, and a sense of identity that

---

52. The contrast between the Megalesia and the March festival—and so also between the "respectable" Roman and "wild" Phrygian elements of the cult—is a common theme in modern studies. See, for example, Scullard 1981:98–99 and Wiseman 1984:117–19 (stressing the "popular"—that is, frenetic—versus the "official"—that is, elite Roman—involvement in the cult).

53. For a review of theories on the taurobolium, see Duthoy 1969. Specific problems on the galli and archigalli (often—and improbably—assumed to be two quite different types of priesthood, the former prohibited to Roman citizen, the latter not) are raised by Lambrechts and Bogaert 1969 and Thomas 1971.

together adds up to "the state."[54] These two subjects may relate in very different ways—from outright conflict to peaceful coexistence. The precise details of their definition may be a matter of sharp dispute. But any discussion about relations between shamanism and the state normally implies from the start that both are identifiable agencies, capable of interaction with each other.

Any attempt to analyze the interaction between the cult of Magna Mater and the Roman state ultimately breaks down in paradox. It is not that we cannot suggest plausible patterns of relationship between the two. The problem is that there appear to be two equally insistent, contradictory, and coexistent models: the first defining the cult of Magna Mater as a political and religious challenge to the routinized forms of state religion at Rome, which were embedded in (and legitimated) the political and social hierarchy of the city; the second suggesting the assimilation of the most potent symbolic forms of the cult by the dominant religious and political order at Rome (in particular the emperor)—so making Magna Mater a support rather than a threat to the state. In the short term, perhaps, it might be reasonable to imagine a situation in which the challenge of the cult to the state coexisted with its assimilation, or one in which there was a constant oscillation between those two poles. But in the long term, as a model for understanding practical and political relations between cult and state over the centuries-long history of the Roman empire, it is necessarily unsatisfactory, even absurd. It attenuates the ideas of assimilation or challenge to the point of nonsense to imagine that they were mutually compatible over hundreds of years.

The underlying difficulty with trying to cast Roman history and religion in these terms is that it implies the existence of a definable Roman state capable of a relatively coherent response to the challenge posed by the cult of Magna Mater. At first sight, there is perhaps nothing implausible about such an implication. The Roman imperial administration has often been seen as a classic example of the kind of centralized control that can be obtained in a preindustrial empire.[55]

54. I have been much struck by Nicholas Thomas's article (1988). In many ways, my sense of the sheer impossibility of analyzing Roman shamanic activity (and its relation with political authority) in those terms led me to reach the conclusions I have in this chapter.

55. For an introduction to the administration of the Roman Empire, see Millar 1981:52–80; Garnsey and Saller 1987:20–40.

But I would suggest that for all its highly developed administrative mechanisms, the sense in which we can talk about a Roman state is very limited. If Rome is to be seen as a state, it is a state at whose center lies dark uncertainty about its own cultural, religious, and political identity. This uncertainty is necessarily implicated in Rome's treatment of foreign, shamanic cults, such as the cult of Magna Mater. At stake here is not the state's reaction to such shamanic activity; much more important are the ways these cults provided a symbolic focus for defining the identity of the state. State and shamanism were not, I argue, two opposing poles. The discourse around shamanic activity was one of the contexts in which Roman identity could be defined.

This claim must be seen against the background of the history of the Roman Empire and of Rome's character as an imperial power. Apart from the geographical extent (which I noted in my introduction), two particular points need to be stressed. First is the speed of Rome's expansion. In 300 B.C. Rome was still in most respects a simple, independent city-state in Italy and had only recently begun to expand beyond its natural hinterland. Less than 250 years later, it had conquered most of the Mediterranean basin and was geared for further conquest in the land mass of Europe and Asia. Rome's transformation into a world power took place within just a few generations.[56] Second is Rome's favored method of dominance. Although we have today a popular image of the Romans as brutish imperialists, Rome controlled her conquered territory by assimilating (rather than annihilating) the cultural and religious traditions of her subjects, and by striking openness with her political rights and privileges. For example, from the earliest stages of her expansion, Rome began gradually to grant full Roman citizenship to her conquered peoples—a process culminating in A.D. 212, when the emperor Caracalla formally granted citizenship and its privileges to all non-slave inhabitants of the empire. In the religious sphere, not only did Rome find a place in the imperial capital for the deities of her subjects (such as Magna Mater or Isis from Egypt), but in provincial territory,

---

56. For the process of Roman expansion, see the clear, popular account in Errington 1971 and the more technical discussions in the relevant chapters of Walbank et al. 1989 and Astin et al. 1989. The underlying causes and the political consequences are discussed (briefly) by Beard and Crawford 1985:72–80 and Hopkins 1978:1–74.

native deities, far from being obliterated, were merged with Roman deities in a complex process of syncretism.[57]

It would be intensely naive to deduce from this that Rome was a particularly gentle or liberal imperial power. Religious syncretism and the expansion of citizenship can be just as effective (probably more effective) weapons of domination as political exclusivity and the destruction of native religious traditions.[58] But this kind of openness (particularly when combined with the extraordinary speed of Roman imperial conquest) had clear consequences for the definitions of Roman cultural identity and Roman power. It strategically blurred the opposition between ruler and ruled, between Rome and her subjects, and between foreign and Roman cultural and religious traditions.

These problematic consequences have often been recognized—at least from the point of view of the conquered peoples and the periphery of the empire. Scholars have been sensitive to the tension and ambivalence that must have accompanied the entry of a member of a "native" provincial aristocracy into the world of central "Roman" politics.[59] They have also seen the importance of religion in the provinces (whether "Roman" religion or a syncretistic amalgam of "Roman" and "native") for negotiating the complex character of Rome's dominance over local systems of power.[60] Particularly impressive has been recent work on the imperial cult (the cult of the deified Roman emperor) in the cities of the Greek world—showing how emperor worship could be incorporated in the traditional forms of civic life in Greece and Asia Minor and at the same time could represent to the conquered Greeks the now overweening power of Rome.[61]

Attention has rarely turned from the periphery to the center. Even when Roman authors stridently deride the wild, uncivilized customs of the conquered peoples or lament their presence in the city

---

57. The full story of the expansion of Roman citizenship is provided in immense detail by Sherwin-White 1973. For an introduction to some of the main issues, see Balsdon 1979:82–96. Ferguson (1970:211–43) offers numerous examples of religious syncretism in the empire (though with little convincing analysis). North (1976: esp. 11) explores the structural connection between religious openness and Rome's liberal grants for citizenship.

58. For recognition that the process of syncretism was far from innocent, see Gordon 1990a:242–44.

59. This is a recurring theme in the work of Sir Ronald Syme (himself a "colonial outsider" in the British elite). See, for example, Syme 1958a, 1958b:585–624.

60. Note, for example, the important study of Février (1976).

61. This is one major theme in Price 1984.

of Rome, modern scholars have found it easier to see this as simple (perhaps understandable) racism or ethnocentricity, rather than to explore the roots of such a hostile representation. Roman culture—with its panoply of law, rhetoric, literature, art, and public ceremony—has always seemed so easily definable, so unassailable. For all its apparent self-confidence, the cultural uncertainties of the center more than equalled those of the periphery. There was a necessary and unresolved tension between, on the one hand, a sense of specific identity in the city of Rome, with its language, traditions, political inheritance, and religious forms, and, on the other, a baffling erosion of that identity as political privileges were shared with the outside, as the literary and artistic traditions of the Greek world came to inform Roman expression, and as Roman religious symbols merged with strange foreign cults and ritual practices. What was it to be Roman in any definable sense, when Rome was synonymous with the world?

In the conflicting, shifting, uncertain answers to that question, we must locate the puzzling and contradictory Roman representations of the cult of Magna Mater. Like some other strikingly foreign religious forms imported (at official instigation or, at least, with official tolerance) into the city of Rome, this cult and its priests came to act as a privileged focus of debate on the nature of the Roman and the foreign. It was not so much a question of whether the eunuch priests challenged the established Roman order or were relatively safe supporters of the symbolic power of the traditional hierarchy. Both alternatives are possible. Much more important is the fact that different constructions of their role—their means of access to divine power, their gender and sexual relations, and their position alongside or in opposition to the traditional priestly groups of the city—effectively amounted to different claims and conflicting counterclaims on how the Roman was to be defined; on proper Roman behavior; on the proper exercise of Roman power; and on proper Roman relations with the divine. These claims were part of an unending process of defining the identity of the ruling power.

REFERENCES

Astin, A. E., et al.
1989 *The Cambridge ancient history.* Vol. 8. Cambridge: Cambridge University Press.

Atkinson, J. M.
1989 *The art and politics of Wana shamanship.* Berkeley and Los Angeles: University of California Press.

Balsdon, J. P. V. D.
1979 *Romans and aliens.* London: Duckworth.

Beard, M.
1980 The sexual status of vestal virgins. *Journal of Roman Studies* 70:12–27.
1985 Writing and ritual: A study of diversity and expansion in the Arval Acta. *Papers of the British School at Rome* 40:114–62.
1990 Priesthood in the Roman Republic. In Beard and North 1990.

Beard, M., and M. Crawford
1985 *Rome in the late Republic.* London: Duckworth.

Beard, M., and J. North, eds.
1990 *Pagan priests.* London: Duckworth.

Beard, M., J. North, and S. R. F. Price
Forthcoming   *Roman religion.* Cambridge: Cambridge University Press.

Carcopino, J.
1942 *Aspects mystiques de la Rome paienne.* Paris: L'artisan du livre.

Coarelli, F.
1982 *I monumenti dei culti orientali in Roma.* In U. Bianchi and M. Vermaseren, eds. *La soterologia dei culti orientali neall'impero Romano.* EPRO 92. Leiden: Brill.

Dodds, E. R.
1951 *The Greeks and the irrational.* Berkeley and Los Angeles: University of California Press.

Duthoy, R.
1969 *The taurobolium, its evolution and terminology* EPRO 10. Leiden: Brill.

Errington, R. M.
1971 *The dawn of empire.* London: Hamish Hamilton.

Ferguson, J.
1970 *The Religions of the Roman Empire.* London: Thames and Hudson.

Février, P. A.
1976 Religion et domination dans l'Afrique romaine. *Dialogues d'histoire ancienne* 2:305–63.

Fishwick, D.
1966 The Cannophori and the March festival of Magna Mater. *Transactions of the American Philological Society* 97:193–202.

Garnsey, P., and R. Saller
1987 *The Roman Empire: Economy, society, and culture.* London: Duckworth.

Ginzburg, C.
1990 *Ecstasies: Deciphering the Witches' Sabbath.* London: Hutchinson Radius.

Gordon, R. L.
1990a   Religion in the Roman Empire. In Beard and North 1990.
1990b   The veil of power. In Beard and North 1990.

Graillot, H.
1912   *Le culte de Cybèle.* Paris: Écoles francaises d'Athènes et de Rome.

Hansen, E. V.
1971   *The Attalids of Pergamum.* 2d ed. Ithaca and London: Cornell University Press.

Henderson, J.
1987   Satire writes "woman": *Gendersong. Proceedings of the Cambridge Philological Society* 215:50–80.

Hopkins, K.
1978.   *Conquerors and Slaves.* Cambridge: Cambridge University Press.

Lambrechts, P.
1952a   Attis à Rome. In *Mélanges G. Smets.* Brussels: Editions de la librarie encyclopaedique.
1952b   Les fêtes "Phrygiennes" de Cybèle et d'Attis. *Bulletin de l'Institut Historique Belge de Rome* 27:141–70.

Lambrechts, P., and R. Bogaert
1969   Asclepios, archigalle Pessinontien de Cybèle. In *Hommages à M. Renard,* Vol. 2. Brussels: Latomus.

Metzler, D.
1983   Zum Schamenismus in Griechenland. In *Antidoron* (Festschrift für J. Thimme). Karlsruhe: Müller.

Millar, F. G. B.
1981   *The Roman Empire and its neighbours.* 2d ed. London: Duckworth.

Morgan, M. G.
1974   Priests and physical fitness. *Classical Quarterly* 24:137–41.

North, J. A.
1976   Conservatism and change in Roman religion. *Papers of the British School at Rome* 44:1–12.

Price, S. R. F.
1984   *Rituals and power: the Roman imperial cult in Asia Minor.* Cambridge: Cambridge University Press.

Richard, L.
1966   Juvénal et les galles de Cybèle. *Revue de l'histoire des religions* 169:51–67.

Romanelli, P.
1963   Lo scavo al tempio della Magna Mater e nelle sue adiacenze. *Monumenti Antichi* 46:202–330.

Sanders, G. M.
1972   Gallos. In *Reallexikon für Antike und Christentum,* Vol. 8. Stuttgart: Hiersemann.

Scheid, J.
1985 *Religion et piété à Rome*. Paris: La Découverte.

Scott Ryberg, I.
1955 Rites of state religion in Roman art. In *Memoirs of the American Academy at Rome*.

Scullard, H. H.
1981 *Festivals and Ceremonies of the Roman Republic*. London: Thames and Hudson.

Sherwin-White, A. N.
1973 *The Roman Citizenship*. 2d ed. Oxford: Clarendon Press.

Syme, R.
1958a *Colonial Elites*. London: Oxford University Press.
1958b *Tacitus*. Oxford: Clarendon Press.

Thomas, G.
1971 Flavius Antonius Eustochius (CIL VI, 508) n'était pas un archigalle. *Revue belge de philologie et d'histoire* 49:55–65.
1984 Magna Mater and Attis. In H. Temporini and W. Haase, eds. *Aufstieg und Niedergang der Römischer Welt*. Berlin and New York: De Gruyter.

Thomas, N.
1988 Marginal powers: Shamanism and the disintegration of hierarchy. *Critique of Anthropology* 8:53–74.

Turcan, R.
1989 *Les cultes orientaux dans le monde romain*. Paris: Les belles lettres.

Vermaseren, M. J.
1977 *Cybele and Attis, the myth and the cult*. London: Thames and Hudson.

Walbank, F., et al.
1989 *The Cambridge ancient history*. Vol. 7, pt. 2. Cambridge: Cambridge University Press.

Wardman, A.
1982 *Religion and statecraft among the Romans*. London: Granada.

Welles, C. B.
1934 *Royal correspondence in the Hellenistic period: A study in Greek epigraphy*. New Haven: Yale University Press.

Wiedemann, T.
1981 *Greek and Roman slavery*. London: Croom Helm.
Wiseman, T. P.
1981 The temple of Victory on the Palatine. *Antiquaries Journal* 61:35–52.
1984 Cybele, Virgil, and Augustus. In T. Woodman and D. West, eds., *Poetry and politics in the age of Augustus*. Cambridge: Cambridge University Press.

Shamanic Practices and the State in Northern Asia: Views from the Center and Periphery

Caroline Humphrey

Northern Asia[1] is the region where it is generally supposed that "classic shamanism" used to exist, where shamans in elaborate costume went into trances, mastered spirits, journeyed to other worlds, and retrieved the souls of the dead. A compelling ideal type of Siberian shamanism, defined by the idea of ecstatic ascent to a celestial supreme being, was popularized by Eliade ([1951] 1964) and has been used by countless other authors as a point of comparison for their own regions. In constructing his concept of "shamanism in the strict and proper sense," Eliade turned the inspirational religious practices of north Asia into a timeless mystery. Peoples, of whom no description whatsoever is given, and at no particular date, are cited as providing examples of this or that aspect of shamanism, as though shamanism were some metaphysical entity making its presence felt despite history and societies; it was assumed that only a prototypical form of shamanism located in remote prehistorical antiquity was genuine. Eliade therefore wrote that "nowhere in the world or in history will a perfectly 'pure' and 'primordial' religious phenomenon be found" (1964:11).

This chapter takes the view that, although shamanic practices are undoubtedly very ancient in north Asia, it is not helpful to search

I would like to thank Nicola Di Cosmo, James Laidlaw, Sherry Ortner, Roger Rouse, and David Sneath for helpful discussions about this chapter.

1. This refers to Siberia, Mongolia, North-Western China, Manchuria, and the Altai.

for some Eliadean original Ur-model, because inspirational religious practices have never been independent of context. Rather, they should be seen as reactive and constitutive in relation to other forms of power, and this may be a means by which we can understand, in a broad regional context, their character at given places and periods, and their transformations through history. Such a perspective implies at least two departures from earlier methodology. We should try to discover what shamans do and what powers they are thought to have, rather than crystallize out a context-free model derived from the images they may or may not use (mystic flight, a celestial supreme being, the world mountain, the cosmic tree, the bird-soul, and so on). Following from this, instead of defining only some specialists as true shamans, which is usually done on the basis of the ritual use of such imagery, it is necessary to look at the entire range of inspirational practice, including that of political leaders and ritual practitioners not usually considered to be shamans. Shamanic imagery does not form a coherent system, still less an ideology. It is a collection of representations, parts of which appear here and there in the cultures of the region, and these pieces can be used by anyone in a variety of ways (in rituals, songs, dreaming, prophesy, mythic genealogy, and clan and state ceremonial, as well as in the trance performances usually considered to be shamanic). The use of such imagery does not separate out a particular class of specialist shamans. Nor does it distinguish performative from liturgical ritual, or either of these from everyday contexts. In what follows, the term *shaman* is used for the specialists called by equivalent words in native languages, and *shamanism* refers to their practices and beliefs.[2] But as I hope will become clear, this term is not meant to define a single category.

Leaving the category shaman rather open in this chapter is deliberate. It allows us to avoid focusing on one type of inspirational religious specialist in societies that have several and categorize them differently. More important, it is intended to signal a change in perspective, namely, the rejection of static models in favor of an understanding of shamanism as discourse.[3] This allows us to see shamanism

2. Atkinson (1989) has with good reason written of "shamanship," rather than "shamanism," but I retain the latter term to keep consistency with other chapters in this book.

3. I use this term in the broad sense of socially situated cultural practices employed by Foucault: "Discourses . . . [are] . . . practices that systematically form the objects of which they speak" (1972:49).

as constitutive of social realities in contexts of power, and to antic-
ipate, rather than be puzzled by, its multiplicities, contradictions, and
changes of content, in different historical situations.

Nicholas Thomas (1988), using a similar kind of analysis to the
one proposed above, has suggested that there is a broad opposition
between inspirational agency and the assimilating, encompassing
power of chiefship in eastern Polynesia. Ritual efficacy in that region
is a matter of influencing the divine forces that control agriculture
and fertility. Broadly speaking, when chiefs are powerful in this
matter, shamans are not, and vice versa. Hamayon (1990) argues,
though from a structuralist point of view, that Siberian shamanism
is essentially dualistic, as well as being practical, undogmatic, and
individual, and is therefore incompatible with hierarchical ideology.
She claims that shamanism in any hierarchical system, let alone a
state, becomes marginalized, feminized, and fragmented.

This chapter argues that shamanism has not always been in contradiction with the state: different manifestations of shamanic practice
may support or undermine political authority and may even emerge
from the core of the state. We need to know more about the purpose
of shamanizing (the interests of its practitioners) and the forms of
power at issue before useful generalizations can be made. I suggest
here, using the example of twelfth- and thirteenth-century Mongols,
that inspirational practices were deeply implicated in the formation of
Inner Asian states.[4] Even after such states were bureaucratized and
their ritual made liturgical, "the marginal" was still necessary for the
legitimation and identity of the center, just as the imperial court was
for the self-definition of the peoples on the periphery. Shamanic and
inspirational practices were contexts for the making of such links. The
example used here is the last of the inner Asian states that took power
in China, the Manchu Qing Dynasty (1644–1911), in which the imperial family and court retained a quasi-shamanist cult until the twentieth century. This chapter is only a preliminary sketch in an area that
requires more research, but I suggest here that the character and social

---

4. This refers to the states that arose among the peoples of the inner Asian
hinterland and later took power in China, not to the properly Han Chinese states.
Thus, "inner Asian states" include the Liao Empire (946–1125) founded by the Khitan
people, the Jin Empire (1115–1234) founded by the Jurchens, the Mongol Empire
(1206–1368), and the Manchu Empire (1644–1911), but not the T'ang, Sung, Ming,
or other Chinese dynastic empires. The dynastic name adopted by the Mongols after
the conquest of China was Yuan, and that of the Manchus was Qing (Ch'ing).

importance of such shamanic practices may have varied, depending not only on stance or point of view of the actors (center, periphery) but on what one might call the political phase of the state (foundation, consolidation, decline).

Shamanism has changed over these centuries or, to be more precise, the aims of inspirational specialists and therefore the content of their practices have responded to the different configurations of power in changing historical circumstances. I suggest that during the formation of the Mongol state, when political power was very much up for grabs, shamanic practitioners entered the fray with a characteristic discourse of prophesy and interpreting omens, often using the imagery of natural events (hailstorms that would defeat an enemy and the like). After a state had been consolidated, taking the Manchus as an example, we find prophecy retreating in significance, to be replaced by discourse concerned primarily with interpersonal power and identity. In this kind of discourse, preoccupations with kinship, ancestry, and geography colored the traditional cosmic imagery of shamanism, and I will show that it had different registers in the center and periphery of the Manchu state. I do not suggest that there was a total transformation of shamanism over the centuries. Rather, these kinds of discourse represent possibilities, which were actualized in different circumstances as the energies and interests of shamans engaged with particular situations of power. Shamanism in north Asia seems to preserve memory traces of previously active discourse in the form of archaisms that might be revivified. Research on the history of shamanism in north Asia is exceedingly patchy. If more information emerges in the future, it may be possible to investigate whether archaic and latent elements in shamanism can be related to the cyclical aspects of the sequence of polities in the hinterlands of China and Russia.

North Asia: States, Societies, and Religions

In the late nineteenth and early twentieth centuries, which is the period from which most of Eliade's materials derived, a synchronic picture of northern inner Asia would look as follows. Two great empires, the Russian and the Chinese, governed the entire region, using various forms of direct and indirect rule. The vast inner hinterland was occupied by peoples one could call in some sense marginalized: Xalx Mongols, Buryats, various Tungus groups, Daur, Barga, Manchu, Uriangxai, and many others. The Manchus, who had governed the Chinese Empire since the seventeenth century, were by this time socially divided. A sinicized elite lived in Peking and in various regimental Banner garrisons, and Manchu peasant farmers and hunters continued to live in the forested margins of the northeast. In the Russian and Manchu empires, there were a host of subpolities of various kinds, ranging from quite elaborate princedoms and monastic fiefdoms in Mongolia, through petty chiefdoms and tribal systems, to simple clan-based societies living by hunting, fishing, and reindeer herding. Buddhism of the Tibetan Lamaist monastic kind dominated in the princedoms. Institutionally, shamanic practice reached its heights of elaboration in the relatively wealthy, yet disunited, tribal societies of the steppe-forest borderlands, such as the western Buryats or the peoples of the Altai. By contrast, shamanism was simpler in hunter-fisher societies and in the princedoms dominated by Lamaism, where it was virtually eliminated in some places.

The geographical extent and social influence of Buddhism and shamanism varied through history. Put simply, the accepted picture is as follows. The Inner Asian states were built up in a context of shamanism. Once a ruling dynasty had been established, it introduced and propagated Buddhism (together with a cult of imperial ancestors). Shamanism was pushed to the margins and interstices. With the collapse of these states, Buddhism retreated, and shamanic practices, which had never entirely disappeared, reemerged. This accepted view requires some further thought if we accept that shamanism was not a particular kind of object to be pushed around but a fluid set of attitudes and practices that had a part in forming many different contexts of social life.

The devolution, or more accurately the disintegration, of Inner Asian states in this region is well documented. It is not always realized what follows from this, that many of the tribal peoples of Eliade's time had been imperial rulers some centuries before. The Mongols are the most famous of these. There also are the examples of the Khitans and Jurchens, the ruling elites of the Liao (tenth through twelfth centuries) and Jin (twelfth and thirteenth centuries) empires respectively, whose descendants became the impoverished peripheral tribes of early twentieth-century ethnography. Such imperial antecedents were not entirely forgotten. There were occasional attempts to revive past glories, and in the seventeenth century, the scattered Jurchen tribes of Manchuria succeeded. Their leader, Nurgaci, assembled a powerful union of tribes, which he declared to be a new dynasty, the Later Jin. His successor, Hong Taiji, renamed the Jurchens as Manchus and the dynasty as the Qing, but in the process of formalization of Manchu imperial legitimacy, there was insistence on reference to the ancestral Jin dynasty, even in the eighteenth century (Crossley 1987:761–90).

This chapter stresses the changing nature of the states that arose in the hinterland of China and of shamanic practices. Particularly interesting are the periods of state formation, when it seems, at least from the case of the Mongols, that political actions and inspirational religious practice were inseparably intertwined. It is suggested here that the Inner Asia states, prior to their conquests of China and subsequent bureacratization, were examples of what Sahlins (1985:42–43) has called "hierarchical solidarity," characterized by common submission to a ruling power. A polity of this kind devalues tribalism and the relationship to particular lands, because the collectivity is defined by adherence to a given chief or king, rather than by distinctive cultural attributes. It arises by a "heroic" mode of clan formation as distinct from the classic segmentary lineage system: the state emerges as the structural means of some "personal project of glory" and is "regarded as little more than the property of the individual" (Sahlins 1985:45–46). The divisions in the ruling family structure the division of the state. In such polities the legitimacy of the chief or king rested in large measure on his ability to represent the social whole vis-à-vis the supernatural forces providing prosperity, fertility, and military success.

Although the Chinese and the peoples of the hinterland were culturally very different, one idiom of the legitimation of political power linked them. This idiom was a concept of heaven (or more simply the sky) as the all-encompassing principle of cosmic order and human destiny. The various peoples under discussion had different understandings of heaven—it could be seen as a single whole, as a family, as two warring camps, and as a vertically layered series of skies—but every single group in the region at all periods had some idea of this kind.[5] The essential political idea was that of the ruler

---

5. Rachewiltz (1973:21–36) suggests that the idiom of the "mandate of heaven"

on earth who governed and succored his people by virtue of the destiny accorded by heaven. This is important in a heroic state organized by hierarchical solidarity: for the military hero's family to rule over every and any other people, it was required to have an all-encompassing divine legitimation. Inscriptions of the Eastern Turkic (seventh and eighth centuries) and Mongol (twelfth through fourteenth centuries) states refer to the "good fortune" of the emperor, and this good fortune was to be destined by heaven to rule, which was manifested by military victory.

A claim by shamans that they are able to ascend to the sky, or otherwise to know the will of heaven, is a politically highly charged matter. Eliade's concept of an Ur-shamanism, based on the idea of the shaman's ascent to celestial abodes, looks rather different when it is realized that this very ability was contested by political leaders. It seems that claims by shamans to communicate with the sky (or skies) occurred only in particular historical circumstances, because this was in effect a politically significant act giving access to information about the fate of human actions. After consolidation of the state, unsupervised shamans specializing in such a regular practice are found exclusively in safe backwaters, far from centers of imperial power.[6]

Varieties of Shamanism

Everything I have written above would suggest that any particular instance of shamanism is not more than that and cannot be seen as

---

is Chinese in origin. It reached the Mongols through the Orkhon Turks (seventh and eighth centuries), who had used an identical expression, "blue heaven above," for the deified sky. De Rachewiltz, who does not mention the role of shamans, argues that among both the eastern Turks and the Mongols this idea had been propagated by state ministers with Chinese education, as a form of ideological propaganda. However, it is noted here that this idea, whatever its origin, was very early internalized by the peoples of the hinterland, that shamanic cosmologies also included the sky as the source of power, and that the "heroic state" type of polity required some such notion of legitimation from its own internal dynamics.

6. Shamans of the Altai and the Yakut regions in the late nineteenth century are examples of this. Both were subordinated in the fringes of the Tsarist Empire and had rituals of symbolic ascent to deities of the sky. It is worth noting that these ascents were normally made not for the purposes of prognostication but more simply to accompany a sacrificial animal's soul across the dangers of the cosmos to the deity's location in the sky.

characterizing shamanic discourse in general. However, it is possible to say something about the place of shamanism in the religious life of the region as a whole and to posit the existence of recurrent varieties of shamanism.

In no society of Inner Asia, including even the smallest tribe, was trance shamanism all that was going on in religious life. This fact is not always realized and the impression has been created by some authors using secondary or tertiary sources that there were many societes in the region where the shaman was the moral, spiritual, and ritual center of all religious life (see, for example, I. M. Lewis 1971). If we look more closely at the small peoples of south Siberia in the early twentieth century, we find that shamans took no part *as shamans* in several major rituals of social reproduction, and in many cases they were specifically excluded. For example, shamans were not allowed to attend the mountain cults of the Daur in the Hailar region, and they were excluded from the great bear-festivals of the Ul'chei, Nivkh, and Orochen. In the case of the Hailar Daurs, this can be explained by the fact that the mountain cult had been taken over by Buddhist lamas acting as priests for local political leaders, and lamas were notoriously jealous of shamans, but in other regions there was no trace of Lamaism, so we must look for some other explanation.

At this period in the Inner Asian hinterland, society, to be outrageously brief, was the object of two kinds of representation of social reproduction. One was focused on the continuation of patrilineal clans or feudal subpolities as ongoing, homogenous corporations, standing above the lives of the individuals comprising them at any one time. The second focused on biological reproduction, sexuality, and gender difference. The continuance of society was represented as a matter of achieving births and overcoming death, through metamorphosis and rebirth.[7] Shamanism could be involved in both these kinds of representation, but it did not assume an exclusively dominant position in either of them. Both were contested areas where shamans (or more generally, inspirational practitioners) had to struggle for preeminance among other contenders.

The analyst can posit two varieties of shamanism that were

---

7. Maurice Bloch has pointed out, for a somewhat similar system in Madagascar, how such representations contradict one another, and how even in the rather different culture of Taiwan, the contradiction is constructed in the same way (1987:335–36).

engaged in the construction of these conflicting views of social reproduction (though it should be stressed that these varieties were not
native categories and are introduced here only for explanatory purposes).[8] One may be termed "patriarchal," because it concerned shamanic involvement in the symbolic reproduction of the patrilineal
lineage, clan, or polity. The conceptual constructs and metaphors
tended to be vertical or hierarchical, but not exclusively so. This
version focused on sky-spirits (often called "father"), which were the
cause of good fortune, life-giving rain, and successful destinies. The
cults were accompanied by games and festivities to promote virility
and strength. Shamanic practices involved divination, offering, sacrifice, and prayer, and these forms of communication with supra-
natural forces meant that shamans did not transform themselves into
other beings and that they used trance mainly to "call down" spirits
to receive offerings. In this ritual arena, shamans were often sub-
ordinate to or replaced by elders of clans or Buddhist lamas. However,
when chiefs and elders were politically weak and demoralized, as
among the colonized Buryats in the nineteenth century, local leaders
would hope to be recognized as shamans, too, because this would
add to their efficacy in clan rituals.[9]

The other variety of shamanism can be called "transformational."
It operated by participation in all the forces thought to be immanent
in the world (in natural physical entities, animals, humans, and manufactured things). Shamans were defined by their possession of some
of these powers and their ability to become the vessel or embodiment
of others. The trance was the means by which such manifestations

---

8. The distinction between "patriarchal" and "transformational" forms of shamanic practice is similar to categories introduced by Thomas, Hugh-Jones, and
Hamayon in this volume. However, the terms *vertical* and *horizontal* would be
misleading in the north Asian context in my view, since they imply particular cosmologies, when in fact shamans acting in the two ways I have outlined above could
use a variety of cosmological models. For this reason, I have preferred to emphasize
what the shaman does (or what his or her concerns are).

9. Mikhailov (1987:98–119) writes that in the Verkholensk district in the mid-
nineteenth century Buryat clan leaders regarded it as a privilege to become a shaman.
He also observes that some shamans, of both the "white" and "black" varieties, took
political positions in the Russian system of indirect rule. The Verkholensk region was
badly affected by poverty and Russian peasant settlement on Buryat lands. In other
more prosperous regions, chiefship alone seems to have been sufficient unto itself,
and chiefs or elders often supplanted shamans at the great communal rituals. This
Buryat example supports Thomas's (1988) argument, but it is only one variant in a
range of other possibilities.

of power took place. Gender and other kinds of difference were the separate sources of energies that had to be made manifest and that had to be negotiated and balanced to restore harmony to the world. Rituals were performance-centered, rather than liturgy-centered (see Atkinson 1989; Humphrey and Laidlaw, in press). Shamanic practices included exorcism, substitution (of one energy by another), bribery, exchange, and the luring and entrapment of spirits. It might be thought that this context, which recognized biological difference, would be the undisputed terrain of shamanism, but this was not invariably so. Shamans could be undercut here by midwives, curers, casters-of-spells, and others attributed with magical powers. Furthermore, in northern Manchuria and eastern Mongolia, there were cults concerned with female fertility and child development that had their own special practitioners, who were not called by native terms for shaman, even though they often used trance. The cults may have had a Chinese origin, but they existed far beyond Han settlement areas. They became part of native cultures and took over aspects of religious activity that elsewhere were carried out by shamans.

The various inspirational practices called shamanism should be seen as intervening in religious life, as struggling to construct meaningful parts of it, rather than as simply being it. These contests were waged in different ways, from the parole of individual shamans in competition with one another, to what we may call registers of comparatively stable local discourse.[10] I use the term *register* in an extended sense to include types of shamanic language, imagery, and practice manifest in particular contexts of political discourse. In the following sections of this chapter, I discuss three such registers, and inevitably they can be no more than the equivalent of snapshots in the multifarious array of changing forms. Shamanic registers seem to be relatively short-lived, even if they contain archaic elements that might some day be revived.[11] Nevertheless, these localized and time-

---

10. I use the term *register* here as an extension of the linguistic concept. The idea derives from the work of Halliday (1978), who distinguished register, which is determined by the social activity one is engaged in, from dialect, which is determined by geographical and social affiliations, especially one's place of origin. The concept was taken up by Judith Irvine (1990) to discuss a series of coherent distinctions in speech and pragmatics made by Wolof people of different ranks in the context of expressing emotions.

11. There are substantial differences, for example, between the range of spirits, invocations, and so on that Shirokogoroff (1935) observed among rural Manchu

specific registers of discourse can tell us something about how shamanism has interacted with the state and smaller polities.

Inspirational Practices and the Founding of the Mongol State

In the twelfth century in the region now called Mongolia, aristocratic
warriors and their followers made sacrifices to heaven (*tenggri*), sending up animals' souls and praying for *tenggri*'s blessing (Munkuyev
1975; Bese 1986). Exclusion from such rituals had political significance, as can be seen from the episode in the thirteenth-century *Secret
History of the Mongols* (par. 70), in which Temujin's (the young
Chinggis Khan's) mother was turned away from a sacrifice, which
marked the start of the long-lasting war between her group and the
Taychiut. Temujin started out as poverty-stricken and cold-shouldered
by other Mongols, though he had illustrious forbears. With increasing
power, the military leader became patron of sacrifices on behalf of
ever-widening conglomerations of people. The will of heaven was
evident from success, such as a military victory or accession to the
khanship. Discovering heaven's will before an endeavor became a
matter of crucial concern. It appears that certain people claimed
privileged access to heaven and that others declared that they received
signs, but there is not clear evidence from Mongol sources of the
existence of professional shamans at this early period.[12] There are
several Mongol accounts of the will of heaven being revealed by
warriors, such as Qorchi, who exacted a price for his favorable
omen.[13]

---

shamans in the 1910s and those in use in Manchuria today (Lisha Li, pers. comm.).
Registers are also locally specific. This is evident from the range of different traditions
documented by Shirokogoroff among various groups of Tungus in the early twentieth
century and from valley by valley differences among the western Buryats at the same
period (Mikhailov 1987).

12. The term *ja-arin* (*jaarin*) in the *Secret History* is translated by some scholars
as "heavenly sign," while others gloss it as "shaman," perhaps because of the similarity
with the later Mongol/Buryat word for great shaman, *zaarin* (the Mongol historian
Dalai supports this view, 1959:21–22). The phrase in the *S.H.* (par. 206) "*Muqali-
da tenggeri-yin jaarin jaagsan uge temdeg-un tula...*" ("Because of the prophetic
edict and sign of the *jaarin* of Heaven to Muqali...") suggests that *jaarin* could
perhaps have meant a person as opposed to an omen (Dashtseren 1985:151).

13. In the *S.H.* (par. 121), when the quarrel between Temujin and Jamuqa
threatened to split the confederacy, one of the commanders, Qorchi, made a prophesy.

Because later, non-Mongol sources have described shamans among the Mongols, the literature on the period has generally identified some personages from the *Secret History* as shamans. The most famous of these is Kokochu, son of the military leader Munglig of the Qongqotad clan, a close ally who had saved Chinggis's life. The Persian historian Rashid-al-Din wrote of him:

> His habit was such that he uncovered secrets and fortold future events and he said, "God talks to me, and I visit the sky!" . . . In the heart of winter in Onan-Keluren, which is the coldest of those countries, it was his custom to sit naked in the middle of a frozen river, and from the heat of his body the ice would melt and steam would rise from the water. (Rashid-al-Din 1952, 1 (1):167)

Kokochu came to Chinggis Khan and told him, "God willed it that you be the master of the world," and he also gave Temujin the title Chinggis Khan, saying, "God willed it that you be called this" (Rashid-al-Din 1952, 1 (1):167). According to a later Mongolian source, Chinggis invited this same Kokochu, now entitled *arsi*, "sage," to meet him on the southern slope of a snowy mountain, and Chinggis,

> having asked him the manner in which one might support and hold the government and how one might protect and support living beings, and having praised him approvingly, conferred upon him the title Teb Tngri[14] and honored him in accord with the manner of a *bagshi*. (quoted in Cleaves 1967:254)

He said, "We would not have left Jamuqa, but a sign from heaven came to me." He reported that he had seen with his own eyes a yellowish-white ox harness itself to Temujin's tent-cart and pull it along, bellowing: "Heaven and Earth agree, let Temujin be the nation's master! Bearing the nation, I am bringing it to him!" Qorchi then asked Temujin what he would give for revealing this omen, and Temujin replied that if it really was like this and he became commander of the nation, he would give Qorchi ten thousand men. Qorchi replied that he wanted the freedom of the country's most beautiful women, too, and thirty of them to be made his wives. Later (par. 207), after Temujin has been made Chinggis Khan, he keeps his promise to Qorchi. This is a clear example of prophecy as politics by other means. Qorchi fixed the price of his allegiance, and the legitimacy provided by the omen may have significantly affected Temujin's chances.

14. The meaning of *Teb* has much perplexed Mongol scholars. One opinion is

So the warrior-king Chinggis and the "shaman" Teb Tenggri respectfully conferred titles on one another. But soon they fell out. This is not surprising when we realize, from separate, non-Mongol sources, that Chinggis was able to discover the will of heaven himself. He seems to have been as inspirationally able as the legendary Teb Tenggri. An Islamic history records of Chinggis:

> He was adept in magic and deception, and some of the devils were his friends. Every now and then he used to fall into a trance, and in that state of insensibility all sorts of things used to proceed from his tongue, and that state of trance used to be similar to that which happened to him at the onset of his rise, and the devils which had power over him foretold his victories. The tunic and clothes which he had on and wore on the first occasion were placed in a trunk and he was wont to take them along with him. Whenever this inspiration came over him, every circumstance—victories, undertakings, the appearance of enemies, the defeat and reduction of countries—anything which he might desire, would all be uttered by his tongue. A person used to take the whole down in writing and enclose it in a bag and place a seal upon it, and when Chinggis Khan came to his senses again, they used to read his utterances over to him one by one, and according to these he would act, and more or less, indeed, the whole used to come true. (Boyle 1977, 22:181)

Furthermore, Chinggis, it seems, was no gullible fool when it came to other people's prophesies. He used to check them. According to a contemporary Chinese source:

> Each time before he set out on a punitive raid Chinggis Khan necessarily ordered his excellency [a shaman?] to divine in advance about success and failure. The Emperor also burnt a

---

that Teb is an intensifying particle, so the compound Teb Tngri (Tenggri) would mean "the perfectly heavenly one"; another is that Teb derives from the Turkic Tab, meaning cunning or clever. Later generations of Mongols, not knowing the meaning of Teb, substituted Tob (center). All the variants are discussed in Cleaves (1967), who notes that this title was bestowed on the Daoist monk Ch'ang Chun, who made a famous journey to advise Chinggis Khan during his campaigns, and on a magician who counseled the Sechen khan.

sheep's femoral bone so as to compare the results with him. (Munkuyev 1975:79)

In the end, Chinggis's desire for uncontrovertible control of the heroic polity necessitated a decisive defeat of Teb Tenggri. The final falling-out came when Teb Tenggri declared that heaven had willed that Chinggis's younger brother Qasar could well soon succeed him as khan. Upon hearing this, Chinggis immediately set out to capture Qasar, but he was stopped by his mother, who was outraged at this unbrotherly act. By this time, Teb Tenggri had attracted to his Qongqotan group a great many followers, including some of Chinggis's people, and furthermore, he insulted the emissary sent to get them back. For this, Chinggis had his stalwarts put Teb Tenggri to death by breaking his back.

With all the obfuscation of ecstasy and so on that surrounds the topic of shamanism, it is instructive to note the matter-of-factness of the Mongol account of Teb Tenggri in the *Secret History*. It is baldly recorded that he knew heaven's will, and that three days after his death, he ascended bodily through the smoke-hole of the tent in which his corpse had been left (*S.H.*, par. 246). Nothing is made of the supernatural aspect of these events. The Mongols were practical people, and they wanted to know what really would happen. In the end the text indicates that Teb Tenggri was someone who made one prophecy too many. He and his Qongqotan group had attempted to destablize the khan's supremacy. Of the ascent through the smoke-hole, the classic shaman's move, Chinggis says flatly, "Because Teb Tenggri laid hands and feet on my brothers and spread baseless slander among my younger brothers, he was not loved by Heaven, and his life—as well as his body—has been taken and sent away." After Chinggis had disposed of Teb Tenggri, we read, "The morale of the Qongqotan was withered" (*S.H.*, par. 246; Onon 1990:139–40).

All this suggests that at the turn of twelfth and thirteenth centuries, when Chinggis was in the process of building up his state, inspirational practices, particularly prophecy, were part of the activity of the war leaders themselves. The stakes were high and the activity dangerous. Get it right and the rewards could be great, as they were for Qorchi (see n. 13); but prophecies that went against the turn of power incurred the risk of death and political defeat. In the heroic polity, the psychological power of shamans over individuals at the center was refracted outward, through the familial structure of the state itself, so that it came to have incalculable influence at large. Other quasi-inspirational practices involved symbolizing the concept of the political center, as can be seen in the role of the "many-leaved tree," an image that recurs sporadically in patriarchal variants of shamanism.[15] The *Secret History* is overwhelmingly practical in tone. It emphasizes Chinggis's military strength, justice, and respect for loyalty. It does not mention his prophetic trances. The will of heaven really appears in it only as another factor to be taken into account. This matter-of-factness perhaps also reflects the nature of the *Secret History* as a source: it was written in the mid-thirteenth century, after Chinggis's death, as a history of the Mongolian imperial line. By that time it would not have been appropriate to represent the emperors as themselves straining to know heaven's will, because by attaining their very status as world conquerors, they had proved it to be in their favor. The confident assumption of acting by the mandate of heaven is written in numerous Mongol edicts of the generations subsequent to Chinggis. Not only is Chinggis presented in the *Secret History* as inevitably fulfilling the pursuit of pure power, but after he had removed the only rival who was both a shaman and a political leader, shamanic discourse could no longer be *the* discourse of the state. It was no longer appropriate to find out about something that had to seem evident (the imperial destiny).

Nevertheless, there is abundant evidence of a variety of shamanic involvement in lesser issues during subsequent reigns. Apparently the Mongol successors to Chinggis never set out on a campaign without consulting diviners, and they predicted lucky and unlucky days for all undertakings. The Persian historian Juvaini says that the Mongols would have returned to attack Hungary if the diviners had allowed it (Boyle 1977, 5:340). Persian and European visitors

---

15. Reference is made to the "many-leaved tree" of Qorqonag forest in paragraphs 57, 117, and 206 of the *S.H.* At this spot, Chinggis's ancestor Qutula was raised up as khan (par. 57), and the Mongols "danced around the tree until they made tracks up to their chests, until they made dust up to their knees." Qutula himself had magical powers according to Persian sources (Boyle 1977, 22:182). Also at this tree, Temujin and Jamuqa declared themselves sworn brothers (par. 117), and Temujin made a pledge to Muqali (par. 206). The dance around a ritual tree, of which the many leaves have often been said to signify offspring of the group, has been important in the mountain cult; in the Buddhist version of this cult (seventeenth and eighteenth centuries onward), the leaves no longer occur, and the tree is represented by a pole or mast stuck in the sacred cairn.

mention shamanic healers, called *kam* (*shaman* in Turkic languages). The Mongols also made models as vessels for the spirits, which they kept in their tents (Vitebsky 1974), and used magical stones for producing rain and storms at strategic moments, both of which are practices known from later shamanism (Mikhailov 1987:32–36). Mongol shamans held séances, closed to outsiders, at which they went into trances and invoked spirits.[16] The *Secret History* contains many passages suggesting metaphorical thinking of the kind characteristic of transformational shamanism. A range of practices broadly similar to later shamanic activities were present in Mongol society during the Yuan dynasty, though they had less raw political import than at the time of the formation of the state.

Some clues on this can be discovered by investigating the use of the title *bagshi*, with which Chinggis invested Teb Tenggri. *Bagshi* (*bakshi*, *bagch*, and so on) has come to mean "teacher," "guru," or "master" in Mongolian, and perhaps it had this meaning even in the early thirteenth century. After the murder of Teb Tenggri, Chinggis avoided giving clear precedence to any particular religious practitioners. He toyed with the merits of various religions, inviting monks and priests to compete in disputations. However, in subsequent generations, the Mongol emperors mainly patronized Buddhism, as the rulers of earlier "barbarian" empires had done before them. A series of chosen high lamas, who came to be seen as giving religious legitimation to the ruler-patron, were given the title *bagshi*.

Marco Polo, who arrived during Quibilai's reign after the conquest of China, says almost nothing about shamanism, but he mentions Tibetan, presumably Buddhist, *bagshis* at the court and attributes magical abilities to them.[17] Now, the Daurs, who have kept many ancient Mongol terms in their vocabulary, use the term *bagchi* differently from other contemporary Mongols; the Daurs use it for

---

16. The European envoy William of Rubruck was sent to the Mongol court in 1253 by Louis IX of France. "The shaman who is calling the spirit begins to recite his song, takes a drum and strikes it hard on the ground. After a while he begins to rave and has himself bound. Then the demon comes in the darkness, and the shaman gives him meat to eat, and he gives replies" (quoted in Vitebsky 1974:37).

17. It is perhaps significant, though Marco Polo's idiom of exotic travel reportage was often sensationalist, that these *bagshis* were described as creating darkness, hailstorms, and lightning; clearing a pool of sunshine over the emperor's palace on a gray day; and making cups of wine and milk rise of their own accord (Vitebsky 1974:30). Such abilities could be attributed to shamans.

precisely the patriarchal kind of shaman mentioned earlier, that is, the person who conducts sacrifices at the mountain cult and who is a diviner, but who cannot master spirits or enter a trance. Altogether this suggests that during the Mongol empire the term *bagshi* may have denoted any religious practitioner in a client relation to a political patron. A later Mongol source, also ascribes this title to Teb Tenggri (though he was nothing like a client), but materials on the Mongol imperial court *after* the move to China suggest that shamans were by then induced into such positions.

Chinese sources mention shamans right through to the fourteenth century (Heissig 1980:7). They continued to divine about the outcome of wars, but their main activity was now more retrospective, making sacrifices to the soul of imperial ancestors as the guardian and inspiration of the state.[18] Endicott-West (1991) writes that shamans and diviners continued to have a favored status under Mongke (r. 1251–59), but that during and after Qubilai (r. 1260–94), they were subjected to several government restrictions because of their penchant for stirring up trouble. The solution, in the case of some shamans, was to incorporate them into the civil bureaucracy; others could not be successfully controlled and gravitated to the courts of the imperial princes, where they were deemed a dangerous influence by the central government.

Early Mongol shamanism is differentiated by the conceptual worlds and interests of the various reporters. It is to be expected that the Franciscan envoys would discuss the Mongols' belief in God, that Marco Polo would note magical happenings, that Persians would also introduce the idea of God and describe Chinggis's prophetic episodes in terms similar to Muhammed's revelations, and that the Chinese annals would note ancestor cults. But these writers' particular categories and lacunae are not all that is at issue. The fragmented picture

---

18. The official record of the Mongol dynasty, the Yuan Shih, records, "In the 9th lunar month of every year and also on a day after the 16th of the 12th lunar month there are used (for the sacrifice) in the courtyard where the food is burnt: one horse, three sheep, mare's milk, spirits and wines, as well as three rolls each of red fabric, gold-embroidered silk, and coarse silk for underwear. At the Emperor's command, a high Mongol official, accompanied by Mongol shamans and shamanesses, has to dig a hole in the ground to burn the meat in. They also burn spirits and wines mixed (with the meat). The shamans and shamanesses call out the personal names of the dead rulers in the national language and make the sacrifices" (Boyle 1977, 23:13).

we receive may also reflect reality: shamanism was not one thing but many. I hope that I have provided enough evidence here to show that during the rise of the Mongol state, there was a distinct register of shamanic discourse, involving prophesy, omens, and other interventions that affected the outcome of political events. It seems to have been relatively spontaneous and unritualized. This high prophetic discourse may well have existed alongside other kinds of inspirational practice. After the empire was established, it seems to have been replaced by a very different register, which was ritualized, even liturgical, and backward-looking.

The Manchu State: Shamanism at Court

After the fall of the Mongol Yuan dynasty and during the Chinese Ming dynasty (1368–1644), Buddhism continued to flourish in China but was upheld for a while in Mongolia only among the scattered aristrocracy (Jagchid 1972). It is supposed (Heissig 1980:7) that shamanism experienced a resurgence in Mongolia, as Thomas's argument would predict, but unfortunately not much is known about this. Equally unclear is the situation among the Jurchen tribes, who gathered strength in Manchuria during the early sixteenth century. It seems that they set up their first state north of China in a shamanist ambience, but rapidly also introduced Buddhist cults.

We do know that in the political thought of the Jurchen Manchus, as with the Mongols earlier, military success was regarded as a sign of the will of heaven.[19] Crossley notes that the expression *Abkai fulingga* ("Heaven's intentions manifest,") was created as a reign-title of the war leader Nurgaci when he became head of state (*fulingga* means "the actualization of thoughts into reality," and *abka* is "sky/

---

19. Nurgaci's successor, Hong Taiji, wrote in 1627, when justifying his successful attacks on the Ming dynasty, which was still in power in China: "The reason why our two nations have sent armies against one another was originally because the officials quartered in Liaodung and Guaning [i.e., the Ming Chinese] considered their emperor to be as high and mighty as Heaven itself, considering themselves like those who live in heaven; and the khan of another nation merely created by heaven was unworthy of any degree of independent standing. Not able to bear the insults and contempt, we have taken our case to Heaven, raising troops and beginning war with you. Since Heaven is in fact just and heeds not the magnitude of the nations but only the rightness of the issue, it has considered us in the right" (quoted in Crossley 1987:773).

heaven"). Crossley comments, "A sense of luck or natural superiority, rather than moral cultivation, is at its heart" (1987:772).

The early Manchus drew on other Mongol traditions, including the organization of banner regiments, a hereditary elite of men trained in military skills. The ideology of the banner was based on servitude and loyalty. However, the early Manchu rulers were not timid conservers of tradition. This is evident in Hong Taiji's revolutionary repudiation in the 1630s of the twelfth- and thirteenth-century Jurchen Jin heritage. He wrote to the enfeebled Chinese still holding on in the capital:

> You Ming nobles continue to see events in the mirror of the Song emperors and have no response at all to us. But you Ming emperors are not the scions of the Song emperors, and we are not the scions of the previous Jin emperors. That was one season, and this is another. This heavenly season (*abkai erin*) and the mind of man have become completely distinct [from the past]" (quoted in Crossley 1987:773–74).

It is quite possible, though I have no evidence, that this new "heavenly season" was something proclaimed by inspirational prophesy. Be this as it may, the new mind was soon manifest in the renaming of the Jurchens as Manchus and in the establishing of the Qing dynasty. The ethnic background of the Jurchens was mixed, and when they were renamed Manchus in 1635, some of them also were designated Chinese or Mongolian. Such categorization rested on ancient criteria of way of life, civilization, and urbanization. Since Jin times, the Chinese had distinguished between "tame" ("cooked") Jurchens and "wild" ("raw") Jurchens. The new order of the banner system comprised Manchu, Mongolian, and Chinese regiments, but ethnically these categories were unclear. The essential idea was that of a state based on functional structural position in relation to the emperor, rather than on ethnicity.

However, Nurgaci soon began a bureacratization that had far-reaching consequences. One of his first acts was to order the writing down of clan genealogies and to make any clan in working order a hereditary company within the banner system. A script for Manchu, borrowed from the Mongols, was introduced at this time. Its creator Nara (Erdeni) was literate and multilingual, for which qualities he

was titled *bakshi* by the ruler (Crossley 1987:763–64). This writing
of genealogies marks the beginning of a transformation of the Manchu
polity away from Sahlins's heroic model. Nurgaci as supreme leader
had drawn all the northern tribes he thought reliable into the banner
system, including the Daurs and some Tungus; they were later called
New Manchus or given the general name Solon, which covered several
different ethnic groups (Lattimore 1935:189). But the setting-up of
permanent banners and the extension of written geneaologies gradually bureacratized and thus undermined the independent political
role of clans. Furthermore, it was now possible to draw sociohistorical
distinctions within the state: there were these people with this ancestry
and those people with that ancestry, and simple allegiance to the
emperor was no longer all that mattered. By the eighteenth century,
these policies, controversially called "racial" by Crossley, were definitely oriented to the differentiation of Manchus from Chinese, especially by the preservation of a pure Manchu homeland in the
northeast, forbidden to Chinese settlement (1987:779–81).

As Shirokogoroff (1935) pointed out, the creation of written
genealogies had an effect on shamanism. Shamans of both patriarchal
and transformational kinds act for their social groups. In the preconquest period, Jurchen Manchu social organization seems to have
been tribal and relatively fluid. Little is known about preconquest
shamans, though there is evidence that Manchus thought of them as
war-leaders.[20] Shirokogoroff suggests that like the other tribal people
of the region, the Manchus had picked up spirit-powers all over the
place. Now, however, with the new emphasis on geneaology, they
were called ancestors. The Manchu clan lists of ancestral spirits contained such beings as Flying Cuckoo, Bodhisattva, White Pheasant
Ancestor, and Stooping Old Woman. By the nineteenth century, their
content was long since bled of the power they might once have had—
for example, the white pheasant became just a heraldic device used
on Manchu uniforms (Shirokogoroff 1935:146). However, the lists

---

20. A myth of the first shaman is quoted by Shirokogoroff (1935:276). During
the Jin dynasty there was a war between the Manchus and the Chinese. The Chinese
emperor took hold of *cooha janggin* (literally, "soldier's commander") and ordered
him to be beheaded. So he was. But even beheaded, the shaman-warrior did not fall
down, and the Chinese emperor then called him *weceku* (guardian spirit). Shirokogoroff (1935:392), also notes that Gantimur, the war-leader who chose the Russian
rather than the Manchu side in the seventeenth-century clashes on the Amur River,
was supposed to have been a shaman.

also contained actual ancestors (*weceku*) whose real names were preserved in the genealogies. These were organized in a pyramid, like
an ideal exogamic lineage, and headed by a clan chief. The effect of
conflating the external spirits with real ancestors was the internali-
zation, or the making ancestral, of a whole range of positive and
negative spiritual forces. This effected a change in the definition of
self-identity and gave impetus to the patriarchal type of shamanism.
Cultures without these genealogies, such as the Tungus and the rural
Manchus of the far northern forests, continued to recognize the exter-
nality of powers in the universe, and hence the transformative shamanic requirement to go beyond the normal social self to engage
with them.

For the urban, "cooked" Manchus, virtually the whole cosmology, including the Buddha and "heaven's children," was ancestralized.
They had a saying, "As many exogamic units and chiefs, so many
(complexes) of spirits" (Shirokogoroff 1935:143). The clan ancestral
lists, which were kept secret in case outsiders should manipulate their
powers, required the existence in each clan of special shamans who
had charge of their cult. These were the *p'ogun saman*s (family or
clan shamans), as distinct from the *amba saman*s (great shamans)
who remained in the forested hinterland of northern Manchuria as
masters of nonlineal, animal and foreign spirits. *Amba saman*s disappeared entirely from the imperial court after the mid-seventeenth
century.

The *p'ogun saman*s rapidly became different from what Shirokogoroff calls "real shamans." They did not undergo the psychic
sickness and spiritual rebirth of shamanic initiation but were chosen
mundanely by the clan-chief (*mokun-da*) at clan meetings or else
proposed themselves for service. The main one, the *da saman*, was
elected annually at the autumn sacrifice. Almost all of them were
unable to introduce the spirits into themselves in trance or to master
any spirits (Shirokogoroff 1935:146). In effect, Shirokogoroff maintains, they became priests. At the court in Peking, they became a
largely hereditary social class, responsible for maintaining the regular
sacrifices for the well-being of the government and empire. The female
shamans were the wives of court officials and ministers. By the mid-
eighteenth century, if we are to believe what the Qianlong emperor
Hongli wrote, the court shamans, who could hardly speak Manchu,
had lost touch with earlier traditions and confined themselves to a

ritualistic repetition of half-understood formulae. The members of the imperial family personally preferred other religions. At this point, Hongli launched his great project of "remembering," that is, the researches to revivify Manchu cultural differences from the Chinese. Histories were written, or rewritten, to establish a direct relation between the present emperor's clan, the Aisin Gioro, and the imperial clan of the Jurchen Jin, and to establish its ancestral claims over the sacred Changbaishan Mountain in northeast Manchuria. As part of this project, in 1778, the emperor issued his famous edict to renew shamanist ritual, together with some preliminary discourses about the need to transmit the correct forms to posterity (Langlès 1804).

The emperor wished to revitalize shamanism, and I suggest that a central motive for this was the renewing of the link between the imperial clan and the forces of regeneration and vitality. But we shall see that his edict in the long run probably had the opposite effect. He complained that the shamans did not agree about how to say the prayers and that there was no conformity in their rituals or any uniformity between the rituals of the palace and those of the ancients. This was due, he said, to the correct forms not being written down. The emperor provided long lists of the mandarins charged with going out to the northeastern homelands to find out the correct prayers and rituals, with ordering and compiling them, with inspection of the written forms, with presiding over the drawings of the ritual objects to be used, and so forth. He also declared that he himself had decided what must be changed and that he had invented a new word for the sacred tree to be erected at the New Year, because there was no existing word for it in Manchu (Langlès 1804:24).

The imperial edict on shamanism also suggests that by the eighteenth century a change had occurred in the cosmology. Shirokogoroff, in his eagerness to press the idea that shamanic practices in the Manchu court had ceased to be "true shamanism," advances the following argument (1935:123–24). Heaven (abka, apka), worshiped by the early "genuine" Manchu shamanists, took second place in Emperor Hongli's new rite to the Buddha and furthermore was renamed shangsi enduri, which Langlès (1804:36) identifies with the Chinese shang di (the term chosen to represent the Christian God). At the beginning of their rule in China, the Manchus had already abandoned the idea of apka as heaven in the sense of the impersonal order of the sky-universe, and they used instead the form apkai *enduri,* an anthropomophized idea of god. This was replaced by *shangsi* as one of a group of deities (*enduri*) in which the first place was occupied by Buddha. However, *shangsi enduri* did not reach the "raw" Manchus still living in the hinterland in Aigun district, and they continued to use the old abstract idea and term, *apka,* into the twentieth century.

Shirokogoroff's picture is tendentious. It is not so clear that the court ritual was much different from what I have termed patriarchal shamanism. In this sense we can talk of a kind of shamanic state religion until the end of the dynasty. It was elaborated and split into different elements, among which the monthly cult of *shangsi* was not the most important. On the cosmological changes, it seems that the Buddha took first place in only one of the temples at the court, the Kun-ning-gung, and that in the ritual enclosure (*tangse*) that was the main site of the imperial cult, *shangsi* (heaven) had precedence (Harlez 1896:47–48). Furthermore, though *shangsi* was a non-Manchu term, it probably meant something very similar to the old *abka.* Unlike other spirits and ancestors of the Manchus, *shangsi* was not represented (for example, by an idol or painting), and shamans did not take part in its worship. It was given offerings, libations, and prayers, by guards and officials under the patronage of the emperor (Harlez 1896:55). We see here a participation by the political ruler in shamanism, analogous to examples mentioned earlier among the thirteenth-century Mongols and the nineteenth-century Buryats (see n. 9).The most splendid rituals of the Manchu court, however, were the grand spring and autumn sacrifices in honor of the imperial clan at the dressed pole or mast. These, and numerous other ceremonies, were conducted by shamans. Their presence was necessary to invoke the spirits, to conjure and address them, to make libations and prayers over the sacrificial pigs and wine, and actually to kill the animals. The emperor was present at the ceremonies, but his part was limited to bows and genuflections (Harlez 1896:60–61). Thus, taken together, we see a range of practices in the patriarchal mode. There is no reason not to call them shamanic. The court ceremonies may be compared with their local reflections, the Mongolian and New Manchu sacrifices at the *oboo* (the mountain cairn with mast), which were increasingly conducted after the seventeenth century by Buddhist lamas under the patronage of political leaders, but which continued in the periphery to be performed by shamans and (or) clan elders. When we know that Buddhist variants of such cults existed, it seems perverse to refuse the term shamanism to an intentional practice by people actually called *saman*.

Inspirational and performative elements were perhaps not totally absent. The shamans at the Manchu court, if they did not go into trance, certainly invoked the spirits and "invited the ancestor spirits to enter the sacred space," and they used drums and other characteristic shamanic instuments (Langlès 1804:44). Prayers were distinguished from other kinds of more enraptured speech. In further sequences, with the light extinguished, the shamans "murmured in the dark" (*furbure*) and then prostrated themselves and sought "to appease the spirits and to attract their favour by flattering words (*forobure*)" (Harlez 1896:54).

In the court shamanism of the eighteenth century, there does not seem to have been a clear distinction between the public seasonal sacrifices or the cult of heaven and other more sporadic shamanic activities.[21] Manchu court shamans and their assistants were in charge of an assortment of rituals: invoking the spirits of the imperial clan; giving thanks for blessings received and asking for new ones; ritually washing the Buddha statue; making sacrifices for the prosperity of saddle horses and of horses in general (this took two days); driving away evil spirits, especially the exorcism of smallpox; praying over offerings, such as chickens, a goose, a fish, or a pheasant; burning incense and paper money for the spirits; parading the statue of Buddha and the tablets of ancestral spirits; and playing official music. A large number of court shamans were women, but the main shamans were men. Shamans in the capital also conducted private curing rituals that were analogous with similar activities all over north Asia.[22] But

21. This is to judge from Harlez's (1896) account of the shamanic ritual proclaimed by Emperor Hongli.

22. Harlez (1896:63) writes: "When anyone is ill and his life despaired of, papers are cut in the form of money or of men, which are burned, rice is scattered and water is sprinkled. If the illness continues, a Shaman is called in, who cuts papers of five colours, an equal number of each, and attaches them to a willow-tree planted upright, then he beats vigorously on the magical tambourine, to drive away the *hutus* [evil spirits] who are beseiging the sick man. . . . Another way of dismissing maladies and their supernatural cause is to vow the immolation of a pig; then, when the animal is killed, to take the skull, put it on the end of a high pole set in the earth, and thus present it to the spirits. . . . During epidemics the spirit of tigers is invoked. Offerings are made to it, the tambourine is beaten, and so on. When anyone is supposed to be possessed by *hutus*, which is frequently the case among the Tatars, a Shaman is called in; with the children of the house, he applies himself to crying so loudly that the evil spirit is frightened and takes flight."

whatever was inspirational in the new register of shamanism introduced by Hongli's edict almost certainly atrophied thereafter. One of the aims of the emperor was not only to distinguish and petrify Manchu shamanism, ("If we do not take care things will gradually change," he wrote), but to give it the civilized manners of Chinese Confucian ritual (Harlez 1896). The shamanic inspirational capacities of invention and imagination must have struggled under the weight of formally prescribed written prayers, decorous gestures, and delineated movements and sounds.

Why did the emperor decide to revivify shamanism when he could have simply substituted Confucian ritual? By the mid-eighteenth century, the court was aware that the urban Manchus and even most of those in the banner garrisons were losing their culture. Many could no longer speak the language. Yet at this same period, the Manchu Empire experienced a rapid expansion, not only to the Yunnan-Guizhou regions of southern China, but into the huge and alien fastness of Islamic Xinjiang. Precious Manchu bannerman, the most loyal soldiers of the empire, were sent from the northern regiments to conquer and guard this distant western frontier. In this situation, the regeneration of the imperial vertical link with heaven on behalf of the polity as a whole is not surprising.

A different and not incompatible argument is advanced by Nowak and Durrant (1987) and Crossley (1987, 1990). Loss of Manchu cultural identity was seen as a threat to the legitimacy of Manchu rule over their vast territory. The Manchu clans, which had been bureacratized and subordinated to the banners by Hong Taiji, had lost social vitality, and their members were scattered all over the empire. Only among the "raw" Manchus left living in the forests of the north was the culture preserved. Increasingly, the emperor came to see the clans and shamanism as the central features of Manchu identity. Unlike his forbears, the emperor now insisted on the direct descent of the imperial clan from the Jin dynasty, and geographically his edict on shamanism sought to draw into the center the true rituals preserved on the periphery. Romanticization of the pristine manly strength of the frontier was prominent in compositions he sponsored or wrote himself, such as the elegiac *Ode to Mukden*, and in the numerous other ethnographic researches of his officials, such as the *Record of One Hundred and Twenty Stories from an Old Man* (1791). A succession of emperors took an almost spiritual pleasure in journeys to wild reserves set aside for the imperial hunt. This nostalgia for old ways and ancient northeastern culture continued throughout the nineteenth century and into the twentieth (Crossley 1987:782–83). The history of the Qing court is the precarious balance of the processes by which the dynasty attempted to solve the contradiction between Manchu rural culture, which still was viable on the frontier, and the political institutions and classical traditions of conquered China. In effect, the court preserved an archaic ideology of Manchuness at odds with the sinicized institutions of government. Shamanism was chosen to revitalize the core of Manchu society because it engaged directly with the principles of social identity (the ancestor spirits) in a Manchu idiom. The trouble was that ethnic differentiation was not a principle that helped the Manchus to rule, as the deeply sinicized urban Manchus perhaps realized.

In the long run, the emperor as shamanic initiator was tragically unsuccessful. The imperial endorsement of the concept of cultural differentiation had far-reaching consequences, the wild and brutal resentment of the Chinese expressed in the Taiping Rebellion in the nineteenth century. The Manchu soldiers isolated in their garrisons were unprepared for the rebellion, and by this time they themselves had become suspicious of inspirational religion (a militant version was fermenting in the secret societies of the rebels themselves). Edicts designed to control shamanic practices were issued during the nineteenth century, and even the rural Manchus' own *amba* shamans of the periphery came under government repression.

The bureacratization of the Manchu state in the seventeenth century, the subordination of clans to the banner system, and the decorous idiom of court ritual expelled the great "wild" shamans from metropolitan religion and tamed the patriarchal clan shamans who remained. Nevertheless, in the discourse of ethnic exclusiveness that came to be seen as necessary for preserving the legitimacy of Manchu rule over a vast and rapidly expanding empire in the eighteenth century, shamanism had a key role. It was the context in which "pure" culture from the frontier revivified the center. Incorporation of external powers to the cult of ancestors provided a centralist ideology that was at the same time an identity for the Manchus. But the means chosen by the emperor, prescribed ritual and written liturgy, served only to negate the strength of shamanic practice, its ability to deal with new forms of power.

In the Manchu State: A View From the Periphery

The Manchu state, like the Mongol one before it, energetically promoted the Tibetan form of Buddhism, though in this case not so much for the court itself as for the Mongols and other people of the hinterland whom it was hoped to pacify. But many peoples on the periphery, including the Daurs, the various Tungus tribes, and the Manchus themselves in some rural areas, remained shamanist. How did they imagine the state? The following material comes from present-day Daurs of the older generation.

The Daurs are a Mongolian-speaking agriculturalist people, but they separated from other Mongol groups probably even before the Yuan dynasty. From Chinese sources, we know that the Daurs descend from people who were rulers in the Liao confederacy. But they do not remember this. They have stories about how they had writing and lost it, but historical memory goes back only as far as the seventeenth century, when they fled from Russian incursions on the Amur and were incorporated into the Manchu banners. In the early twentieth century, the localized banner units, which did not include all males, were crosscut by the still vital clans that mapped society. There were many ways in which such peoples related shamanically to the state. I do not want to give the impression that there was just one form of shamanic reaction to state power, or within one people just one way of thinking about it, but for reasons of space, only one case is given here.

Among the Daurs, as among the rural Manchus, the patriarchal kind of shamanism was regarded as secondary. It was centered on the *oboo*, the mountain cairn that was the site of propition of land spirits. These rituals were served by the *bagchi*, who was otherwise employed as a minor diviner and assistant to the main shaman. Each localized clan had its own *oboo*, where the clan chief ordered rituals at irregular intervals,[23] when a drought threatened. There were also banner *oboo*s set up by the state and banner authorities. This whole cult and its terminology was male (women and *yadgan* shamans were excluded). It was regarded as not very important: the Daurs were successful farmers, there was plenty of land, and the rains did not often fail.

---

23. The clan chief also decided when various communal agricultural activities were to take place.

Spiritual power was manifest in another kind of Daur shaman, the *yadgan* (or *saman*). The *yadgan* could be either male or female, though most of them were men. They were regarded as infinitely more powerful than the *bagchis*. Yadgans were "chosen" by spirits; experienced initiatory death and rebirth; were capable of mastering spirits, transforming them from one kind to another, and renewing their powers; and were able to travel to the "other world" to rescue souls. Most of their activity was concerned with curing people of physical and psychological troubles, but they also held a complex ritual every few years for the revitalization of the relation between society and the entire range of spirits. There were two kinds of *yadgan*, those called clan shamans (that is, those whose helper spirits were clan ancestors), and those who were independent (that is, their spirits came to them nonlineally, through women, and in other ways). There were also female shamans called *otoshi* who had charge of a group of spirits concerned with childbirth, growth, and certain diseases. All these kinds of shaman were similar in that they operated in what I have called the transformational mode. On the periphery, when the empire had been long since bureacratized and distanced, the divinatory and patriarchal activities so important when the state was being fought for and established, faded into relative insignificance, and the creative transformational variant of shamanism flourished even to the extent of taking over the sphere of clan ancestry.

The state was represented in two major ways in Daur shamanism. One can most simply be translated as "hell"—that is, as a cosmological vision, located underground, the world of the dead, which people called *ukel-un gurun* (the empire of death). This state was reachable by going down through the bottom of wells or through caves. When already underground, one had to cross a river, rowed by a lame boatman, and then to penetrate through the encircling walls, where the gatehouses were guarded by fearsome soldiers. Once inside, there were palaces and prisons, multistory buildings with glass windows, towers, barracks, and cities. The light was dim and yellowish. The state had a ruler, Ilmu-Khan, who was surrounded by numerous ministers and scribes. In the registers of Ilmu-Khan were written the destinies, the years of life, and the numbers of children of all people and animals in the living world. Ilmu-Khan was a just judge: he put the souls of the dead in prisons or gave them other punishments, or he allowed them to be reborn in the world. Animals and all living creatures could take their cases to him for judgment. From him or one of his subordinates, the shaman had to beg for renewed life for a dead soul.

This vision of the underworld as an urbanized state is undoubtedly influenced by Buddhism, particularly the idea of punishment for misdeeds in this world. It is part of a vertical cosmology, though one in which heaven is not visualized as a city or called *gurun* (state or empire). The sky (*tengger*) was imagined in layer after layer, vanishing into ethereal nothingness; it was personalized as one all-seeing, benevolent, universal "father"; or, at the most elaborate, it was seen as peopled by a kingly family of *tenggris*, with other sky-beings (*enduri*) floating on clouds and with dragons rippling in the far distance.

Stories about shamanism (for example, the epic of Nisan Saman, which was popular among all the rural peoples of Manchuria) often use this statelike image of the world of the dead. But as far as we can tell, Daur shamans did not operate with this vision, which was indeed explicitly repudiated by some people because of its alien preoccupation with cause and effect, whereby the soul becomes enmeshed in the results of previous actions. In shamanism, they maintained, action is free and is the manifestation of one's nature. In shamans' songs, which are not about shamanism but an active part of its practice, the "other world" seems to be the unseen powers of this world; the state is the Manchu dynasty in actions it never knew it undertook. This shift has the effect of horizontalizing the cosmology.[24] The "road" or "way" of the spirit becomes essential. The path between this world and the other is along a river or is represented as a transversal of real, named, geographical places. The spirits are envisaged not only, or even primarily, as ancestors: they include Tiger Spirit, Fox Spirit, birds, numerous female spirits, and Town Spirit (*xoton barkan*), who possessed soldiers in barracks. In the concept of ancestry, the Daurs were midway between the urban Manchus, who drew in diverse spiritual forces and had long since absorbed them with the human ancestors, and the Tungus peoples, who acknowledged the fleeting powers of the existential world in numberless spirits, among whom ancestors were relatively insignificant. This cosmological difference in emphasis may be related to the extent

---

24. More precisely, it had the effect of producing a horizontal version of the cosmology, which coexisted with the vertical one.

to which these peoples were actually engaged/disengaged with perpetuating state structures,[25] though it may just reflect the degree to which they were influenced by the Chinese cult of ancestors.

That a given spirit is called an ancestor tells us that the people see something of themselves in it, and we then need to know what this idea of ancestor contains. For the urban Manchus, ancestors were names on a written, though secret, list. For the nonliterate, rural Daurs, ancestry as imagined in shamanism had an extraordinary shattering violence. There were several multiple ancestor spirits. The main one, which was the earliest and therefore was ancestor to everyone, was Holieli, often called *Da Barkan* (the "great deity").[26] People made images of this spirit, which they kept in a box in their houses. It consisted, in the best known example, of fifty-eight separate parts: bald monsters, nine-headed monsters, half-people, single legs, left-side cripples and right-side cripples, some different kinds of turtle and tortoise, a leather softener, nine fishes, a hunting gun, a dragon, and nine dancing boys and nine dancing girls.

There are many versions of the story of this spirit, and the components of the images also vary. In a *story* of the Nonni River Daurs, the Holieli ancestor is an antelope that emerged from a rock split asunder by lightning. It ran straight to Senyang, where it began to harass the people. The Manchu government had it seized, placed in a bag of cow leather, and thrown into the river. It drifted down the river till it met the flood dragon, where the bag burst on the dragon's horn. The antelope pushed its way out of the bag, gained the bank, and once more began to harass the people. The Manchu court again had it seized, placed in a bag, loaded on a horse, and sent off. The horse followed its nose to the Amur River, where it was

---

25. The Tungus hunters and reindeer-herders discussed by Shirokogoroff (1935) were outside the Manchu banner system and were called "wild" and "primitive" by such peoples as the Daurs. Little is known about the shamanism of those Tungus included in the banners (known as Solon and New Manchu).

26. This spirit was also known among the various Tungus groups of northern Manchuria and south Siberia. Shirokogoroff classifies it as "non-ancestral" for the Tungus (1935:150–53). It was known as Malu Burkan and was said to have come to its present worshipers from the Daurs, though it was of Tungus origin (the Daurs stole it from the Tungus and subsequently gave it back, but half of it did not want to leave and stayed with the Daurs). It is perhaps significant that the origin of Malu was thought to be the spirit of a specifically nonbannerman, "wild" Tungus. The separate parts of the spirit cause various diseases, including mental illness, listed by Shirokogoroff (1935:151–52).

captured by a tribe of strange Tungus. They thought there must be something very nice in the bag and opened it. The antelope leapt out and took to the forests. It was chased by the lightning, which struck and struck, and many creatures were killed, but the deer escaped by sheer luck. It got to the Nonni River, near the Eyiler and Bitai villages. A man was ploughing. When the antelope spirit ran beside the man, there was a great crash of thunder, and everything was smashed into ninety-nine pieces. Since then, the antelope's spirit and those of all the people and animals killed by lightning joined forces for haunting and possessing people. First, it was worshiped by the Tungus, and then it was recognized as a spirit by the Manchu court, people say (*Daur. Soc. Hist.* 244).

In a shaman's *song* for Holieli, the ancestor is smashed to pieces by lightning and becomes the half-people and crippled people. It starts from the end of the earth, which is at the source of the Ergune River. It is an old man, then it becomes a fish, traveling down the Jinchili River, gathering as it goes all the people of the clans and all kinds of animals. Its aim is the southern sea, the entourage of the Dalai Lama (*dalai* means ocean in Mongol). It raids the city of Peking and occupies the seat of orthodoxy. It is a loud voice yelling in the palace. It is given a jade throne, a pearl restingplace. From there it begins its journeys again, crossing all borders, passing through all boundaries; it reaches the Daur and becomes hidden in the plow-blade of the farmer. Again it is honored by the people. It is in its original place. It is given a two-dragon throne on the western wall of the house and offerings—all kinds of silks, damasks, and satins. In a robe of grass, it tramples on the clean satins. Again it seems to set out on its metamorphic journey. The song continues:

> Where the rivers flow together
> Where they flow down is a dug-out canoe,
> The Tungus who live in the dense forest
> Kill the boar and are skilfull master-hunters.
> [It is] the tracks they do not find,
> The footprints they do not see,
> The gold-colored tortoise,
> The silver-colored frog,
> A buzzing biting wasp,
> A creeping spider,

> The wriggling lizards and snakes,
> The sound of a shaken bell,
> A cuckoo calling loudly,
> The leopard growling,
> The huge and fearless wild boar . . .
>
> (*Daur. Soc. Hist.* 248–49)

The ancestor in a sense becomes the spirit-emperor, masterfully transcending the etiquette of the court and the boundaries of the empire. Effortlessly, it swims as a fish to the palace, where it yells; unhindered, it returns to the Daur. It cannot be pinned down: it is manifest both in the domestic sphere of the plough and the house and in the wilderness of the forests, where the best hunters cannot see it.

The ancestor Holieli has many powers because it has many transformations. It does not have all powers perhaps, because there are other spirits, with other metamorphoses. But specifically, it takes the power of the imperial ruler. Yet it seems that this is transcended by the idea of metamorphosis itself: the signs and marks of imperial rank are desecrated and abandoned as the spirit takes to the forest as a wasp, changes to a spider, and changes to the sound of a bell. In the practice of ordinary Daurs, the pacification of this spirit, which caused very great harm and mental illness, involved furnishing its representation with imperial imagery (silk, dragons, special wood for the carved models, and so on). Shamans used to order people who had costly embroidered or damask clothing, the very means of imitating the courtly Manchus in real life, to offer them to this spirit. The spirit seems both a violent rejection of and a homage to the imperial state.

This spirit was considered a burden. Not all shamans could master it. The *bagchi* certainly could not, and he did no more than make small offerings. A *yadgan* was required for large sacrifices and the invocation of the spirit, and even so many felt themselves powerless before it. A story says that the people of the Dengteke clan near Hailar tried unsuccessfully to get rid of it because the sacrifices of cattle it demanded were so burdensome. They threw the box of images in the river, but it would not move, and soon the young men and women began to suffer nervous disorders.

My interpretation of this is that Holieli Barkan represents a forgotten and repressed imperial past. I am not borrowing the term repressed from psychoanalytic theory but using it in an attempt to explain a Daur idea. Perhaps punished would be a better term. The striking of the ancestor by lightning means, according to Daurs, the anger of heaven. This is the vision of those who know they are powerless, that they have not been born with the good fortune to rule. But in the semiforgotten past, the real ancestors of the Daurs were (or might have been) ruling peoples in the far off dynasties of the Liao and the Jin. The ancestor, or origin (Da *hujuur*, literally root), in Daur and Mongolian culture is a way of thinking about the self. There are many other spirits that are not thought of as ancestors. So in this case the Daurs in a sense are the smashed and dislocated people, half-people, monsters and limbs, and people who died and will take revenge unless placated, because those ancestors are what they came from. But at the same time, this spirit of Holieli Barkan survives and unites all the shattered parts. In the end, it is one spirit, not many, and it is like a wayward emperor and slips hither and thither and escapes from the bag in which the Manchu state tries to entrap it.

The imperial dynasty had recourse to the periphery in its attempt to define its identity and reaffirm its power. The people on the frontier, too, people who were not even Manchus, had at least one shamanic idiom of self-definition that spanned the distance between the village and the capital city in metaphors of effortless travel and self-transformation. It is a mistake to suppose that the practice of shamanism in face-to-face social groups limits its concerns to the local or restricts imagination.

Conclusion

Studies of north Asian shamanism have consistently ignored the ways in which it engages with politics, not simply politics in the narrow sense, but the power to have effect on the reproduction of particular forms of society. For millenia, north Asia has been a region of empires that ebbed and flowed over the land, but people here were not ignorant of hegemony, challenge, and independence, circumstances whose contours determined the kind of society in which one lived. For most of this history, the central interest was military, that is, war, not as an episode with a beginning and an end and interspersed with periods of peace, but as a permanent way of life necessary to reproduce the social group in the face of challenges from others. It is curious, therefore, that observers have noted how north Asian shamans dress like animals or birds but have generally ignored the more obvious ways in which the shaman is a warrior, wearing armor and bearing symbolic weapons. The shaman negotiates and fights with the spirit threats to the social group, even those conceived as ancestors. A shaman can do this in many ways: as an actor in the struggle for power, or, after the establishment of temporal powers, on their behalf, against them, or in some ambivalent relation to them.

In this chapter, I have tried to show how different aspects of shamanism took part in the rise and fall of north Asian states. It has not been possible to provide more than sketchy suggestions here, but my intention was to indicate a recognizably common stock of ritual activities, accompanied by a conglomeration of cosmological ideas, some of which are transmitted and acted out according to particular historical circumstances. Actual shamanism depends on the concerns of the participants, both patrons and shamans, and on the point of view from which they act. Although shamanism, being orally transmitted and performance-based, manifests its agency in small groups (the local clan, the village, the imperial court), there seems to be no justification for the idea that its interests or its view on the world are thereby confined or intrinsically archaic. It also does not seem right to attribute shamanism with one essential cosmological idea, such as the Eliadean ascent to celestial abodes, and then to say that this is distorted, hidden, or revealed according to the prevalence of outside influences. In shamanism, as the discussion has shown, "ancestry," "the other world," "the state," and indeed "heaven" (or "the sky"), are not invariant ideas; they do not take form or become concepts except from a particular standpoint. This is more the case for shamanism than with other religious phenomena, because shamanism is not so much reflection about the world as it is action on the world.

In the case of the rise of the Mongol state, we can perceive a visionary shamanism that denied or confirmed political action and whose interest and point of view was that of an actor and potential competitor. For this very reason, it had to be suppressed by the emergent supreme ruler. In the middle stages of the Manchu dynasty, the semipetrification of shamanic activity at the court did not prevent it from being deliberately sought as a solution for the regeneration of an empire in risky expansion. Just as the diverse spirits of nature were reassembled as "ancestors," the far-flung rituals of the "uncooked" peasants were diligently researched and brought to the capital as authentic links with all-powerful heaven. In the forested periphery of the empire, the Daurs enacted a shamanism that objectified and somehow made terrifying a historical sense of punishment, survival, and escape. Even here in the outback, the sense of self invoked in Daur ideas of ancestry was not localized and disengaged but vividly activated in the geographical distances and history of the state. Purists might say that only the last of these is "real shamanism," but it is more interesting to see it as one possibility, quite specific in time and place, and not unrelated to the others.

REFERENCES

Atkinson, J.
1989   *The art and politics of Wana shamanship.* Berkeley: University of California Press.

Banzarov, Dorzhi
1955   *Sobraniye sochinenii.* Moscow: Izdatel'stvo Akademii Nauk USSR.

Bese, Lajos
1986   The shaman term *jukeli* in the *Secret History* of the Mongols, *Acta Orientalia* 40 (2–3):241–48.

Bloch, Maurice
1987   Descent and sources of contradiction in representations of women and kinship. In Jane Fishburne Collier and Sylvia Junko Yanagisako, eds. *Gender and kinship: Essays towards a unified analysis.* Stanford: Stanford University Press.

Boyle, J. A.
1977   *The Mongol world empire: 1206–1370.* London: Variorum Reprints.

Cleaves, F. W.
1967   Teb Tenggeri. *Ural-Altaische Jahrbucher* 39.

Crossley, Pamela Kyle
1987   Manzhou yuanliu kao and the formalization of the Manchu heritage. *Journal of Asian Studies* 46(4):761–90.
1990   *Orphan warriors: Three Manchu generations and the end of the Qing world.* Princeton: Princeton University Press.

Dalai, Ch.
1959   *Mongolyn boogiin morgoliin tovch tuukh.* Studia Ethnographica 1(5). Ulaanbaatar: Erdem Shinzhilgeenii Khevleliin Gazar.

Dashtseren, T., ed.

1985 *Mongolyn nuuts tovchoo*, Corpus Scriptorum Mongolorun 21, fasc. 1, Ulaanbaatar: Academy of Sciences.

Eliade, Mircea

[1951] 1964 *Shamanism: Archaic techniques of ecstasy.* Trans. William R. Trask. Reprint, Princeton, N.J.: Princeton University Press.

Endicott-West, E.

1991 Notes on shamans, fortune-tellers, yin-yang practitioners, and civil administration in Yuan China. Typescript.

Foucault, M.

1972 *The archaeology of knowledge and the discourse on language.* New York: Pantheon.

Gumilev, L. N.

[1970] 1987 *Searches for an imaginary kingdom: The legend of the kingdom of Prester John.* Trans. R. E. F. Smith. Reprint, Cambridge: Cambridge University Press.

Halliday, Michael A. K.

1978 *Language as social semiotic.* London: Edward Arnold.

Hamayon, Roberte

1990 *La Chasse à l'Ame: Esquiésse d'une theorie du chamanisme sibérien.* Nanterre: Société d'ethnologie.

Hangin, John Gombojab

1973 *Köke Sudur (The Blue Chronicle).* Asiatische Forschungen 38. Wiesbaden: Harrassowitz.

Harlez, C. de

1986 The religion of the Manchu Tartars. *The New World* 5:43–66.

Heissig, Walther

1980 *The religions of Mongolia.* Trans. G. Samuel. London: Routledge and Kegan Paul.

1984 Shaman myth and clan-epic. In M. Hoppal, ed., *Shamansism in Eurasia.* Göttingen: Edition Herodot.

Humphrey, Caroline, and James Laidlaw

In press *The archetypal actions of ritual.* Oxford: Oxford University Press.

Irvine, Judith T.

1990 Registering effect: Heteroglossia in the linguistic expression of emotion. In Catherine A. Lutz and Lila Abu-Lughod, eds., *Language and the Politics of Emotion.* Cambridge: Cambridge University Press.

Jagchid, Sechen

1972 Buddhism in Mongolia after the collapse of the Yuan dynasty. In *Traditions religieuses et para-religieuses des peoples altaiques.* Communications of the thirteenth PIAC congress. Paris: Presses Universitaires de France.

Langlès L.

1804 *Rituel des Tatars-Mantchoux redigé par l'ordre de l'empereur Kien-Long.* Paris: L'Imprimérie de la Republique.

Lattimore, Owen
1935   The Mongols of Manchuria. London: George Allen and Unwin.

Lewis, I. M.
1971   Ecstatic religion: An anthropological study of spirit possession and sha-
       manism. Harmondsworth: Penguin Books.

Mikhailov, T. M.
1987   Buryatskii shamanizm: Istoriya, struktura i sotsial'nyye funktsii, Novo-
       sibirsk: Nauka.

Mostaert, Antoine
1953   Sur quelques passages du L'Histoire Secrète des Mongoles. Cambridge,
       Mass.: Harvard-Yenching Institute.

Munkuyev, N.
1970   Zametki o drevnikh mongolakh. In S. L. Tikhvinskii, ed., Tataro-
       Mongoly v Azii i Evrope. Moscow: Nauka.
trans. 1975   Men-Da Bei-Lu "Polnoye opisaniye mongolo-tatar." Pamyatniki
       pis'mennosti vostoka 26. Moscow: Nauka.

Nowak, M., and S. Durrant
1977   The tale of the Nisan shamaness, a Manchu folk epic. Seattle and London:
       University of Washington Press.

Onon, Urgunge
1990   The history and the life of Chinggis Khan. Translation of The Secret
       History of the Mongols. Leiden: Brill.

De Rachewiltz, Igor
1973   Some remarks on the ideological foundations of Chinggis Kahn's empire.
       Papers on Far Eastern History, 7 March. Australian National University
       Department of Far Eastern History.

Rashid-al-Din
1952   Sbornik letopisei. I (2) Trans. O. I. Smirnova. Moscow-Leningrad: Aka-
       demiya Nauk.
1954   Sbornik letopisei. I (1). Trans. L. A. Khetagurov. Moscow-Leningrad:
       Akademiya Nauk.

Sahlins, Marshall
1985   Islands of history. Chicago: University of Chicago Press.

Serruys, Henry
1987   The Mongols and Ming China: Customs and history. Ed. F. Aubin. Lon-
       don: Variorum Reprints.

Shirokogoroff, S. M.
1935   The psychomental complex of the Tungus. London: Kegan Paul, Trench,
       Trubner and Co.

Thomas, Nicholas
1988   Marginal powers: Shamanism and the disintegration of hierarchy. Critique
       of Anthropology 8:53–74.

Vitebsky, Piers
1974 Some medieval European views on Mongolian shamanism. *Journal of the Anglo-Mongolian Society* 1(1):1–17.

Wittfogel, Karl A., and Feng, Chia-sheng
1949 *History of Chinese society, Liao 907–1125.* New York: Macmillan.

Contributors

Tamsyn Barton was, until recently, a Research fellow in Classics at Newnham College, Cambridge. She is currently completing a book on astrology in antiquity, *Power and Knowledge*, before moving on to work with a development institute in South India.

Susan Bayly is a Fellow of Christ's College, Cambridge. She is the author of *Saints, Goddesses and Kings: Muslims and Christians in South Indian Society, 1700–1900* (1989).

Mary Beard is a lecturer in Classics at the University of Cambridge. She is a Fellow of Newnham College, and the author (with John North) of *Pagan Priests* (1990).

Maurice Bloch is Professor of Social Anthropology at the London School of Economics and Political Science. His books include *Marxism and Anthropology* (1983) and *Ritual, History and Power* (1988).

Peter Gow, Lecturer in the anthropology of art in the School of World Art Studies and Museology at the University of East Anglia, has conducted field research in eastern Peru and western Brazil. He is author of *Of Mixed Blood: Kinship and History in Peruvian Amazonia*, and has published in *Man, L'Homme, History and Anthropology*, and other journals.

Roberte N. Hamayon is an ethnologist, specializing in Mongol and Buryat studies. She is a *docteur ès-lettres*, director of studies for North-Asian religions at the École Pratique des Hautes Études, (Religious sciences), Sorbonne, and the author of *La chasse à l'âme: Esquisse d'une théorie du chamanisme sibérien* (1990). Since 1988, she has also been the director of the Laboratoire d'ethnologie et de sociologie comparative (CNRS-University Paris-X).

Stephen Hugh-Jones is a Lecturer in Social Anthropology at the University of Cambridge. He has a long-term research interest in the indigenous peoples of Colombia and is the author of *The Palm and the Pleiades*.

Caroline Humphrey is a lecturer in Social Anthropology at the University of Cambridge. She is the author of *Karl Marx Collective: Economy, Society and Religion in a Siberian Collective Farm* (1983) and has recently completed a book on the shamanism of the Daur Mongols.

Nicholas Thomas is a Senior Research Fellow affiliated with the Australian National University. His publications include *Out of Time* (1989), *Marquesan Societies* (1990), and *Entangled Objects* (1991). His current research is on contemporary art and cultural politics in New Zealand.

Index